THE FRAUD IDENTIFICATION HANDBOOK
Fraud Avoidance Through Knowledge

George B. Allen

First Edition
PP Preventive Press L.L.C.
Highlands Ranch, Colorado

THE FRAUD IDENTIFICATION HANDBOOK
Fraud Avoidance Through Knowledge
By George B. Allen

Published by:
PP Preventive Press
2343 W. Hyacinth Rd.,
Highlands Ranch, CO 80126

First Printing May 1998
Printed in the United States of America

Allen, George B.
THE FRAUD IDENTIFICATION HANDBOOK: Fraud
Avoidance Through Knowledge/George B. Allen --1st ed.

Includes bibliographic references and index.
Preassigned LCCN: 98-92302
ISBN 0-9669160-0-X

ACKNOWLEDGMENTS

The unspoken inspiration for this handbook came from Dr. Stephen J. Reynolds, Professor of Geology, Arizona State University and from Donald G. Farmer, US Department of Energy Office of Inspector General. Dr. Reynolds was my principal thesis advisor at the University of Arizona. He showed me the value of compilation and the power of synthesis. My former investigative supervisor, Don Farmer, opened my eyes to investigative methods and to their role in society.

A number of individuals helped to shape and edit this Handbook. My wife, Dr. Janet L. Slate, lent her support, editorial eye, and scrutiny to the entire work. My father, Dr. Hubert Allen, reviewed the medical portions of the Insurance Section. My sister, art appraiser Lisa Barnes, reviewed the Art Fraud Section. Brother and biostatistician Hubert Allen Jr. reviewed the Science Fraud Section. Dave Ingersoll, climbing partner and real estate broker, reviewed the Real Estate Section.

I made all final editorial and stylistic decisions.

Warning—Disclaimer

This Handbook is designed to familiarize individuals and businesses with fraud prevention. It is not designed to render legal, accounting or other professional services with respect to any one scheme or system of fraud identification. If legal or other professional services are required, then the services of an attorney, accountant or other professional should be retained.

It is not the intent of the author to reprint all of the material pertinent to the subject. Rather, the Handbook is intended to outline and organize the various forms of fraud. You are urged to consult original sources, including books, periodicals, the Internet, and other media to refine your fraud education. For more information, see the Bibliography at the end of the Handbook.

Fraud prevention is not a self-taught skill. You are urged to take classes and to retain professional help in your efforts to avoid fraud.

Every effort has been made to make this Handbook as complete and accurate as possible. However, there may be either content or typographical mistakes. Therefore, this text should be used as a general guide, not as the ultimate source of fraud-prevention information.

The purpose of this Handbook is to educate. The author shall have neither liability nor responsibility to any person or entity with respect to any loss or damage caused, or alleged to be caused, directly or indirectly by the information contained in the Handbook. The Handbook is specifically **not intended** to inspire, cajole, or assist those who wish to commit fraud or those involved in ongoing fraudulent schemes.

If you do not wish to be bound by the above, you may return this book to the publisher, distributor, or bookseller for a full refund. The publisher will reimburse all wholesalers or retailers.

TABLE OF CONTENTS

Things are not always as they seem.
Aesop

PREFACE

WHY WRITE A FRAUD IDENTIFICATION HANDBOOK?
The inspiration for this book comes from my experience as a federal investigator and from my perception that there is need for an accessible, widely available, fraud handbook. During the early 1990s I spent three years working as a special agent for the US Department of Energy Office of Inspector General. Much of my job focused on investigating research scientists who had allegedly committed fraud. Although proving that the scientists committed fraud turned out to be a detailed and difficult task, the essence of their schemes was simple: using government equipment for non-government projects; charging time for work not completed; misappropriating money from a well-supported project to an unfunded project. In nearly every case, the scientist presumably knew his actions were improper. Even so, most of the scientists were surprised when confronted with a criminal investigation. They recognized misconduct, but not fraud, and certainly not criminality. While some may find the scientists' attitudes brazen, I found it disheartening. After all, if well-educated scientists could not recognize fraud, what hope did the rest of us have?

I have also been a victim of the fraud. Over a ten-year period I actively bought-sold and traded mineral specimens. I did not set out in this hobby as a self-taught amateur. Actually, my background was quite extensive: I had received about five years of geology education during two degree courses; I had worked for years as a professional metals-exploration geologist, and I had even co-authored one, well-received, mineral collecting paper. Even in the face of this extensive preparation, I have been the victim of mineral-specimen fraud on three or four occasions. In retrospect, my technical background was no match for my ignorance of fraudulent schemes.

Sensing a need, I set out here to create an affordable Fraud Identification Handbook, one that provides a global view of fraud perpetrators, their schemes, and their victims. The idea is that by categorizing fraudulent schemes and showing the broad framework of fraud, individuals can offset schemes before they do their damage—anticipation begets avoidance.

HANDBOOK'S DESIGN

There are ten chapters in the Handbook. The Introduction defines fraud and gives a historical perspective. Following the Introduction, roughly half of the book focuses on schemes that target individuals: the Confidence Games, Consumer Fraud, and Investment Fraud Chapters. The other half of the book focuses on fraud that primarily effects institutions: the Government Fraud, Operations Fraud, and Public Interest Fraud. The Science Fraud and Financial Fraud Chapters describe schemes that effect institutions and individuals equally. The final chapter, a Summary and Conclusion, gives an overview of fraud and suggests a universal method to foresee and avoid fraudulent schemes.

Bracketed by the Introduction and Summary-Conclusion, the core of the Handbook chapters are ordered alphabetically. This serves the target audience well, placing the historically oldest frauds, confidence games, first, and the most esoteric frauds, science, last. In-between are descriptions of the schemes that target everyday personal, business and government life.

HANDBOOK AUDIENCE

In order of priority, there are three general audiences for this book:

■ The savvy individual who knows that there are innumerable resources to guide him or her, but lacks the time to seek out each source.

■ The novice professional who lacks a basic knowledge of the frauds involved in their prospective or new job. For this person, such knowledge may be critical to a pending interview, to a successful new career, or to avoid committing fraud.

■ The established professional who needs a handy resource to flag the many frauds that may come his or her way. This audience includes business people, doctors, scientists, engineers, and even lawyers.

USE OF THE BOOK
This book makes sense when read as a whole, by individual chapter, or when used as a quick reference to see if a life situation matches a documented fraud. As a whole the Handbook is intended to develop a thematic or conceptual understanding of fraud and its place in society. Thematic or conceptual understandings are realized when people see both internal relationships and external relationships surrounding a scheme. The internal relationships tie the perpetrator to the scheme and to the victim(s). The external relationships of a scheme put it in context with other schemes and to society in general. Abundant examples of real-life schemes illustrate the internal mechanics of schemes. The structure of individual chapters serves to show the external relationships between schemes. For example, the section on Stock Fraud traces schemes through underwriting, to the customer's first contact with a broker, and on to the execution of trades and internal management of customer funds. The Science Fraud Chapter shows how fraudulent schemes are executed through experiments, publications, and into other aspects of scientists' life.

Achieving a thematic understanding of fraud and fraudulent schemes is a critical skill to anticipate new schemes as they emerge. In this vein, forensic accountants or fraud investigators may also benefit from a complete reading of the Handbook because these professionals must anticipate where an enterprise could be hiding fraud. I have attempted to show the continuum of fraud in different human enterprises so that the reader can develop an intuition as to when a set of circumstances may evidence fraud. Without a thematic or conceptual understanding of fraud, there is no hope of detecting every scheme, because new schemes emerge each day, making a compendium outdated the instant it is completed. Therefore, no compendium can describe every fraudulent scheme.

The savvy individual can use this book as a primer before buying, investing, entering into contracts, paying taxes, and voting. The Handbook is not intended to be definitive, so any specific guidance would have to be arrived at through the individual's own due diligence and through the appropriate assistance of an attorney, accountant, or other professional.

Of course, with the knowledge-base, an individual can save money by preparing him or herself prior to entering the professional's office.

The novice professional can use the Handbook in preparation for job interviews or prior to starting work in fields such as lending, real estate, stock brokerage, civil service, medicine, and law enforcement. The Handbook would be a good introduction to the nefarious side of each of these careers. For those who are new to law enforcement, this guide can fill in the gaps left by most academies. Also, the Handbook serves cautionary tales for those who consider committing fraud.

The harried professional may use this book, in conjunction with advice from accountants, attorneys or other professionals, to fortify him or herself against unfamiliar fraud. For example, the stock broker may wish to read the Real Estate section prior to entering a real estate deal or a growing service business may wish to review the Contract Fraud section prior to signing a major service contract.

The person whose interest lies only in identifying suspected schemes that arise from time to time can refer to the index where keywords direct the reader to descriptions of previously documented frauds. For many, seeing a scheme in writing is enough to bolster their suspicion that they have been targeted by schemers or that they are about to be enticed, or self-deceived, into perpetrating a fraud themselves.

George B. Allen

...And there is nothing new under the sun.
King Solomon
    Ecclesiastes

CHAPTER ONE - INTRODUCTION

FRAUD DEFINED

Fraud is a loaded word. To be useful here, it must un-bundled and then rebuilt. The loading of the word fraud comes from its wide currency—unlike most technical terms, it enjoys everyday use with people throughout society as well as specialized use in law and science:

■ Random House (1997) shows wide latitude, "deceit, trickery, or breach of confidence, used to gain some unfair or dishonest advantage."

■ Codified federal law defines and uses the word variously. One important statute, Fraud and False Statements, § 1001, gives the following:

"Whoever, in any matter within the jurisdiction of any department or agency of the United States knowingly and willfully falsifies, conceals or covers up by any trick, scheme, or device a material fact, or makes any false, fictitious or fraudulent statements or representations, or makes or uses any false writing or document knowing the same to contain any false, fictitious or fraudulent statement or entry, shall be fined not more than $10,000 or imprisoned not more than five years, or both."

■ From case law: Fraud "...consists of any false representation of a matter of fact, whether by words or by conduct, by false or misleading allegations or by concealment of that which should have been disclosed, which deceives or is intended to deceive another so that he shall act upon it to his legal injury (Baker v Rangos 1984)."

■ One science-fraud scholar defines fraud this way: "...serious misconduct with intent to deceive" (Goodstein Website).

Perpetrators, their schemes, and the victims form the essence of this book. To develop this elemental view of fraud, the Handbook adopts the following definition: "The intentional or unintentional gaining of something of value from a person, persons, or organization by a person, persons, or organization by use of deceit, false statement, understatement, or omission."

This definition consists of five elements: (1) the perpetrator; (2) the victim; (3) the use of deceit, false statement, understatement, or omission; (4) the presence, absence, or degree of intent; and (5) the thing of value.

This definition gives license to look at fraud committed by people, businesses, organizations, and government; with or without intent; and with great, modest, or intangible gain. Making intent optional includes all misrepresentations that could be attributed to accident or misunderstanding. In law, these misrepresentations are civilly actionable. Including intangible losses as well as tangible gives license to describe ethical fraud important in the Science and Public Interest Chapters. These Chapters show that people are motivated to commit fraud by things other than money— reputation, jealousy, political pressure, laziness, and indifference.

In the larger perspective, fraud is a category of social behavior— a form of misconduct: any deviation from laws, regulations, rules, protocols or social norms.

FRAUD CONTRASTED

Fraud is generally associated with, or related to, white-collar crime and theft. White-collar crime is criminal conduct that does not involve violence or the threat of violence and usually takes place in a professional work place. Fraud overlaps with white-collar crime, but the two are not the same because fraud spills over into other areas of misconduct—actions seldom treated as crimes. Also, white-collar crimes include acts which do not involve deception. The simplest way to see the relations is with a table:

	FRAUD	**WHITE COLLAR**
LOCATION	Anywhere	Office-business
PERPETRATORS	Anyone	Business people/ Profesionals
ALWAYS CRIMINAL?	No	Mostly criminal
INVOLVES SOMETHING OF VALUE	Not necessarily	Yes

Non-criminal frauds include personal misconduct, business misconduct, and scientific misconduct. For example, lying to one's spouse about how you spent money is a deception involving something of value—personal misconduct—but it is not criminal. Lying to employees to diminish their salaries is deception to gain money, and is business misconduct, but it is not criminal. And excluding a co-worker from proper recognition in a scientific publication is deception, but once again, it is not criminal. Analogously, white-collar crime includes acts like regulatory violations that are criminal, but not necessarily fraudulent—so, fraud and white-collar crime do not completely overlap. Confidence games are another class of frauds that often lie outside of the white-collar crime domain. They frequently do not involve business people and they often occur in a non-office environment.

To contrast fraud with other non-violent crime, consider the other major classes of white collar crime: theft, regulatory violation, and embezzlement; with embezzlement being the most closely related to fraud.

- Embezzlement is the conversion of something of value to one's own use, or to the use of another. The embezzler has lawful custody over something, but he or she is not entitled to convert its use. Although actual conversion is not fraud, many embezzlements include falsification of records or false statements, and these deceptive acts are fraud.
- Regulatory violations are any civil or criminal violations of government regulations. Failing to pay a toll or illegally dumping chemicals are examples of non-fraudulent, white-collar crimes.
- Theft is closely related to fraud in that thieves often rely on some concealment or fraudulent ruse, but strictly, theft is the non-consensual taking of something where there were no custodial rights.

HISTORY OF FRAUD

Fraud in Antiquity

Hoving (1996) makes the case that fraud is as old as history and that it pervades human activity. Art and artifact fraud are excellent gauges of the amount of fraud in history because the earlier epochs of human history left abundant art and artifacts, but few written records. A former director of the Metropolitan Museum of Art, Hoving traces art and artifact fraud from pre-history to the present, estimating that at least 40% of all art objects are frauds. The earliest frauds he identified are Phoenician, dating from the "second millennium until the sixth century B.C." Interestingly, he depicts ancient Rome as a veritable *faux* art factory.

The International Chamber of Commerce (1985) cites a shipping fraud dating to 360 B.C. "Zenothemis and ...[a] shipowner, Hegestratos, convinced a buyer to advance money to them in Syracuse upon declaring that their vessel was fully laden with corn... However, the vessel was empty, and three days after sailing, Hegestratos went down into the empty hold and tried to cut through the ship's timbers in an attempt to scuttle the vessel. He was caught by the passengers and in his panic jumped overboard and drowned. The ship scuttling failed."

Even science may have a long legacy of fraud. Modern researchers speculate that scientific patriarch Claudius Ptolemy may have committed scientific misconduct in the second century A.D. Archaeoastronomical studies found that Ptolemy's observations could not have been made in ancient Alexandria, but rather had to have been made in Rhodes. Therefore the astronomical readings attributed to Ptolemy were taken by Hipparchus of Rhodes (Broad and Wade 1982).

Fraud in the Middle Ages

Durant (1950) called the middle ages, A.D. 325 -1300, *The Age of Faith*. During this epoch, Europe wallowed in ignorance, creating an environment full of fraud. Presumably, the pall of ignorance set a stage where deception and self-deception were a way of life. Alchemy, astrology, superstition, magic, quackery, and occultism formed the basis for everyday beliefs. Counterfeiters and coin clippers plagued Twelfth Century currency (Durant 1950).

Fraud in the Renaissance and Reformation
The Renaissance and Reformation span the period from 1321 to 1648 (Durant 1950). While the Renaissance saw rationality again blossom as it had in ancient Greece and Rome, the majority of people carried forward with their Medieval ignorance. Evidence of this irrationality comes from the literature of the time. Grimmelshausen's (1669) *Simplissimus* (which recalls events from the first half of the seventeenth century) and Cervantes *Don Quixote* (1604) are both filled with fantasy and deception. For example, Grimmelshausen was so preoccupied with deception that his varied works used a "... bewildering array of pseudonyms..." for himself (Postscript in 1963 ed.).

Beyond literary interpretation, there are also substantive examples of fraud in Renaissance and Reformation art. One of the best-known historical artifacts is the Shroud of Turin, Christ's purported death shroud. Allegations of fraud taint its authenticity. Hoving (1996) details many of the steps modern investigators went through to authenticate or debunk the shroud. Relying on radiocarbon age determinations, Hoving concluded that counterfeiters made the shroud in 1356, an age consistent with a historical reference to its manufacturing date, and one that makes the Shroud of Turin a fake. For art historians, the Shroud may be emblematic of rampant Renaissance fraud. The era was full of Roman-era coin, carved gem, medal, and inscription fakes (Hoving 1996).

Fraud in the Eighteenth and Nineteenth Centuries
The Medieval and Renaissance tradition of ignorance begetting fraud continued into the Eighteenth and Nineteenth Centuries as shown by abundant confidence games in the United States. As with

the Middle Ages, fiction serves as a useful gauge of Nineteenth Century fraud, and none is more apt than Mark Twain's (1885)*The Adventures of Huckleberry Finn*, with its charlatans, The Duke of Bridgewater and the Dauphin, the purported lost King of France. These two characters perpetrate a litany of frauds from pretending to be preachers to extended quackery in the form of phrenology and "layin on o' hands...for cancer."

Sifakis's (1993) book *Hoaxes and Scams,* is probably the best compendium of Eighteenth and Nineteenth Century fraud. The scams from this era are a continuation of old schemes that target the average person: quackery, gambling, and mysticism; new schemes that target the wealth of the era—the miners and ranchers in the New World; and scammers who pretend to come from Old World families so they could con people out of loans and into fake business deals. Sifakis details Eighteenth and Nineteenth Century frauds which focus on land swindlers, gold mine salters, coin counterfeiters, medical quacks, and heir and heiress impostors.

Twentieth century criticism of Nineteenth Century science shows that fraud existed in rigorous disciplines too. Recent research has shown the German biologist Earnst Haeckle altered the appearance of embryos in sketches. The alterations gave undue support to his theory of evolution: the idea that the development of an individual mirrored the evolution of the species—ontogeny recapitulates phylogeny (Pennisi 9-5-97). Another pioneering scientist, Louis Pasteur, reportedly committed ethical fraud by not giving due attribution to one of his predecessors, a chemist who laid the groundwork for Pasteur's anthrax vaccine (Geison 1995). This qualifies as fraud because Mr. Pasteur, presumably, intended to enhance his reputation by intentional deception.

Modern Era Fraud
The modern era saw the transition of fraud from small-time confidence games, petty grifters, and medical quackery, all of which were mostly completed by speech, to banking, contract, procure-

ment, telecommunication, credit card, lending, securities, tax, insurance, accounting, futures, and, among too many to list, entitlement fraud. Rather than using a beguiling smile and quickly-won trust, contemporary frauds rely on technological veils—the use of computers, the Internet, cellular phones; the perversion of complex contracts; and the evasion of complex laws—all of which make modern fraud a sophisticated, cutting-edge, multi-hundred-billion dollar per year enterprise. Notwithstanding new technology, the long-standing, pre-modern era deceptions remain alive as incarnations in telemarketing fraud and a great variety of confidence games.

Anecdotes of contemporary fraud compose the bulk of this text and illustrate that fraud touches every aspect of modern life.

In the tenth gulf of the eighth circle lies forgers, counterfeiters, and alchemists, moaning with varied ailments; a stench of sweat and pus fills the air, and groans of the sufferers make a terrifying roar.

The Inner-workings of Hell, in Dante's *Inferno* (Durant 1950)

CHAPTER TWO - CONFIDENCE GAMES

INTRODUCTION

It is hard to believe any kind of fraud could go by the appellation "game," but in many people's minds confidence games are the quintessential frauds. In a confidence game the perpetrator establishes trust with his or her victim prior to depriving the victim of something of value. Trust can be established by pretending to be a government or business official, or by developing rapport during a brief conversation or during on-going contacts. The trust, combined with the victim's ignorance, greed, or preoccupation with other matters, facilitate the crime. Mark Twain's *The Adventures of Huckelberry Finn* portrays a classic "con man" in its character The Duke of Bridgewater. *The Grifters* (Thompson 1990) is another apt fictional portrayal of the con man (and woman) lifestyle. Two recent books, Jay Robert Nash's *Hustlers and Con Men* (1976) and Carl Sifakis's *Hoaxes and Scams* (1993), give detailed descriptions of famous and infamous scammers and scams. Don Wright's *Scam, Inside America's Con Artists Clans* (1996) fully portrays contemporary confidence games through the lives of Travelers, migratory

Scottish, English and Irish clans that specialize in trailer and home repair rip offs.

As hard as it is to believe that fraud could be described as a game, it is equally hard, and sad, to believe that people fall for these scams. The most disheartening part of the scams is that those most likely to be victims also appear to be those least likely to read cautionary words like those that follow and like those found in innumerable consumer outreaches. Notwithstanding the naïveté of victims, no Fraud Handbook could be complete without a confidence games chapter, so here we go.

(As an aside to those who are unlikely to fall for confidence games, it is worthwhile to understand the techniques behind these schemes: If you have ever bought a used car, you know that the confidence game style is still used by otherwise legitimate businesses to nudge buyers. Being aware of this can be helpful in day-to-day consumer life.)

The two principal categories of confidence games are: (1) those targeting businesses and organizations, and (2) those that target individuals or families. Nash (1976) uses an alternative classification where he distinguishes between elaborate cons called the "Big Store" and quick or "Short" cons. The Big Store often involves extensive role playing and props used over days, weeks, or months. "Short Cons" usually are immediate or day-long confidence games. The business versus individual system is used here, because it allows readers to more quickly focus on their own fraud exposure.

For more on con games see CHAPTER THREE'S Home Repair Section details the Traveler's home-repair con games. Varied other Sections in CHAPTER THREE also include snippets of confidence games: In particular, the Auto Section and the Telecommunications Section go into depth about confidence games in contemporary settings.

CONFIDENCE GAMES THAT TARGET BUSINESSES AND ORGANIZATIONS

Introduction
Confidence games that succeed against organizations do so most frequently by taking advantage of the ignorance of lower level employees, by taking advantage of the greed of management, or by taking advantage of the overall fast-moving nature of today's business.

There are six classes of confidence games that specifically target businesses and organizations: i. advanced fee schemes, ii. impersonations, iii. money changing schemes, iv. money transfer schemes, v. office supply orders, and vi. outliers.

Advanced Fee Schemes
Some confidence games target businesses and organizations and some target individuals, but advanced fee schemes target both. Consequently, both of the victim classes, business-organizations and individuals, have their own discussion of advanced fee schemes. Advanced fee schemes involve a criminal asking for an advanced payment on the future delivery of goods or services. These qualify as confidence games when the perpetrator assumes an identity or an affiliation that creates trust with the victim, or when the perpetrator goes to some length to build confidence with the victim before asking for the advance. Here are a few schemes:

- Referral Journal Fraud: A telemarketer defrauded professionals by collecting a fee from them to place their name and service in a journal directed to AFL/CIO union members. The perpetrator never placed the ads, defrauding victims of $35,000 (USPIS Summer/Fall 1992).
- Classified Ad Fraud: An individual submitted false invoices for classified ads that never ran (Fitzgerald 10-94). In a bit of a

stretch, the use of the advertising pretext makes this a confidence scheme.

- Ten Percent Down Fraud: Sikafis (1993) describes a scheme in which a salesman induces buyers to pay an advanced fee when offered 10% discount on an item. The item is never delivered. In Sikafis's example, the sale items are magazines.

Prevention: Don't pay advances for anything of significant value unless you have credit references and a credit report to show the reliability of the vendor. Try to always use credit cards to pay for non-routine items.

Impersonations play a peripheral role in a great variety of frauds. CHAPTER FOUR - Financial Fraud describes the highest impact impersonations in the Check Fraud Section. The following are more nuisance than anything else:

- Injured Boss Fraud: Criminals posing as hospital or law enforcement officials call hotels asking employees to provide quick cash for an emergency situation. If the employee agrees to forward the cash, the criminal or his accomplice come by or ask the employee to drop off the money at another location. Of course, there is no injured boss or other emergency (Western 11-19-95).
- Tow Truck Scam: Criminals identify themselves as the boss of a business, say that their car has broken down and they need the employee at the business to pay a truck driver a towing fee. Later, an accomplice comes by to pickup the towing fee ($100 or more). As a variation, the perpetrator asks that the money be brought to a third location, like a gas station (Robinson 4-17-98).
- Reprinted Classifieds: A small print shop photocopied classified employment ads out of national newspapers, reprinted them in a cheap format, and then billed businesses for the unauthorized ads (USPIS Summer 1998).

Prevention: Independently confirm the identity of anyone asking for money or financial information. For example, if someone says the boss is hurt, ask the name of the ambulance service and call the service.

Money Changing Frauds, largely short cons, are a nuisance more than anything else. But they can seriously impact a small business:

- Counterfeit Currency Fraud: Sikafis (1993) describes three techniques involving counterfeit deception:

    * The criminal passes a $20 bill to a clerk, and lingers so the clerk will later recognize him. After leaving, an accomplice comes in flashing false law enforcement credentials, saying the person who passed the bill was a counterfeiter. The accomplice asks for the $20 bill back for investigative purposes, thereby defrauding the store of about $20.
    * A criminal passes a counterfeit bill by asking for change for a $50. Once the criminal has the confidence of the clerk, he replaces one of the $20 bills he was given with a counterfeit one. Upon receiving change for the counterfeit, the criminal successfully passed the bad bill.
    * Two dollar bills have been altered with the pasted-on corners of $20 to allow them to be passed as twenty-dollar bills. In this scheme, the perpetrators tries to get change from someone who is too busy to notice the alteration.

- Short Changing the Business: Con artists defraud cashiers by repeatedly asking for change, ultimately confusing the cashier into giving away more money than they received (Sifakis 1993).

Prevention: Educate employees in counterfeit currency identification and instruct employees to be leery of those who repeatedly ask for change.

Money Transfer Schemes are all variations on the basic advanced fee scheme, but here, the victim puts up his or her own money in anticipation of some big business deal going through. If they work, these are no short cons—many of these qualify as the Big Store and can be disastrous for the victim. Often, these schemes involved wire fraud: The perpetrators use fax machines.

Money Transfer schemes are particularly popular with foreign nations, and Nigerians are the masters. The US Secret Service describes Nigerian-based money transfer schemes as "4-1-9" fraud after the section of the Nigerian penal code which addresses fraud schemes (USSS Web site). Here are a few of these money transfer schemes:

- Blocked Fund Fraud: Criminals, often based overseas, entice victims into paying an advanced fee, purportedly to assist in the release of blocked funds. The "investor" never receives any return on his investment (NFIC Web site).
- Capital Development Money Holding Scheme: By fax, Nigerians asked oil companies for access to the companies' bank accounts so the *Nigerian Oil & Mineral Producing Area Development Commission* could deposit a portion of its annual capital development fund in an offshore account. The faxes promised to give the company 30% in exchange for use of the account. Once the Nigerians obtain the account numbers, they make withdrawals, not deposits (Knott 3-6-95). A variation of this scheme has the Nigerians asking for the victim's account number so that they can transfer money. In this scheme, the Nigerians promise an advanced fee, but instead use the account number to make unauthorized withdrawals (Knott 3-6-95).

Prevention: Do not send money to anyone without independent confirmation of the person or organization's credit worthiness and identity, and do not reveal personal or business account numbers to anyone unless you know them well.

Like Money Transfer Schemes, **Office Supply Cons** often involve extensive planning and staging. When successful, they can cause significant damage to the victim. Here are the common ones:

- Order-by-Trick Scam: A deceptive billing scam in which the seller convinces the buyer to order supplies (or, potentially, services) at inflated prices. The perpetrator: (1) convinces the buyer that the seller is an authorized vendor who has been in-active in the recent past; (2) "...misrepresents the quality, type, package size, price, or brand name of the merchandise"; (3) "...uses high pressure tactics to rush the buyer into a decision and [to] keep the buyer from getting information about prices, quantities and brand names; or (4) "...misrepresents the purpose of the call, claiming that he or she is calling to send a promotional item such as a cordless screwdriver, a heavy duty flashlight, free samples, or a catalog... (FTC Website)."
- Inflated Billings: Perpetrators misrepresent office supplies as being available at a discount, then, after the victim-company begins to order the supplies, the criminal increases the billing prices by multiples of the original price, hoping the victim will pay the invoice without examining it. The criminal may also use bribes, in the forms of gifts sent to the company purchasing agent's home, in order to induce the purchasing agent into overlooking or furthering the scheme (USPIS Summer 1990).

Prevention: Audit office supply billings. Limit the amount of goods shipped to any one buyer until you have a credit history on them.

Outlier Scams

Notwithstanding how handy it is to pigeonhole every scheme in its own category, some just don't fit. It is a testament to the ingenuity of confidence men and women that so many schemes cannot be lumped together:

- Bust-Out Scheme: A procurement-fraud in which a new business establishes good credit with suppliers. With the credit, the new business then makes very large supply orders. Once the new business receives the large inventories, the goods are shipped "out the back door" to associates and the suppliers are left unpaid. To cover the criminal trail, records are destroyed, fires set and robberies are faked in an effort to hide or disguise what actually took place. The business files bankruptcy and the crime is complete (FBI 1989). In one example of a bust-out scheme a perpetrator "...created fictitious computer companies and then ordered computer parts and accessories from several legitimate computer companies throughout the United States. The subject paid for the merchandise with non-sufficient funds checks, sold it, then left town and started over again in another state (USPIS Fall 1990)."

- Equipment Loan For Review Fraud: A computer magazine editor defrauded suppliers of their equipment by asking to borrow it for the purpose of an article, then, rather than returning the equipment, he sold it through classified ads (USPIS Winter/Spring 1994).

- Timely Frauds: Criminals latch onto current business trends. They take advantage of emerging problems, technologies, or practices to entice business into frauds. For example, one regulator expects a variety of fraudulent schemes to arise from businesses offering year two thousand (Y2K) computer solutions: (1) Frauds soliciting for money to finance Y2K consulting ventures, and (2) Business that pretend to offer the service, but in fact, do not remedy their customer's Y2K computer problems (Landwehr 2-27-98).

- Tool Sales Fraud: Some career criminals are itinerant tool salesmen who target mechanics. They sell poorly-made tools as discounted high-quality tools, enticing the victim by implying that the tools were stolen (Wright 1996).
- Violent Crime Fraud: In a classic "big store" scam, a well-known crime family staged a rape at Disney World to try to collect a major liability pay off (Wright 1996).
- Protection Fraud: Organized crime figures have extorted money from business for protection, then expanded the extortion by staging a false threat to obtain a one-time additional payoff (Sifakis 1993).

Prevention: Obtain a deposit from anyone who borrows from a business. Conduct reference checks on any computer or other consultants. Be leery of door-to-door sales outfits that purport to offer deep discounts. Investigate any suspicious liability claims. Report extortion to law enforcement.

CONFIDENCE GAMES TARGETING INDIVIDUALS

Introduction
Since individuals usually have less money than businesses, and no insurance against theft, any confidence game can cause significant damage to the victim. Most schemes that target individuals fall into one of seven categories: i. advanced fee ii. impersonations, iii. pigeon drops, iv. gambling, v. prisoner scams, vi. cults and religions, and vii. wholesale and retailing.

Advanced Fee Schemes are one of the most common frauds perpetrated against consumers and businesses. Perpetrators, often telemarketers, falsely promise "gifts," discount items or services to be delivered after the purchaser pays a small "advanced fee." In this scheme, the promised good or service is never delivered. Often the perpetrator covers his tracks by using shell companies or "bust-out" tactics that have him leaving town before anyone can catch up to him. Here are some common advanced fee schemes:

- **Business Opportunity Fraud:** A general class of advanced-fee schemes where the perpetrator inflates the promise of a business, or otherwise deceives prospective investors. When nothing of value is exchanged for the investor's initial payment, these businesses opportunities are merely fronts for advanced fee frauds. See CHAPTER THREE for a detailed Business Opportunities discussion.

- **Front Money Fraud:** Criminals proclaim to have a winning lottery ticket (Wright 1996), a business payoff, a large debt to be paid back to them, or some other extraordinary future payoff. The criminal then induces a victim to loan some "front money" until the extraordinary payoff comes in. Instead, by various devices, the criminals run away with the victim's money. These large-sum schemes often involve repeated contacts to prep the victim. For more examples, see the Money Transfer Scheme discussion above.

- **Lost Pet Fraud:** Criminals may respond to lost pet-owner's ads and claim to have the pet. For a fee, they promise to deliver the pet, but in fact, they never had the pet in the first place (Thatcher 2-8-98).

- **Prayer Book Scam:** A con man defrauded charity donors by pretending he was collecting money to buy prayer books for soldiers fighting in the Gulf War. The con man told "pastors he had been asked by the military to distribute prayer books to American soldiers stationed in Saudi Arabia during Operation Desert Storm. Allegedly, the con man used the donations for personal expenses and failed to deliver any prayer books (USPIS Winter/Spring 1994)."

- **Puzzle Playing Advanced Fee Scheme:** Marketers target seniors with idle time and bait them with puzzles. The victim is told that he will receive a large dollar amount once he returns and completes the puzzle and sends it in along with a small fee, $10 to $50. The victim never receives a prize. One woman lost $11,000 (Hays 5-21-95).

- Ten Percent Down Fraud: Sikafis (1993) describes a scheme in which a salesman induces buyers to pay an advanced fee when offered 10% discount on an item. The item is never delivered. In Sikafis's example, the sale items are magazines.

Prevention: Don't pay advances for anything of significant value unless you have credit references and a credit report that independently confirm the supplier's representations. Check-out small businesses by calling the local Better Business Bureau or other community sources. Use a credit card for sight-un-seen payments and delay payment until the goods or services are received. If the goods or services are not delivered as promised, don't pay and write a letter to your credit card saying that the goods or services were not rendered as promised.

The **Pigeon Drop** has the confidence shark spinning a tale requiring the victim (pigeon) to drop-off or pick-up money at a specific location. During the course of the drop-off or pickup, the criminal deprives the victim of their money. This genre of fraud typically involves some impersonation and lost or found funds:

- Criminals defraud people, especially the elderly, by telling them they are "bank examiners." The criminal asks the pigeon to withdraw his money from the bank and give it to the "examiner." The impersonator uses the pretext that he or she are involved in an embezzlement or counterfeiting investigation at the bank.
- Con men or women orchestrate a scene where the target finds a wallet or case stuffed with money—counterfeit money. The victim is then convinced by the perpetrators that the best course of action is to hold onto the money for awhile to see if anyone claims it. If no one claims it, the perpetrators say all of the finders will split the money. In the interim, the perpetrator ask the pigeon to give a small deposit of their own money to the others to show their good faith. The criminals run off with the

35

victim's real money, leaving the victim with a handful of counterfeits (Nash 1976).

- A perpetrator may deliberately misplace a document-filled wallet or bundle. The documents suggest a promising business venture. An honest finder of the documents is then lured into investing in the fraudulent scheme. The finder feels comfortable making his investment because he "stumbled" upon the opportunity. The criminals run off with the pigeon's money after he makes his investment (Nash 1976).
- In the Jamaican Con "... a swindler pose[s] as a foreigner who didn't trust banks. He convinced the woman to hold his money in a handkerchief and for her to <u>put up some of her own money</u> as a gesture of good faith. When the man left, promising to meet her later, she opened the handkerchief and discovered that it contained rolled up newspaper (Wright 1996)."
- In the Envelope Switch the victim is defrauded by switching a paper-stuffed envelope in place of one with cash. While the victim thinks he has finally been paid off for his initial investment, he actually receives a worthless bundle (Nash 1976).

Prevention: Don't engage in any venture that requires large cash transaction: Transactions involving more than $10,000 or constructively amounting to more than $10,000 must be reported to the IRS. Conduct a due diligence study of any investment. Be wary of any deal that involves drop offs or pickup in unusual places such as parking lots or alleys. Don't engage in off-the-books money transfers or loans. Confirm the identity of anyone who presents themselves as a law enforcement or government official.

Gambling
It is difficult to find much sympathy for those who loose money in illegal gambling, but no Fraud Handbook is complete without some discussion of gambling:

- <u>Spinning Coin Game</u>: Confidence artists can alter a coin to make it always fall toward one side. They defraud gamblers by wagering on the outcome of this fixed game (Sifakis 1993).
- <u>Gambling Wire Fraud</u>: Bookies and organized gambling rings with off-site betting, defrauded betters by tapping the wires from race tracks and then rigging the bets against their customers (Nash 1976).
- Illegal gambling houses rig games by marking cards or by making all of the players, save the one victim, co-conspiring actors.

For more descriptions of gambling scams see Sifakis's *Hoaxes and Scams* (1996).

Prevention: Don't engage in illegal gambling. When so much is legal, why bother going off the books?

Impersonation plays a peripheral role in a great variety of frauds. CHAPTER FOUR - Financial Fraud describes the most high impact impersonation frauds in its Check Fraud discussion. CHAPTER SIX -Investment Fraud, describes broker impersonations in its Real Estate and Stock Sections. The following examples include both devastating and trivial impersonation con games:

- One interesting variation on impersonation-confidence games comes from law enforcement and private investigators. Both government and private agents use impersonations, which they euphemistically call "pretexts," to obtain information from or about their targets. Although the courts have generally not objected to pretexting, there are some circumstances when these impersonation are illegal: If the subject of an investigation has an attorney representing him or her, it is a violation of attorney-ethics rules for an attorney's representative to talk to the subject of an investigation.

- <u>Pretend IRS Agents</u>: Perpetrators impersonate IRS Agents. Targeting the elderly, the perpetrators tell the victim if they pay a tax, they will receive a prize. Another scam involves telling a widow her deceased spouse left a tax bill, and if she does not pay it in cash, she will loose her house. IRS Agent impersonators also try to obtain Social Security numbers or credit card numbers for credit card or identity fraud schemes (AARP January-February 1995).
- <u>Grandson Gimmick Fraud</u>: Pretending to be a grandson, a man defrauded a grandmother. The impostor said he needed money to make bail from jail. The grandmother sent the check by Western Union Money Transfer (*Albuquerque Journal North* 9-1-95).
- <u>Debt Collector Impersonation</u>: Some bill collectors impersonate law enforcement officials or lawyers in order to fraudulently convince debtors that criminal or civil sanctions are pending if the debtor does not pay off their loan (Hudson Fall 1993).
- <u>Bank Official Impersonation</u>: Criminals, impersonating bank officials tell "... the elderly...that a particular bank teller is giving out counterfeit bills and that the bank needs help in catching the teller. The elderly person goes to the teller's window and withdraws a large sum of money. The victim then gives the money to the "bank official" to be examined. The "bank official" assures the customer that the money will be deposited in his/her account; of course, it never is (Information Plus 1994)."
- <u>Energy Audit Fraud</u>: Criminals posing as utility company workers gain entry into a victim's home, whereupon they steal as much as they can (Wright 1996).
- <u>Lost Friend of Family Scam</u>: A perpetrator tried to defraud a middle-aged man by exclaiming he was a friend of the victim's brother, and the brother said, "If I was ever in town to look you up." The "friend " asked for money. The perpetrator had been a former postal employee, and he obtained the victim's name by

reading the victim's correspondence with his brother (USPIS Spring 1990).

- Grave Plot Fraud: Perpetrators send letters to the survivors of overseas, deceased relatives, asking for maintenance fees. The fees are never used for the deceased's grave (Nash 1976).
- Movie Casting Fraud: A career confidence man defrauded people in two towns during the 1970s by pretending to be a movie producer and using the facade to pass bad checks (Nash 1976).
- Home Entry Fraud: Some sneaky criminals enter homes-for-sale by posing as potential buyers. Upon entry, one criminal tours the house while the other steals from it (Wright 1996). Other pretexts, such as the need to use the phone, or to look at the utilities are used for the same criminal purpose.
- Contaminate and Steal: Career criminals orchestrate a theft where they "accidentally" spray a victim with insecticide during a staged termite treatment. The perpetrator then instructs the victim to put all of his or her jewelry in a glass filled with milk to neutralize the pesticide. By slight of hand, the criminal then steals all of the jewelry under the victim's nose (Wright 1996).
- Shared Ride Fraud: Criminals may pretend to offer benign rides to attract victims. They use ride boards to entice victims into low cost shared-car rides. Instead, the driver makes off with the passenger's luggage and money at the first convenient spot (Sifakis 1993).

Prevention: Confirm the identity of anyone who presents themselves as business representatives, law enforcement or government official.

Money Exchange Schemes are mostly nuisances to individuals. The most serious loss exposure comes to those engaged in illegal activities like counterfeiting or black market money exchanges.

- ◆ Criminal Money Exchanges
- Black Market Money Exchanges: Nash (1976) describes well known criminal, Abram Sykowski, who defrauded victims by promising to give them black market, inflated, exchange rates on French Francs after they deposited money in Swiss accounts. After receiving the deposits, he would renege on his promise.
- Green Goods Fraud: A scheme involving criminals on both sides of the deal—someone who thinks they are buying high quality counterfeit bills actually receives poor quality ones (Nash 1976).

- ◆ Ordinary Money Exchanges
- Cab Fraud: Cab drivers can shortchange passengers by pretending to give the proper change. If the passenger is in a hurry he or she might leave without checking the change (Sifakis 1993). Alternatively, by simply refusing to make change, the cabby may hope the passenger will just leave an extraordinary tip.
- Short Changing: Dishonest cashiers may shortchange by counting bills twice to gain a customer's confidence. Once the customer is at ease, the cashier palms one bill as he or she passes the change to the victim. The perpetrator expects that the victim's suspicion is down after seeing the change counted twice (Sifakis 1993).

Prevention: Do not engage in counterfeit or black market money exchanges. Give exact change to cabbies. Be leery of those repeatedly ask for change or count change more than once.

Prisoner Scams befall those who become overly enchanted with amateur rehabilitation. Consider the following:

- Prison Pen Pal Scam: Jailed criminals trick victims, who are befriended as pen pals, into cashing falsified U.S. Postal Money Orders with the victims' bank accounts. After the deposits go through, the criminal instructs the victim to withdraw most of it. Soon thereafter, the victim receives a "Dear Joan" letter from the criminal, and an official letter stating the victim owes the bank the amount withdrawn because the deposits were worthless (USPIS Winter/Spring 1993).

- Prisoner Help: A convict defrauds victims by promising to reveal the location of hidden assets if the victim will help him or his family. Invariable, the help is not rewarded with a payoff. Also called "Spanish Prisoner Fraud (Nash 1976)."

Prevention: Don't conduct business with the incarcerated.

Cults and Religious Scams target those looking for redemption or those whose circumspection is left at the door of the house of worship. In brief, here are some:

- Cult Fraud: Cults target and recruit the elderly [and others] in order to take their money. Many cults "...flourish in the nursing homes and sunnier climes where senior citizens are clustered (Hays 5-21-95)."
- Doomsday Cults: Purveyors of Armageddon "...urge elderly recruits to surrender money, cars and houses on the theory that since the world is about to end, they will lose it anyway (Hays 5-21-95)."
- Religious Investment Fraud: A Chicago Savings Club owner defrauded "...fellow Christians by promising high rates of return on investments he told them were placed with "...churches and other religious causes...Instead [he] loaned the money to relatives, funded personal business ventures and invested in struggling companies (USPIS Winter/Spring 1995)."

Prevention: Families might counsel members who fall into cults.

Wholesale and Retailing Scams

In these schemes, the perpetrator puts the target at ease by offering seemingly good deals and by pretending to be a legitimate business. The problem with these purveyors is that, even if they deliver, the goods may not be what they seem, and the fly-by-night nature of the businesses diminishes the chance for returns.

- Overstock Sale Fraud: A somewhat complex scheme where the perpetrator claims to have excess items like TVs for sale at deep discounts. The criminal insists the items must be paid for in cash. After receiving the cash, the criminal instructs the buyer to go meet a nearby truck where the items are supposed to be waiting. When the victims arrives at the truck, he or she find that there is no merchandise and the truck has nothing to do with the perpetrator who just ran away and committed the fraud (Wright 1996).
- Stuffed Flat: Unscrupulous furniture sellers may use an apartment as a front for selling used, or low quality furniture to unwitting buyers. The store continually replenishes the apartment, deceiving buyers into thinking they are getting a good deal by buying furniture at distressed prices (Sifakis 1993).

Prevention: Be leery of those who sell wholesale or retail items out of non-traditional sites. Ask to see a sales license or sales tax ID number, if none are available, don't buy.

Caveat emptor.
(Let the buyer beware.)

A Latin proverb

CHAPTER THREE - CONSUMER FRAUD

INTRODUCTION

Anytime someone or some organization buys something or receives a service for their own use, as opposed to resale, they are a consumer. Although no dollar amount is available to characterize the total cost of consumer fraud, the great number of anecdotes and the known impact on individual industries demonstrates consumer fraud has a profound impact on Americans. The telecommunications industry alone estimates $40 billion annual consumer losses to telecomm marketing fraud (Marvin Sept 1994).

The two hands of consumer fraud are criminals posing as businesses and otherwise legitimate businesses defrauding consumers. Of these, criminals posing as businesses obviously pose the greater threat because consumers have few recourses against criminals— they often conceal or fritter away assets and they are hard to pin down.

This Chapter, along with CHAPTER SIX, Investment Fraud, have the highest potential for benefiting the average American.

AUTOMATIC TELLER MACHINE (ATM) FRAUD

More theft than fraud, criminals use a variety of techniques to steal from bank customers who use ATM machines:

- Criminals steal ATM cards then defraud banks by quickly make withdrawals (Baum 2-11-95).
- Automatic Teller Machine Shoulder Surfing: Thieves glance over ATM user's shoulder's to steal their account numbers and passwords (Judson 1994).
- Criminals in Connecticut defrauded bank customers by installing a fake ATM, collecting the ATM card numbers, creating fictitious ATM cards, and withdrawing over $50,000 from the customer's accounts (Holland and Eng 5-31-93).

Prevention: Safeguard ATM cards and numbers. Report any ATM card or number theft or loss immediately to the issuing bank. Be wary of ATM machines in strange locations.

BUSINESS OPPORTUNITY FRAUD

Some criminals capitalize on individual's desires to be their own boss or on some people's unemployment. These criminals offer "can't fail" business opportunities. Many of these are advanced fee schemes (see CHAPTER TWO - Confidence Games and the Telecommunications section in this CHAPTER). The perpetrator inflates the promise of a business, or otherwise deceives prospective investors. Deceptions include: understating the initial cost, overstating the potential return, or understating the amount of sales work required for success. The following are some of the common business opportunity scams (FTC Jan 1998):

- Vending machines.
- Display racks.
- Franchises.
- Medical billing businesses.
- Envelop stuffing.
- ATM machines (Choquette 7-6-98).
- Multilevel marketing.
- Water purification system sales.

- Popcorn vending machines (Lynch 7-19-95).
- Pay phones (Lynch 7-19-95).
- Invention Marketing: Firms promise to promote the new products, but almost never successfully gain anything for the inventor (Boselovic 11-16-97).

Some business opportunities are actually illegal pyramid schemes. One example involves businesses that rely on participation fees from future vendors instead of relying on product or service sales to customers. The initiator of the pyramid is paid first, and eventually, those at the bottom are paid nothing and lose their initial payments to the tier above them. Chain letters and multilevel sales organizations are variations on pyramid schemes (SEC no date and Palmeri 8-14-95).

Prevention: Conduct a background investigation of the offerer. Conduct a due diligence study of the business offer. Enlist the advice of an accountant, attorney or other business professional. Remember, FTC rules give you a ten day right of return on any business opportunity purchase.

CREDIT CARD FRAUD

As central features of contemporary life, credit cards also feature greatly in fraud. One estimate puts world-wide annual credit card losses at $3 to $5 billion, making somewhat over 1% of customer interest costs directly attributable to fraud (Leiren Jan 1996). There are three basic credit card fraud schemes: i. false credit card charges, ii. false card applications, and iii. fraudulent credit card services.

False Credit Card Charges
To illegally make charges on another person's credit card without making a counterfeit card, a criminal must obtain four pieces of information: i. the card holder's name, ii. the card number, iii. the expiration date, and iv. the cardholder's address of record. Even

without the card, the criminal can make mail-order charges and have the goods sent to the address of record, or in some cases to another address.

◆ Criminals obtain card information in a variety of schemes:
- Credit Reports: Employees of a legitimate business, like a car dealership, have access to credit reports and can steal card numbers to rack-up charges. At one New Jersey dealership, employees used access to run up $800,000 in fraudulent credit card charges (Davis August 1995).
- Every Day Card Access: Cashiers, retail clerks, bellhops, company employees, maids, mail thieves, airline cargo handlers, couriers for bank services, workers at presort houses, postal clerks, postal carriers, and credit card company employees all have access to other people's credit card numbers. They may simply write the numbers down, or run multiple copies of charge slips, keeping some for themselves while servicing the customer (USPIS Service Fall 1991).
- Dumpster Diving: The **legal** practice of scouring dumpsters to gain personal and private information about a person or company (Judson 1994).
- Purchasing credit card numbers from mail order companies and then placing the numbers on other cards (Judson 1993).
- Stealing Mail: Thieves follow mail carriers, steal from rural mail boxes, open the letters to obtain confidential information, keep credit card applications, and then seal up and return the mail to avoid detection. The thieves then continued to steal the mail until the new credit cards arrived (USPIS Summer 1998).

◆ More advanced criminals can use the card information to make counterfeit cards. Typically, the criminals encode card numbers on blank, discarded, or expired cards. Credit companies try to thwart these schemes by using code verification values: Numbers that credit card companies embed in magnetic strips on their cards to allow vendors to differentiate between fraudulently fabricated cards and the genuine cards (Information Plus 1994).

◆ Alternatively, criminals may simply alter someone else's card (Graves 11-20-94):

- Dip the cards in hot water, flatten the embossed numbers, then empress new numbers on the card.
- Use an iron to flatten existing numbers, then emboss new numbers.
- Cut off the numbers with a sharp knife, then rearrange the numbers.
- Use computers to decode the magnetic strip and install a new code with a new number on the card.

Prevention: Safeguard credit cards and card number. Do not let shopkeepers or other take the card out of sight. Do not reveal the card number to anyone or to any company that is not known to you. Completely destroy any purchase receipts or other documents with credit numbers on them prior to throwing them out. Review all monthly charges and report questionable charges immediately to the credit card company.

False Card Applications

Once a criminal has sufficient background information on another individual, he or she can apply for a new credit card in the name of another. The overall scope of this scheme is described in the Identity Fraud Section (below). The critical information an identity thief needs for a credit card application includes: i. name, ii. date of birth, iii. social security number, iv. addresses (previous and current), v. phone number, vi. job history. There are two sources of false applications: a. insiders who convert their legitimate access to consumer information to their own use, and b. outsiders who are information thieves.

◆ Insider False Applicants

As is true in the False Charging discussion, all those (listed above) with access to a card-holder's card or card information may use the data to make false applications. In one case a former Citibank employee used his position of trust to replace the names and addresses of two Citibank cardholders with his own name and address. He fraudulently obtained the cards and charged $11,641.91 on them (USPIS Winter 1989-90).

◆ Outsider False Applicants

A criminal can obtain this information by conducting his or her own background investigation, by stealing someone's mail or other privileged documents, or by hiring a private investigator to conduct a background investigation. A typical background investigation involves searching public records such as arrest records, court records, and water utility records. Records like divorce proceedings commonly have all of the information needed to apply for credit.

With all of the information in hand, a criminal then applies for the card and either has it sent to an alternative address or steals the mail as it comes in. Mail thieves simply follow the mail person on their rounds and clean out mail boxes after delivery. One way of getting the new cards to an alternative address is for a criminal to apply for a "Change of Address" in the victim's name (Love 5-27-98). Alternatively, criminals can create drop boxes: Empty houses, rented mail drops, or un-related people's houses as locations to divert victim's credit cards so that the criminal can use them (NFIC Website).

Prevention: Review all monthly charges and report questionable charges immediately to the credit card company. Make annual reviews of all three credit bureaus' files on your credit history to see if anyone is making inappropriate inquiries or making applications in your name.

Fraudulent Credit Card Services
A third way for criminals to defraud consumers by means of credit cards is to induce consumers to pay for fraudulent services. Obviously, almost any fraudulent service could be charged to a credit card, so this discussion will focus only on card-related services. Fraudulent services come in two varieties, credit protection and credit repair:

◆ Credit Protection
Fraud Insurance: A telemarketing firm defrauded credit card holders by selling them "fraud insurance policies" to cover potential fraudulent charges against their credit cards. The charges were exorbitant, far exceeding a cardholder's liability (Monealegre 12-12-97).

◆ Credit Repair
Marketers deceive credit-impaired consumers by offering credit cleaning and a variety of restricted credit cards with the promise that these services can enhance someone's credit rating:

Credit Cleaning is a euphemism for altering credit histories so that borrowers can deceive lenders. Also known as "skin-shedding," this is an illegal practice (Staples Website). A second scheme involves promises of a new, clean credit history by means of "File Segregation." File Segregation is another term for identity fraud. The credit "repair" company encourages the debtor to apply for a new IRS Employee Identification Number and to use it to apply for new credit (FTC 6-97).

Restricted-use cards come in two varieties, those that are useable only in highly-limited mail-order catalogs, and those that require deposits:

- In one scheme, limited use credit cards are sold as premium credit cards—gold or platinum—but these do not turn out to be Visa or Master Cards. Instead they are off-brand cards usable only in over-priced catalogs (FTC 10-96b).
- Deposit-contingent cards may well be Visa or Mastercards, but these offers can also be fronts for advanced fee schemes that required the victim to make high-fee calls to a toll-charging "900" number or ploys to entice consumers into non-ordinary cards that were valid only for use with limited-merchandise, over-priced catalog shopping (CreditComm Services Website).
- The card-offers can be advanced fee schemes to defraud consumers by requiring a "processing fee" which invariably never leads to the issuance of a card (USPIS Winter 91/92).

Prevention: Use credit-counseling services, not credit repair services, to improve credit worthiness. Do not pay for credit repair. Do not subscribe to limited-use credit card services. Do not use any credit card service that involves applying for credit under another name or using another number identification.

EDUCATION FRAUD

There are two primary categories of education fraud, degree fraud and funding fraud. CHAPTER FIVE'S Education Section covers the latter. Degree fraud is largely the production of "diploma mills," non-accredited institutions that sell degrees without requiring class attendance and without imposing standards. One scheme grossed more than $1 million per month from unwitting students and from those who want to inflate their resumes (Lord 9-28-98).

Prevention: Check the accreditation of a school before enrolling. Schools should be recognized by the US Department of Education and listed on the Council on Higher Education Accreditation's Website. Ask professions in your field of choice if the school has a recognized program (Lord 9-28-98).

FRAUDULENT DEBT COLLECTION

The Federal Trade Commission regulates a number of fraudulent collection practices. The debt collection frauds generally involve collectors impersonating others, making false threats, or misrepresenting facts:

- Collectors illegally <u>pretend</u> : a. to be attorneys, b. to represent a government agency, c. to represent a credit bureau, or d. to be another person for the purposes of exaggerating their authority.
- Collectors inappropriately <u>threaten</u>: a. that they can seize, garnish, or attach wages without the actual authority to do so, or b. that the debtor committed a crime or may be arrested.
- Collectors <u>misrepresent</u>: a. the amount due as greater than the actual amount; b. that the papers sent to the debtor are legal documents when they are not; c. that the legal documents being sent to the debtor are not legal documents; or d. that a lawsuit will be filed when the collection agency actually has no intention to do so. Also, it is fraud for a collection agency to disseminate false information about a debtor (FTC Aug 1996).

Another scheme involves service companies that pretend to consolidate debt. In fact, some service companies simply collect the monthly payments from the victim, tack on a service charge, and pay off all of the existing creditors each month (Sifakis 1993).

FUNERAL AND BURIAL SERVICE FRAUD

The death business is prone to fraud because families are emotionally vulnerable when handling a death and because many people find it unseemly to haggle over prices on a solemn occasion. Fraud and questionable sales practices, occur throughout the death business: i. in planning, ii. at the time of death, and iii. and after burial.

Pre-death Fraud

There are at least three questionable or fraudulent pre-death, funeral-business practices:

- The embezzlement of funds by individuals who sold "pre-needed" funeral services. One defendant "allegedly forged notices of cancellation of [funeral service] contracts and converted proceeds from the refund checks for his personal use (USPIS Winter 91/92)."

- The sale of <u>Prepaid Funeral Plans</u> that contain hidden fees or conceal no-refund policies (Horn 3-23-98)

- The mortuary practice of paying off nurses (or others) who are in a position to refer bodies back to the mortuary (Horn 3-23-98). In some cases, the nurses may send the body off to the mortuary without the prior consent of the deceased's family.

Fraud in Funerals

Although it is not fraud in the strictest sense, some mortuaries take advantage of grieving families by price-gauging. In some cases, the funeral charges are hundreds of percent above the mortuary costs (Horn 3-23-98). One example involves the sale of specialty caskets; ultra-expensive sealed caskets which actually promote the decay of bodies. These caskets have been sold without disclosing that they promote rapid body decay (Horn 3-23-98).

Those who target the bereaved are called Death Vultures or Hearse Chasers. They "...victimize the bereaved by selling them flowers, bibles, and other things, falsely claiming that they had been recently ordered or purchased by the deceased. Sometimes they render bills when nothing is owed. Sometimes they claim partial funeral payment has been made by the deceased and endeavor to collect the fictitious balance (City of Denver 9-84)."

Cemetery Fraud

There are a variety of schemes used to defraud a deceased's survivors:

- Multiple Burials: Cemeteries may defraud families by selling the same plot a number of times or by interning more that one person in the same plot.
- Domestic cemeteries may defraud families by failing to use maintenance fees to maintain graves.
- Grave Plot Fraud: Perpetrators send letters to the survivors of overseas, deceased relatives, asking for maintenance fees. With these frauds, the fees are never used for the deceased's grave (Nash 1976).

Prevention: Do not buy pre-paid funeral plans. Discuss death arrangements with the dying well in advance of death. Have a close friend competitively shop for funeral options so that family members are not distressed by the choices. Have someone check grave sites to be certain services paid-for and services rendered.

HOME REPAIR FRAUD

Exterior Frauds
Telemarketing (see section below) and home repair fraud pose the biggest fraud-risk to working-class families who otherwise lack investments and self-owned businesses. This is true because career criminals target assets; and the working class's biggest single investment is their home, so the best way to target them is through the phone, or at their home. Don Wright's 1996 book *SCAM!* is an excellent exposé of home-repair fraud and the organized-crime families that thrive on it. The families, called Travelers, are migratory clans of English, Scottish and Irish ancestry. Traveler's rely on: victims' trusting natures, their interest in a bargain, their lack of knowledge of competitive contract bids, and their ignorance of home repair techniques. The Traveler's favorite frauds involve applying substandard liquids for exterior home repairs: (1) roofs, (2) siding, and (3) driveways. For example, Travelers may coat roofs and driveways with sealant diluted with gasoline. Soon after the

application, the sealant quickly evaporates in the sun or washes off during the next rain. In some cases, the sealant is a mixture of used crankcase oil with other non-sealant. The siding of a house may be painted with latex paint that is highly diluted with water—so diluted that it washes off in the first rain after the application.

One other common exterior home-repair fraud relies on the victim's ignorance of lightening rods. In this fraud, the Traveler makes faulty installations of lightening rods or makes some minimal repair to an existing rod. The faulty installations involve creating only one path for the lightening to go to the ground, rather than the required two paths. Alternatively, the Traveler installs an ineffective grounding rod. In both cases, the faulty installation may cause a home fire. Travelers are known to initiate their work by impersonating government or utility company inspectors while authoritatively insists on the lightening rod repairs or installations.

Aside from using substandard materials and completing faulty work, Travelers also unjustly enrich themselves in home repair by deceptive pricing tactics. They often entice the victim into the home repair by saying that the roof or driveway sealant is leftover from another job and this good fortune affords the customer a deep discount. Alternatively, the Traveler may explain that the labor is free, so the victim need only pay for the materials. In this case, the cost of the materials is not disclosed until after they are applied, and, when the price is revealed, the victims are billed for materials at extraordinary mark-ups. In one fraud, the victim saw a price of $25 on a large bucket of paint, but after the paint was applied and the victim learned of the charges, she saw that small print on the bucket indicated a $25 price for a gallon of paint, not for the entire 5 gallon bucket, so the paint ended up costing $125 per bucket.

Interior Frauds
The most common home interior frauds are: (1) plumbing, (2) termites, and (3) remodeling. Wright (1996) describes a number of

plumbing frauds employed by Travelers. Typically, the criminal insinuates himself into a target's home. Once inside, he pours water around a pipe or down a basement crack to make it look like there is a pipe or tank leak. After getting permission to fix it, he may either just wipe-up the water to dry the area, or he may complete un-needed excavations, ultimately overcharging for the on-the-spot repair.

In termite fraud, perpetrators are known to bring in their own termites, creating an instant infestation. Alternatively, they may bring in a pre-eaten piece of wood, show it to the homeowner, and claim the wood came from the home. The instant treatment will often use cheap or ineffective chemicals, and the bill will be inflated in comparison to customary charges.

Remodeling fraud typically involves using substandard or used materials, and presenting them as first-rate, or starting a small project and enticing the victim into allowing ever-expanding renovations. In the substandard material case, the victim is defrauded when he or she pays retail prices for second-rate materials. In the "expanding project" scheme, the victim is defrauded because the contractor only discloses the cost of the remodeling after it is completed. Much to the homeowner's surprise, upon completion, the Traveler demands a highly inflated fee.

Miscellaneous Home-Related Frauds

◆ Ransacking

The movie *Diehard* depicts a building siege where business employees and a building are held hostage by an organized-crime band. Most people who see the movie sit back and enjoy it as violent fantasy, but in fact home sieges do occur. Sieges are the overtaking and sometime ransacking of premises by force. A ransacking may also occur purely by deception. In the non-violent version, criminals enter a home by deception, and while one keeps the victim entertained, one or more peruse the home for valuables and steal them. The criminals use some kind of pretext to effect the theft. If a house is for sale, the criminals may pretend to be prospective buyers. Alternatively, the criminals may pretend to be government officials, like federal agents or inspectors, to gain entry. In one case, Travelers pretended to conduct energy audits for public utilities (Wright 1996).

In the violent version of the ransacking (the siege), once the criminals gain entry to the premises by pretext, they tie the victim up and then go on to stealing the belongings.

◆ Home-Repair Contract Fraud
Licensed contractors may also defraud homeowners. Upon signing, a contractor can defraud the property owner by falsely certifying: (1) that he/she is licensed; (2) that he/she carries liability insurance; (3) and/or that he/she carries worker's compensation insurance. After signing a contract, anyone of a variety of service providers may ask for an advanced-fee and then fail to deliver the service or a refund of the fee.

There are a number of schemes that take place after the contracting is complete:

- At the close of a fixed-price contract the contractor confronts the homeowner with addition fees. The contractor may say that some costs were outside of the agreed-to contract, that he/she made a mistake in bidding the fixed-price contract, or that cost over-runs force him/her to make additional charges.
- After a contractor is done-and-gone, he/she may fraudulently attach liens to the property, hoping to extract further payments.
- Another post-completion fraud is called lien sharking: A scheme whereby unscrupulous general contractors fail to pay their subcontractors, thereby inducing the sub to file liens against a building owner. The desperate subcontractors may then sell the liens to a consolidator who colors the title to the

property. To clear the title, the property owner is forced to pay-off the liens, in effect paying for the work a second time (Sifakis 1993).

◆ Inspector Fraud

In a somewhat complex scheme, criminals may impersonate government officials, pretending to conduct on-the-spot inspections. During the forced inspections, the impersonators identify made-up building deficiencies, and then they refer the repairs to their accomplices who pretend to make repairs (Sifakis 1993). This also sounds like a good opportunity for the perpetrators to overcharge for work that is actually completed.

Prevention: Avoid snap decisions when considering home repairs. Secure multiple-competitive bids to safeguard against price gauging. Conduct adequate background investigations of potential contractors, including licensing, bonding, and insurance checks. Do not allow work to begin until you have a written contract. At the end of the project, don't pay until everything is complete and check to see that subcontractors are paid. Do not let purported inspectors in until you confirm their identity with their parent organization; the city county, water company, etc..

IDENTITY FRAUD

Introduction

Identity fraud is the limited or wholesale theft of another person's identity for the purpose of: (1) hiding one's own identity; (2) fraudulently using another person's credit; or (3) obtaining benefits entitled to another person. This may be the focus crime of the late 1990s. The idea of someone else using your identity gives people the creeps and intimates the movie *The Invasion of The Body Snatchers*.

A criminal may assume another person's entire identity or just portions of it. Those who assume an entire identity are most likely fugitives from the law or from their past. The most common wholesale identity theft is the assumption of a dead person's identity. To do this, a criminal may search archived obituaries to find the name of a child who died at about the same time that the identity thief was born (USPIS Winter/Spring 1995). With the name in hand, the identity thief may apply for a birth certificate in the deceased's name. Armed with a birth certificate, the identity thief can start to build a dossier with driver's licenses, Social Security cards, and any number of other identifications. With an identity in hand, the thief can then start to build a credit history.

Someone who is just interested in credit and/or asset theft may only be concerned with obtaining identifiers such as a person's Social Security number, birth date, driver's license number and address history. Armed with these, and or credit card numbers, the identity (really credit) thief can begin to apply for credit cards or bank loans in the name of the victim (see above Credit Card Fraud Section for more).

While obtaining another person's dossier may seem difficult to the naïve and non-criminal, in fact it is easy:

- A career criminal solicited resumes from attorneys in order to falsely assume their identities to obtain bank loans and credit cards (USPIS Fall 1990).
- Criminals may a obtain credit profile reports by abusing legitimate means to gain an individual's credit card number or loan history: Employees of a New Jersey auto dealership used the dealer's access to credit reports to fraudulently obtain 2,500 credit files which they used to make more than $800,000 in fraudulent charges (Davis Aug 1995).

- Identity thieves impersonate IRS Agents to obtain Social Security numbers or credit card numbers for credit fraud schemes (AARP January-February 1995).
- A couple stole individuals' identities by finding their names and background in *Who's Who in America.* The couple used the information to obtain credit in the victim's names (Davis July 1998).
- Law enforcement officials, private investigators, or those with criminal intent are routinely successful in using "pretexts" to call banks and other repositories of confidential information. The pretext has the caller pretend to be the customer or someone with a need-to-know. Very often, bank clerks, or other information custodians fail to screen the callers and simply provide the personal information to the caller.

The most clever credit thieves avoid detection by always paying the minimum balance on a loan so that there are never loan calls or foreclosures. In acting like a financial leech, the identity thief avoids the brush-off.

Prevention: Conduct annual reviews of your credit reports from all three national credit bureaus. Instruct all three credit bureaus to place your credit files on "fraud alert" so that anyone requesting your credit history or credit in your name cannot get what they want without your approval. Fraud alert will prevent you from obtaining instant credit, but it will also safeguard you against most identity thefts. Make sure that you are receiving all expected mail, and if not, file a lost mail report with the Postal Service.

MOTOR VEHICLES FRAUD

Introduction
Consumer-fraud related to vehicles effects nearly all Americans 16 years and older. One survey found that complaints about used car sales comprised 80% of all consumer complaints (Hahn 1996). A

1970s study found that 53% of vehicle repairs are unnecessary (Baker and Templin 1995) and a third study, conducted in California, found evidence of fraud in 40% of repairs (Gellene 7-12-94). Fraud occurs in new vehicle sales, in used vehicle sales, in towing, and in repairs. Vehicle sales and services are prime areas for fraud because they are complex and few consumers have the ability to understand the vehicle sales and service industry in detail. Consequently, most people are left to the mercy of the sales and service providers.

The best countermeasure against fraud in the vehicle industry is a knowledge of the common fraudulent schemes, and specific knowledge about the vehicle being bought or serviced.

New Vehicle Sales
Strictly speaking, there does not appear to be a lot of fraud at the retail, new-vehicles-sales level. Vehicle manufacturers are major corporations with well-established programs designed to deter out-and-out fraud.

Many buyers find dealer hard-sell practices to be unethical, bordering on the fraudulent. Even so, they are seldom illegal. The buying game focuses on the customer's desire to know the dealer's cost and the dealer's desire to conceal that cost. Presumably, the buyer wants to know the true cost so that he or she can avoid paying an excessive profit to the dealer. On the face of it, consumers do not treat any other retailer this way, so it is curious that this attitude is so prevalent. For example, when a consumer enters a grocery, few concern themselves with the markup on food.

In any case, the struggle between the customer and the dealer to reveal the base cost has inspired a pat system for new car sales. The salesman acts like the "good cop," saying that he wants to get the buyer the best price. He says that unfortunately, the sales manager has the ultimate approval over the deal, so very quickly, the buyer is in a small office with the sales manager who plays "bad cop." Although the whole process may feel unseemly to the buyer, unless the dealership pulls a bait and switch, sells or offers to sell a specific vehicle at a specific price, and then delivers a different vehicle, substitutes parts, or lies about future service or warranty services, there is little room for fraud in new car sales.

Here are five examples of new car dealers involved in fraud:

- A dealer defrauded the manufacturer by falsely claiming to have installed accessories. The phantom accessories inflated the vehicle values and, thereby, the loanable amount (Burks 8-16-95).
- GM defrauded buyers by switching 5000 engines and misrepresenting the nature of the switches (*NYT* 5-4-78).
- A Grand Jury indicted a dealer for forging and coercing customer signatures that were used to defraud automakers of promotional rebates (Rechtin 8-93).
- Car dealers may delay, or fail to complete warranty work because the work is paid for at wholesale rates by vehicle manufacturers, which is less profitable than retail work (Sifakis 1993).
- In a "bait and switch" dealers may sell the vehicle with inducements like free oil changes for life or other maintenance, but later fail to deliver the services or disclose that they forgot to mention minor costs not covered by the "free" service. Typically, the dealers waive service fees and then charge inflated prices for parts.
- Car Import Fraud: Federal Agents "confirmed that a car dealer had illegally inspected numerous foreign vehicles, made false statements concerning their compliance with DOT/EPA safety and emissions standards, and forged pertinent documents and import records (DOT OIG 4-1-91 thru 9-30-91)."

Prevention: The best safeguard against fraud by new dealers is to research the intended vehicle prior to shopping for it. *Consumer Reports,* available at most libraries, is the most frequently consulted source for new vehicle buyers. Once you strike a deal, get all of the terms in writing, including and especially any offers for free services. For exotic imports, check their safety and pollution certifications with the US DOT and EPA.

If the post mortem reveals some misrepresentation, contact the Federal Trade Commission, and/or the state consumer affairs or state dealer licensing offices.

Used-Vehicle Sales
Used-vehicle dealers are the poster boys of unethical sales practices. Both licensed dealers and private parties may commit used-vehicle sales fraud:

- Unlicensed individuals may defraud buyers when they run unlicensed dealerships out of their homes, and thereby avoid the scrutiny of government regulation.
- Sellers may roll back odometers to make vehicle appear to have less than their actual mileage.
- Unlicensed dealers may convey fraudulent or altered motor vehicle titles, or they may even sell stolen vehicles (Wright 1996).
- Sellers may falsify the bill of sale to indicate that the sales price is much lower than the actual price. In collusion with the buyer, this scheme defrauds states of sales tax revenues, but it also exposes the unwitting buyer to criminal prosecution. In some cases, depending on the state, the buyer may allow the seller to handle the sales tax payment, leaving the seller the chance to underpay it without the knowledge of the buyer (Wright 1996).
- Thieves steal a car, strip it, abandon the shell, and then buy a shell at auction, reconstructing it for resale with a salvaged title (*Car & Driver* 7-94). Alternatively, a seller may salvage a ve-

hicle, present a clean title, and fail to disclose the reconstruction (*ABC* 6-30-95).

- Travelers, organized crime families, have actually "laundered" titles: In Alabama pre-1974 vehicles do not require titles. The Travelers would buy or steal a used vehicle, declare to the state that it is pre-1974 so that they could obtain a new, clean title. This scheme allows the perpetrator to pay no to little sales tax, and then sell it to an unwitting buyer who assumes he or she has a clear title (Wright 1996).

- Unlicensed dealers and private parties, more than dealers, are likely to manipulate a buyer by passing off a fictitious story: "My grandmother owned it, and she only drove to church once a week for five years." The fictitious story is used to deflect any pointed scrutiny of the vehicle at hand.

- Used-vehicle dealers may practice off-lot selling, also known as curbstoning (*ABC* 6-30-95). Dealers curbstone by sending lot-vehicles home with salesmen who then try to sell the vehicles in their time off (City of Denver September 1984). The salesmen may also take out newspaper advertisements, pretending to be an individual owner. In many states, this practice is illegal. The idea of curbstoning is to tap into a market that might otherwise be inaccessible to a dealer—those who prefer not to buy from dealers.

- Criminals can pretended to be brokers. In this scheme two telemarketers promised car sellers to provide a listing which would match them to buyers. None of the sellers were matched to buyers (USPIS Summer 1991).

- Dealers can violate state-specific "lemon laws" that prevent them from concealing known or historic defects.

Prevention: Buyers safeguard themselves by: (1) using references to look up the value of a chosen vehicle; (2) screening dealerships by consulting state consumer fraud divisions and the local Better Business Bureau; (3) conducting a title search on the intended vehicle through the state motor vehicle office; and (4) taking a possible purchase to an independent mechanic for an inspection prior to buying.

If a buyer discovers something very bad about the vehicle that was not disclosed, he or she may be able to return it under the "buyer's remorse" laws that are in force for dealerships in many states. If bought from a private party, after-the-fact discoveries may be beyond quick recompense.

Towing

Vehicle towing services can take advantage of the stranded. Truck drivers may refuse to attempt simple diagnoses that could result in a roadside repair. For example, in older vehicles, the ignition wires pop off from time to time, and a 30-second glance at the distributor could reveal the cause of a stalled vehicle. (Older Jeeps are notorious for this problem.) Another 30 seconds would have the wire back in the distributor cap, but if a wrecker driver refuses to take a quick look, he or she could have inflated a $20 service charge into a much higher towing charge.

Some wrecker drivers pretend to be insurance or American Auto Association-approved. This may cause the stranded vehicle owner to pay towing charges when they otherwise would have been covered by AAA or other insurance (*WSJ* 7-28-95). Alternatively, wreckers may be fronts for car-theft rings. One source estimated that 10% of tow trucks belong to thieves (*Car & Driver* 7-94).

The fraudulent tow service could well be a front-for and a lead-into repair fraud.

Prevention: Having towing insurance through a vehicle insurer or a travel club like AAA and using a cell phone to contact the insurer when in need is the best measure to safeguard against towing fraud.

Vehicle Repairs

As stated above, one survey found that more than 50% of vehicle repairs are unneeded. Since most vehicle owners are positively ignorant about vehicle mechanics, and there are thousands of parts and corresponding potential vehicle problems, the opportunities for fraud are manifold. Vehicle-repair fraud falls into five major categories: (1) estimate fraud, (2) diagnosis fraud, (3) unnecessary repairs, (4) product substitution, and (5) denied warranties.

◆ Estimate Fraud occurs when mechanics inflate the projected cost of materials or the time required to complete a job. In this class of repair fraud, the work is necessary, but the projected charges are inflated. There are three prevalent types of estimate fraud: a. double booking, b. bill round-ups, and c. body shop exaggeration.

- Double booking involves charging book rates for two or more, inter-related services instead of charging the true time. For example, if a mechanic did a brake job one day, and the same vehicle later came back for a brake caliper change, there naturally would be two, one hour charges. However, if both jobs are done at the same time, the actual time should be 1.5 hours. In double booking, the dishonest mechanic charges the time as though both jobs were completed independently.
- In round-up billing the mechanic rounds fractional hourly charges up to their nearest hour. So instead of charging 1.25 hours to change a fuel pump, the mechanic rounds the labor bill to 2 hours (Autosistance/Top Rip Off's Website).
- Body Shop Exaggeration occurs when a body shop: (1) simply falsifies estimates, (2) manipulates car components or body features, or (3) replaces undamaged parts with defective parts to make the insurance adjuster or vehicle owner think there is more extensive damage to a car than really exists. The shop owner then undoes the manipulation, at no or little cost, and charges the insurance company or vehicle owner as though he completed a repair (*CBS* 8-24-95).

Prevention: After a problem has been diagnosed, and before agreeing to a repair, call a couple of shops for multiple repair bids. Also, call parts dealers to compare the proposed parts costs. If the mechanic who completed the diagnosis did not have a repair and parts estimate consistent with other shops, take the vehicle to a competing shop.

◆ Diagnosis Fraud occurs when mechanics employ an un-due number or inappropriate type of diagnostic test in order to inflate their bills. Alternatively, the mechanic may simply misuse an instrument in order deceive a customer about the problem's source. In this class of fraud, the material or service sold is un-necessary because of deliberate misrepresentation of testing or examination results. Here are some areas prone to diagnosis fraud in: a. battery, b. transmission, c. front-end rebuilding, d. oil change, and e. strut sales:

- Mechanics may insists on unnecessary battery replacement after mis-using voltmeters to deceive the car owner that there is no battery charge; or they may state that the car won't start because the battery is dead, when in fact, the battery cables simply need to be adjusted or replaced, a much cheaper repair.
- In a scheme to sell a new or rebuilt transmission, a mechanic may deceive a customer by pointing to metal tailing that came from a transmission pan and saying that their presence necessitates a transmission rebuild. Similarly, a mechanic may falsely attribute sluggish performance to the need for a new transmission.
- Mechanics may offer a flawed explanation of unusual tire wear to induce the vehicle owner to pay for an unnecessary front-end job.
- The mechanic may falsely report the condition or amount of oil in the crankcase to induce the owner into an unnecessary oil change (Sikafis 1993).

- A tire salesman may falsely explain an abnormal tire-wear pattern as resulting from worn struts or shock absorbers in order to induce the customer to buy new struts and/or shock absorbers.

Prevention: Visually inspect the parts that the mechanic said need replacing. Consult the repair manual for your specific vehicle to see if the diagnosis is consistent with the diagnosis given by the mechanic. Call other shops for comparable bids on the parts and repair.

◆ Unnecessary Repairs: There are three classes of un-necessary repairs: a. repairs required because the mechanic disabled or destroyed something; b. overkill repairs, and c. phantom repairs.

Here are three examples of mechanic-induced repairs: i. the deliberate puncturing of tires by dealers to induce the victim to buy a new tire (Sikafis 1993); ii. adding baking soda to the top of the battery to cause foaming and thereby suggest the battery has failed (Sikafis 1993); and iii. adding contaminants to a gas tank to cause bad engine performance. Obviously, the numbers of ways a criminal mechanic can sabotage a car are limitless.

Overkill repairs occur when mechanics correctly identify a problem, but exaggerate the type and/or extent of repairs that are needed. a. Tune-ups, b. accelerated maintenance, c. un-needed preventive maintenance, and d. excessive engine repairs are common targets for overkill repairs. Here are examples of overkill repairs:

- Mechanics overkill tune-ups when one or two simple adjustments would have solved the problem (Mark March 1995).
- Mechanics incur un-needed costs to the customer when they ignore the factory maintenance schedule, accelerate it, and cause more frequent maintenance.

- Mechanics may call for maintenance that is not routinely undertaken until something stops working—like carburetor rebuilding.
- A mechanic may be guilty of excessive engine repair when a head gasket replacement unjustifiably turns into an entire engine overhaul (Sikafis 1993).

The hook for overkill repairs often come from newspaper coupons or other advertising that offers discounted oil changes with free inspections. The shop may use the inspections to push accelerated maintenance schedules or other unwarranted repairs (Autosistance/Top Rip Off's Website).

Phantom repairs are "...work done on parts that don't need attention, can't be serviced, or may not even exist." Examples include adjusting valves that automatically adjust, lubricating chassis that have sealed lubrication points, pretending to adjust timing belts on cars that are automatically adjusted, and charging to clean nonexistent chokes on fuel-injected engines (Kaye and Newman 1992). Phantom repairs may be charged in conjunction with needed repairs to conceal the fraud. For example, a mechanic may say he replaced the alternator when he really only replaced the alternator belt (Mark March 1995).

Prevention: Visually inspect the parts that the mechanic said need replacing. Consult the repair manual for your specific vehicle to see if the diagnosis is consistent with the diagnosis given by the mechanic. Call other shops for comparable bids on the parts and repair.

◆ Product Substitution: There are three common types of product substitutions:
- Installing generic parts and charging for the brand-name item (Autosistance/Top Rip Off's Website).

- Installing used parts and then charging the customer for new ones (*CBS* 8-24-95). Substituting used spark plugs for new is an often-cited example.
- Putting used lubricants in the engine or gear boxes and charging for new lubricants (Sikafis 1993).

Prevention: Prior to letting the mechanic begin his or her work, instruct the shop to supply the removed parts to you upon completion. Put this term on the repair contract. Once you receive the part, if you are suspicious, take the part to a part dealer to see if it indeed came off of your vehicle. If the service involved changing fluids, check the fluids to see if they appear to be clean.

◆ Denied Warranties: Some dealers charge for repairs that should be covered under the warranty (Mark 1995).

Prevention: Review the warranty prior to closing on the vehicle purchase. Keep the warranty in a safe place and consult it before requesting warranty work. If the dealer refuses to honor the warranty, consult the Federal Trade Commission and the manufacturer Zone Representative.

RETAILING FRAUD

Introduction
Retail sales occur whenever a business sells goods to the ultimate consumer. The bulk of retailing fraud has little effect on the individual consumer. Instead, petty frauds have enormous effects when seen on the scale of whole market places. This is the "salami slice" effect where many tiny cuts are imperceptible, but all told, they add up.

In addition to this section, the Handbook addresses retail fraud in a number of other sections including the Gem and Mineral and Auto sections. The Federal Trade Commission and state consumer protection agencies have primary jurisdiction over retail fraud, but their actions generally protect the entire marketplace rather than serving any one individual, so if you want to avoid loss, be careful at the outset of a purchase rather than hoping for recourse after it.

There are five common retail fraud schemes: i. faulty pricing, ii. product substitution, iii. weights and measurements fraud, iv. misrepresented sales, and v. charging for goods not delivered.

Faulty Pricing

Retailers engage in faulty prices when they mis-charge or price-gouge. One common mis-charging scheme involves multiple items for a fixed price such as three six packs of soda for $5. While the consumer assumes that one six pack would cost $1.66, and if asked, that is what the retailer would say, grocery scanners often read the price for a single six pack as $2.50 rather than the discounted bulk price.

Product Substitution

Product substitution comes in three varieties: i. substituting one brand for another, ii. counterfeiting brands, and iii. using inferior ingredients in a product where the contents list high-grade ingredients.

◆ An example of brand substitution includes substituting generic drugs for brand-name drugs. Pharmacists may do this in a scheme to overcharge insurance companies. If the consumer does not check the prescription, he or she will never realize the substitution.

◆ In a counterfeiting example someone bottled inferior shampoo in counterfeit bottles, defrauding leading consumer product manufacturer Proctor and Gamble. The fraud failed when someone noticed that the bottles lacked the triangular recycling symbol which appears in the legitimate product (Sicherman 9-4-95). Counterfeit products are often found in fourth-tier retailers, flea markets, and at third world open markets.

◆ In a well-known <u>inferior product</u> case, some juice manufacturers diluted fruit juices by using low-cost liquids to reduce their costs. The scheme defrauded consumers who thought that they were buying "all natural" drinks (Patel 5-21-94).

The clothing retail business is another sector susceptible to product substitution. In this case, consumers are at a disadvantage because they cannot readily discern one brand from another.

Weights and Measurements Fraud
The fuel distribution business historically had the most widespread occurrence of weights and measurement fraud. Typically, these involve under-dispensing gasoline and diesel. The food industry also has potential for weight and measurements fraud:

- Butcher Shop Fraud: Sikafis (1993) describes a number of schemes used by dishonest butchers to short weigh meat sales by: (1) putting a finger on the scale while weighing; (2) having a forceful fan blow down on the scale; (3) putting tacks (or other weights) on the scale pan to bias the weighing; and (4) tying lead to the shrouded heads of fowl and then cutting the heads off after weighing.
- Freezer Meat Fraud: Some butchers entice buyers with wholesale prices, but these prices may be deceptive, because they represent "hanging weight"—meat weighing in before cutting and trimming where cutting and trimming may represent as much as 50% of the total. The meat sales may also be deceptive in that some of the cuts are not graded (City of Denver September 1984).

Misrepresented Sales
Retailers use a variety of schemes to misrepresent sales: i. bait and switch sales tactics, ii. pretending to have a sale, and iii. deceptive descriptions:

◆Bait and Switch
- "A type of misleading advertising technique. A potential customer is lured by an apparently outstanding bargain ("the bait") but the would-be seller discourages (and sometimes refuses to make) the sale and instead promotes another, higher priced, product ("the switch") (NASAA 1986)."

◆Pretend Sales
- Going-Out-Of-Business Sales: These sales may deceive buyers into thinking bargains are available because the business will close, when in fact the enterprise continually renews itself. This deception can also be used for "Inventory Liquidations (City of Denver September 1984)."
- Retail Sale Misrepresentation: Retailers commonly raise competitive prices, then mark them down in a "sale" to entice consumers into believing there are bargains (NBC 9-12-95).
- Stuffed Flat: Unscrupulous furniture sellers may use an apartment as a front for selling used or low-quality furniture to unwitting buyers. The store continually replenishes the apartment, deceiving buyers into thinking they are getting a good deal by buying furniture at distressed prices (Sifakis 1993).
- Overstock Sale Fraud: A somewhat complex scheme where the perpetrator claims to have excess items like TVs for sale at deep discounts. The criminal insists the items must be paid for in cash. After receiving the cash, the criminal instructs the buyer to go meet a nearby truck where the items are supposed to be waiting. When the victims arrives at the truck, he or she find that there is no merchandise and the truck has nothing to do with the perpetrator who just ran away and committed the fraud (Wright 1996).

◆<u>Deceptive Descriptions</u>
- Battery Free Flashlight: Sikafis (1993) reports consumers have been mislead by offers of battery-free flashlights, when in fact, they are buying flashlights where the batteries cannot be replaced.
- Used Goods Fraud: Rent-to-own stores (and presumably other types of stores) have sold used goods as new (Hudson Fall 1993).
- Stock Splitting: A fraudulent retailing practice in which items normally sold together are spilt. In addition to the customary charge for the core item, there is an additional charge for the contrived accessory. For example, a retailer may take a cord out of a phone set, and then charge extra for the essential cord (NBC 8-2-95).

Goods and Services Not Rendered
Retailers can engage in gross fraud by making promises that they do not keep. For example, a retailer may issue a "rain check" for sold-out items, but never deliver the item. Alternatively:

- A sale may be facilitated with a money-back guarantee that is not honored.
- Sifakis (1993) describes a retail checkout stand scheme. In this scenario, the checker charges the customer for an unwanted, unreceived item. If questioned about the charge, the checker points to a prominently pre-placed item, and offers an apology: "I thought you wanted to buy that item."
- Markets may defraud customers by charging for items which they did not buy (Sifakis 1993).

Prevention: Shop competitively. Pay with credit cards so that mischarges are reversible. Review all charges at the time of payment, rather than at a later time. Read content labels and manufacturer tags. Report suspected violations to the Federal Trade Commission.

SUBPRIME LENDING FRAUD

While banks, savings and loans, investment houses and other main-stream financial service businesses serve those with favorable credit ratings, a host of fringe lending institutions and businesses (most with non-lending profiles) lend to those with less than stellar credit histories: Second mortgage lenders, used car dealers, rent-to-own stores, furniture stores, pawn brokers, and trade schools all engage in subprime lending. These businesses lend money to poor-risk borrowers at exorbitant rates, disguising the extreme interest rates with a number of tacked-on fees such as loan insurance and hidden finance charges. These lending practices generally skirt usury laws and are not criminally fraudulent (Hudson Fall 1993). Subprime lending fringes on fraud when the lender fails to adequately reveal all of the terms of loans, most specifically, the charged interest rate. Subprime lending prospers because of the desperation and ignorance of the borrower. What subprime borrowers fail to focus on is that by borrowing at double digit interest rates, over a period of four to six years, they end up paying twice the asking price for items. For example, if a borrower purchases a $1,000 couch on terms of zero down, 18% interest, over 4 four years, the ultimate cost to the borrower would be $2,000.

One example of the added fees that allow subprime lenders to skirt usury laws is credit insurance, a high-premium policy that is inappropriate for small denomination loans (Hudson Fall 1993).

Prevention: When borrowing any money, ask the lender to write down the total cost of the loan. Make sure the lender itemizes all fees. If you do not understand any of the fees, ask for a written explanation, or make a note of the verbal explanation. Take the loan terms to a bank to determine if they can provide a more favorable loan.

TELECOMMUNICATIONS FRAUD

Introduction

There are three business lines in telecommunications: hard-line telephone service, wireless phone service, and Internet service. Service theft by fraud primarily effects hard-line telephone services and wireless services, and the telecommunications companies are the principal victims of this fraud. In contrast, the other major class of telecommunications fraud, marketing fraud, involves use of the service, not theft of it, and it targets consumers, not service providers.

Various sources give a sense of the magnitude of annual telecommunications fraud losses: $40 billion lost in telemarketing fraud annually (Marvin Sept 1994), $7 billion lost in 1994 to telephone card fraud (Acello 11-3-98), $1 billion lost to annual hard line phone service theft (Sprint no date), and $1 billion lost annually in cellular phone service theft (McFadden 6-26-95).

Telecommunications is a fraud free-for-all—criminals defraud companies, consumers defraud companies, criminals defraud consumers, and companies defraud consumers. Got all that straight? If not, it should all become clear after you read this Section.

Theft of Phone Services

The theft of phone services is, strictly speaking, not always fraud. This is so because telecommunication service thefts do not always involve deception, and without deception, non-consensual taking, gaining, or receiving, the misdeed is simply theft. Even so, the various media lump all telecommunications theft as fraud, so that is the way it is treated here.

There are three principal categories of service theft: hard-line theft, access card theft, and wireless theft. Beyond these two categories, there are also a few outliers in telecomm service fraud: contract fraud and internal fraud. Contract fraud, otherwise addressed in CHAPTER SEVEN - Operations Fraud, involves telecommunications contractors who defraud the telecomm companies. Internal fraud involves telecommunications employees who embezzle phone services.

Without advertising it, the telecommunications industry has taken the position that when a criminal violates company security to steal phone time, the company covers the customer's losses. However, when a customer is beguiled into fraud, by incurring inflated phone service charges, the customer pays. Under this arrangement, the telecommunications companies cover the bulk of fraudulent charges, and men seeking phone-sex cover the rest.

Unauthorized Hard-line Phone Access
Criminals use a variety of schemes designed to steal fixed-line service from telecommunications companies, business, and individuals:

◆ Defrauding Telecomm Companies
- Conspiring criminals can make collect calls from one pay phone booth to another, thereby defrauding the phone company of revenues. In this scheme, two individuals agree to be at separate pay phones at the same time. One makes a collect call to the other at a separate phone. When the receiving conspirator accepts the call, the phone company ends up paying for it. This is especially costly when the criminals make international calls.
- Some phone service thieves, called phone phreaks, specialize in stealing phone access by using a whistle or other device to mimic the tone used by phone company switching systems, thereby tricking the system into granting free phone service. One such device is called a Blue Box. It duplicates phone switching equipment's' 2600-hertz tone so the user can receive long distance phone service without paying for them (Judson 1994).

◆ Defrauding Business Phone Systems

▪ Telephony criminals can gain access to a company's long-distance service by entering toll-free voice-mail systems, thereby obtaining free long distance service (Thrasher July 1994).

▪ PBX Fraud: "A PBX is a small computer that operates as an automatic switchboard for any location that has multiple telephone lines, which includes most companies of more than half a dozen or so employees." Computer hackers break into the system, making unauthorized phone calls which are billed against the victim company (*Information Plus* 1994).

▪ Outside Telephone Line Fraud: Hotel guests have been known to ask for long distance phone access without proving a credit card. These criminals claim that they lost their credit cards and ask for a waiver. Ultimately, they do not pay the toll charges (Western 11-19-95).

◆ Defrauding Private Parties

▪ In a sneaky scheme, criminals, pretending to be phone company technicians, ask phone customers to press "90#" to "help" the technician in diagnostic testing. The "90#" phone sequence gives the criminal access to the service owner's long distance account (Ann Landers 6-23-98).

▪ Criminals obtain free long distance calls by asking the phone company operator to charge the calls to a random third party. If a person at the third party, a home or business, agrees to the charges, their phone account will be billed for someone else's call (Sprint, No date).

Prevention: It's mostly up to the phone companies. As for businesses and individuals, they can avoid being drawn into schemes by: a. confirming a repair person actually works for the service provider; b. reviewing all monthly phone charges; c. reporting any questionable call charges to the phone company; and d. not giving permission for third party phone charges.

Travel Card Access Fraud

As most people know, phone companies issue access codes to their customers to allow account use away from the base phone. If a thief gains the number, he or she can charge calls to someone else's account. Some of the schemes to steal the numbers involve deception:

- Shoulder surfers are individuals who steal telephone credit card numbers by glancing over card user's shoulders to see the card or the code as it is punched into a touch tone phone. Shoulder surfing commonly occurs at airports. The stolen numbers may be used for the thief's exclusive use or to be resold to others. Surfers may work in teams to distract the card user, or they may use binoculars to sight the card from a distance.
- Organized criminals have learned to tap into payphones to steal long distance card numbers. After tapping into the pay phones, the criminal would activate the phone's conference call option. The thief then waits until after an unsuspecting victim enters his or her long distance account number and leaves the pay phone. The criminal would then return to the phone, tape record the dial tone, and then decode it using a dial-number recorder, a device that translates tones to their corresponding numbers (Blair 7-4-98).
- Perpetrators impersonate phone company representatives and ask the victim, over the phone, for his calling card number. Once they gain the number, they sell it or use it themselves to charge long distance calls to the victim's account (Sprint no date)
- Quick-footed phone thieves can take advantage of pay phone call-redial features to reclaim a calling card number. The perpetrator hurries in after a phone card user leaves and presses the redial feature to recapture the calling card code. By tape re-

cording the tone sequence and later decoding, or writing down the numbers on the phone's visual display, the thief can gain the access code.

Prevention: a. Safeguard your remote access number. b. Before leaving a phone booth, tap in random numbers to clear your access numbers from the phone's memory. c. Review all of your monthly toll charges and report questionable ones to the phone company.

Cellular Phone Service Theft
Thieves use electronic devices to steal a cellular phone's unique electronic serial numbers and mobile identification numbers in order to make clones. The clones are then sold at a discount so that an illegal user can charge calls against legitimate cellular phone accounts. During 1994 the losses amounted to nearly $1 billion, almost 7% of the industry's revenue (McFadden 6-26-95). Indicators that you may be a victim of cellular phone fraud are: You receive many wrong number calls; you are frequently, suddenly disconnected; your line has chronic static; you are billed for calls which you didn't make (Conners and Nelson Aug 1995).

Prevention: Review your monthly cell phone bill and report all questionable charges to the cell phone company.

Contract Fraud
Criminals contract to receive wholesale, prepaid cards from telecom companies, then renege on their agreement to pay for them. In response, the telecom provider cancels the cards, denying the retail card-buyer the phone service (*U.S. News & World Report* 7-29-96).

Prevention: To protect yourself, consider buying from the best-established card vendors.

Internal Fraud
Telephone company employees can potentially steal significant quantities of phone service by taking extremely small segments of phone service, like one second, from very many customers. Infinitesimally small thefts, taken by the thousands or millions add up to major theft. These frauds are completed by using computers. The technique is called "salami slicing (Judson 1994)."

Conceivably, a phone company employee could also steal phone service by setting up fictitious accounts or by using phones to make unauthorized toll calls.

Prevention: This is up to the telecomm companies.

Telecommunications Marketing Fraud
There are two major classes of telecommunications marketing fraud: deceptive sales of telecommunications services and deceptive sales of non-telecommunications goods and services, also known as telemarketing fraud. The deceptive sales of telecommunications services mostly effects hard-line phone services. In contrast, the deceptive sales of non-telecommunications goods and services involves using the phones and Internet to commit a nearly infinite variety of frauds. In effect, goods and services marketing frauds use the telecomm companies as shills.

Fraudulent Telecommunication Services Sales
The National Fraud Information Center ranks two phone fraud schemes, slamming and cramming, as the top consumer fraud complaints. Slamming is the unauthorized switching of phone service providers. You have been slammed when a different monthly phone bill comes your way. Cramming is the addition of unwanted or unexplained service charges to a customer's bill (*USA Today* 7-6-98). The FTC names six cramming schemes (FTC 5-98a):

- Contest entry forms that lead to fraudulent charges on a phone bill. The forms ask for your phone billing information, then the criminal uses it to incur charges against your phone account.
- Direct mail sweepstakes that charge your phone bill for unrendered services.
- Instant calling cards that are issued against your phone account. Anyone in your house can pickup your phone, request a card, and then have charges placed against your phone account.
- Dating service calls where the charges are exorbitant and not disclosed prior to billing.
- International calls, often to adult talk-lines, where the charges are exorbitant and not disclosed prior to billing.
- "Free minutes" or 900-free-fixed calls to dating, psychic, or adult entertainment lines that say they will not charge for waiting time, but do.

Prevention: a. Do not give out confidential, financial, or account information to someone you don't know; b. Do not make 900 prefix phone calls prior to knowing the charges; c. Do not make international, 011 calls prior to checking the tolls; d. Do not allow 900 or 011 prefix parties to put you on hold for extended periods; and e. Check your monthly phone bill and call your phone company to identify any calls that you don't recognize or charges that do not seem right.

Interestingly, after slamming and cramming, the third most complained about consumer fraud is the advanced-fee schemes (victim's payment for goods or services that are not rendered), a class of fraud often committed by phone or Internet. So really, the phone and Internet are top spots for consumer fraud.

Fraudulent Use of Telecommunications To Sell Other Goods And Services - AKA Telemarketing Fraud
In the Nineteenth Century confidence game (see CHAPTER ONE - Introduction) men plied their trade by self-taught, beguiling acting

and persuasion. Their ingenuousness and endearing presence allowed them to take from the unwitting. As America grew from a place of county fairs and door-to-door salesmen to a telecomm society, Twentieth Century telecomm fraud took the place of the in-person confidence man.

At earnings of $40 billion a year, telemarketing fraud is a substantial industry. Telemarketing frauds "...have approached an estimated nine out of 10 Americans." A disproportionate number of the victims are 65 years in age or older (Marvin Sept 1994). Telemarketer frauds have taken on Dickensian proportions with a profile of sly criminals who work out of dank-sounding boiler rooms, repeatedly defraud the same elderly victims. *Time Magazine* outlined systematic Elderscams that targets seniors—a "fronter" makes the first attempt to entice the victim—a "closer" finalizes the fraudulent sale—and the "reloader" makes further attempts to defraud the victim (Church 9-25-97).

There are eight common telemarketing schemes, and an infinite number of variations: (1) Advanced-fee Scheme, (2) Cost-inflated sales, (3) Sweepstakes-Contest Scheme, (4), Fraud Recovery, (5) Securities Fraud By Phone, (6) Bank Fraud by Phone (7) Charity Fraud, and (8) Credit Cards Offers. Although most telemarketing schemes transfer unchanged to the Internet medium, a few uniquely emphasize the Internet.

◆ Advanced-fee Schemes are one of the most common frauds perpetrated against consumers and businesses. Perpetrators, often telemarketers, falsely promise gifts, prizes, discount items or services will be delivered after the purchaser pays a small "advanced-fee." In this scheme, the promised good or service is never delivered. Often the perpetrator covers his tracks by using shell companies or "bust-out" tactics that have him leaving town before anyone can catch up to him.

The number of advanced-fees schemes is limitless—any conceivable product or service can be touted to encourage a victim to make an advanced payment. Here are some common ones:

- Amusement Games: Perpetrators sold games that either did not work or did not provide the promised returns. The criminals: "Used toll-free 800 numbers advertised in newspapers—promised high income with little effort—participated in business opportunity fairs—[and then] changed corporate names to thwart regulators (Lynch 7-19-95)."
- Auditor Fee Scam: Telemarketers may entice victims into advanced-fee fraud by saying the victim won a prize which is receivable after he pays a small auditor's fee (USPIS Winter/Spring 1995).
- Automated Teller Machine Fraud: Criminals defraud investors by advertising ATMs for investment on the Internet, in newspapers, and at trade shows (Choquette 7-6-98).
- Free Trip Scam: Telemarketers may entice victims with free trip offers, only to lead the consumer into paying for a variety of additional fees (FTC Website).
- Record Sale Scam: "Mr. Blues" defrauded rare recordings investors in an "Advanced-fee Scheme" where they, "falsely promised record collectors around the globe that he would sell them rare recordings...none of the victims who sent him money ever received an album (USPIS Winter/Spring 1995)."
- Referral Journal Fraud: A telemarketer defrauded professionals by collecting a fee from them to place their name and service in a journal directed to AFL/CIO union members. The perpetrator never placed the ads, defrauding victims of $35,000 (USPIS Summer/Fall 1992).

Prevention: a. Do not buy items from companies that first contact you. Only buy from providers that you find and that have certifiable reputations. b. Check the backgrounds of telemarketers by calling the Better Business Bureau and the Federal Trade Commission. c. Pay by credit card to allow for cancellation of the payment. Never pay by cash, cashier's check, or personal check.

◆ <u>Cost-Inflated Sales</u>. Telemarketers can defraud consumers by pretending to sell discounted goods and services. Instead, the consumer receives low-quality or way over-priced goods and services. Examples include water purifiers, vitamins, and vacations (FTC 4-94).

◆ <u>Sweepstakes-Contest Schemes</u>. Although fraudulent sweepstakes and contests are more commonly pushed by direct mail advertising, they also occur over the phone. These schemes involve promises that the would-be victim has already won a prize—claimed simply by mailing-in an advanced-fee. After payment, the winner will soon receive his or her cash, car, vacation, or other prize. Note well, as a matter of law, no fee can be required to enter a sweepstakes. Here are some of the common ones:

- Sweepstakes Duty Fraud: Telemarketers impersonate Canadian customs officials in a phone fraud. The impersonators inform the victim that he or she won a sweepstakes, but before they collect they must pay a 7% duty on the prize. The criminals instruct the victims to send a cashier's check to a Canadian address (Seniors Site Website).
- 900 Phone Calls: Some sweepstakes or contests illegally require participants to call toll-charging 900- prefixed numbers (*Consumer Reports* Jan 1998).
- Limited Winner Sweepstakes only award prizes if the holders of a limited number of numbers claim their prize. In these cases, the sweepstakes may never award any prizes because winners do not routinely present themselves (*Consumer Reports* Jan 1998).
- Cash Prize Fraud: Telemarketing criminals have promised cash prizes over the phone. They claim to need the winner's bank account number to pay the prize. Once they have the account

number, the criminal prints a counterfeit demand draft using the victim's bank account number. From the printer, it is off to the bank to cash the counterfeit check (OCC Website 1997).

Prevention: a. Don't pay to enter a sweepstakes. b. Don't call 900 prefixed numbers when responding to sweepstakes or prize offer. c. Don't pay any sweepstakes processing fees. Protect others, refer all suspicious sweepstakes and contests to the FTC.

◆ Fraud Recovery. Talk about mean spirited. Career telemarketers re-target the same victims over and over again. The re-targeting occurs in "recovery rooms" (OCC Website 1997) that specialize in hitting up former victims. They even sell "mooch lists" (lists with victim-names) to other telemarketers so that different scams can be played on the previously victimized. The classic recoveries play on the victim's previous losses by promising, for a fee, to work toward getting the old losses back (USPIS Winter/Spring 1995).

Prevention: Report any telemarketing losses to local law enforcement, the State Attorney General, and the Federal Trade Commission and hang up on anyone who offers to recover money from previous losses.

◆ Securities Fraud by phone can entail any of the fraudulent securities schemes detailed in the book's Investment Chapter. Typical securities schemes are: a. selling unregistered securities, b. misrepresenting the nature of the investment, c. misrepresenting the risk in the investment, d. misrepresenting the return on the investment, e. converting investor funds to the broker or another person's use.

Prevention: See CHAPTER SIX'S Securities Section.
◆ Unauthorized Debits: Telemarketers may obtain a victim's bank account number under the pretext of selling magazine subscriptions, only to use the account to overcharge (Sullivan July 1996).

Prevention: Never give out bank account numbers over the phone or to businesses that you do not know well.

◆ CHAPTER EIGHT, Public Interest Fraud, details <u>Charity Fraud</u>. Typical telemarketing charity frauds ask the victim: to buy tickets for benefit shows, to make a donation for handicapped children, to purchase light bulbs, or to buy other household items at inflated prices (FTC 2-94). Another common charity scheme is called "badge-related" fraud. In this scheme, the telemarketer pretends that he or she are representing a police- or fireman-related organization that is seeking donations.

Prevention: See the Book's Charity Section.

◆ Credit Card Fraud is discussed in the Credit Card Section of this chapter.

Internet Scams

By and large, all of the telephone scams lend themselves to direct transfer to the Internet. In addition, there are some scams unique to the Internet medium:

- Internet Registration Theft: One company registered the Internet name of a preexisting company and then tried to sell the name back to the existing business (*Denver Post* 4-18-98).
- Internet Service Fraud: Internet providers can defraud customers with charges for services that were advertised as free, or for failing to deliver services (NFIC Website 1997).
- Trojan Horse: An internet-downloaded computer program that allowed criminals to use the victims telephone lines to charge long distance telephone calls to the victim's phone account. One victim was enticed into downloading the program, and, once in place, the program disconnected the victim's regular internet service provider and connected it to a different pro-

vider (NFIC Website 1997). This is the Internet equivalent to phone service slamming.

Prevention: The same safeguards listed to avoid phone fraud apply to Internet fraud.

TRAVEL FRAUD

Introduction

The American Society of Travel Agents (ASTA) estimates annual US losses to travel fraud in the $5 billion dollar range (Busch March-April 1995). The travel industry is a magnet for fraud because everyone wants a travel bargain, making people predisposed to jump onto something that sounds to good to true. Also, since the service is sold in a location different from where it is rendered, the fraud often becomes apparent after the travel starts, leaving a time buffer between the perpetrator of the fraud and the victim.

There are two basic travel frauds: i. advanced-fee - failure to render schemes, and ii. hidden cost schemes.

Advanced-fee-Unrendered Service Travel Schemes come in three closely-related varieties: i. impostor travel agents sell worthless vouchers and quickly disappear; ii. impostor travel agents defraud airlines and customers by selling valid tickets, never paying the airline for the tickets, and disappearing; and iii. criminals legitimately register as travel agents, sell counterfeit tickets for travel well in the future, and disappear before the date of the scheduled travel (Busch March-April 1995 and *Consumer's Research* 12-94).

Hidden Cost Schemes start by offering free or discount travel as bait. But once hooked, the consumer finds additional fees that often make the trip more expensive than the identical retail travel package. Typical concealed costs include inflated hotel charges attached to free airline flights, club membership dues, companion air tickets at inflated prices, "peak season" premiums, or required meal plans (FTC Website and FTC 4-94).

Prevention: Pay for all travel arrangement with a credit card so that any services not rendered or mis-represented are contestable. Do not pay months in advance. Investigate any offers that appear too good to be true.

Leave no stone unturned.
Heraclidae (quoted by Aristophenes <u>in</u> *The Wasps*).

CHAPTER FOUR - FINANCIAL FRAUD

INTRODUCTION
In its broadest usage, finance covers anything to do with money, investments and debt. A Fraud Handbook could very easily be built around two divisions, finance and contracts, but this would poorly serve the primary targets of this Handbook—individuals. Instead of taking arm around the finance universe, the Finance Chapter narrowly focuses on financial fraud not covered elsewhere in the book—two financial business lines and one financial protocol. The business lines are banking and insurance and the protocol is the financial statement.

For fraud in other divisions of finance see:

- CHAPTER THREE, covering credit card, debt collecting, sub-prime-lending and identity theft.
- CHAPTERS FIVE AND SEVEN for fraud in government finance. These Chapters cover fraud in government programs, contracts, and employee fraud.
- CHAPTER SIX covers Real Estate Lending Fraud and Securities Fraud.

BANKING AND LENDING FRAUD

Introduction
Banking and lending are part of the financial service industries. Banking and lending institutions receive funds from depositors (customers) to: safeguard, invest, disburse, manage, and lend. A great variety of businesses engage in banking-like operations:

banks, savings and loans, brokerage houses, mortgage lenders, insurers, private placement partnerships, and sub-prime lenders. Some financial institutions, like banks and savings and loans, engage in the complete spectrum of banking operations. A rash of changes during the 1990s in regulatory laws have allowed financial institutions to blur the lines between banks, brokerage houses, savings and loans, and insurers, so that increasingly, all of these types of financial businesses offer the full spectrum of products, and in many cases, also invest money for their own accounts. Other businesses, like many discount brokerage houses, focus on providing financial services, avoiding investing on their own behalf.

Like all large, government-regulated industries, the banking and lending industry has four types of fraud exposure: i. internal fraud, ii. external or customer fraud, iii. fraud the business commits against the regulators or against its insurers, and iv. fraud that the lenders (or their impersonators) commit against their customers.

Internal fraud is nearly equivalent to embezzlement, because insider fraud generally involves people who convert, to themselves or others, assets entrusted to them. For internal fraud, see CHAPTER SEVEN'S Employee, Customer, and Competitor section which discusses embezzlements. One internal fraud not addressed elsewhere is trust-account fraud. By example: A trust company executive defrauded two heiresses of nearly $1.8 million by losses in real estate tax shelters and through self-serving interests. "Brown lost nearly all of the trust funds belonging to the ...sisters, but continued mailing statements incorrectly representing the state of the trust accounts (USPIS Fall 1991)."

The Handbook covers fraud against regulators in CHAPTER SIX's Real Estate section. For sub-prime lending fraud and fraud against consumers see their respective sections in CHAPTER THREE - Consumer Fraud Chapter.

After relegating most financial fraud to other sections of the Handbook, only a portion of external fraud and fraud against consumers remain for discussion here. External fraud consists of two major categories, lending fraud and check fraud. CHAPTER SIX'S Real Estate Section explores external fraud, but that discussion is limited to real estate lending, so the following essay discusses lending fraud on non-real estate assets.

Non-Real Estate Lending Fraud

Lending institutions make a variety of loans: i. commercial loans, ii. personal loans, iii. factoring loans, and iv. unsecured personal loans. Lending fraud can occur: i. at the outset, in the loan application, ii. during the life of the loan, and iii. at the time of repayment.

♦ Application Fraud
Fraud in commercial and personal loan applications commonly involves falsifying background information, such as: a. business history, b. lending history, c. credit history, and d. financial statement falsification. This Chapter's Finance Statement Section covers the latter fraud.

♦ Concurrent Loan Fraud primarily involves falsifying financial statements. Financial statements may be falsified by failing to update them or by making overt false statements in them. One example would be in construction lending. A contractor could defraud a lender by saying it met a milestone, such as completing construction on a foundation, when in fact it had not. If the milestone marked qualification for an infusion of cash, falsifying it would be concurrent-loan fraud.

A different example of fraud concurrent with a loan involves factoring, the buying of outstanding accounts receivable. Factoring may be fraudulent when a business sells its accounts receivable without informing the merchant bank that carries the charges. "...As a result, the bank is left exposed when the merchant is unable to cover the chargebacks that occur in subsequent months (USPIS Fall 1991)." A second factoring fraud involves inflated factoring: Businesses may inflate their accounts receivable to receive larger premiums from factoring companies that buy the debts (Jesilow, Pontell, and Geis 1993).

Prevention: Lenders must, and do, conduct independent audits.

♦ Repayment Fraud

Commercial loan fraud, at the time of repayments, can involve both financial statement fraud and bankruptcy fraud. See the Financial Statement Section below for an explanation of those issues. Here are some examples of bankruptcy fraud:

- Some individuals have engaged in liberal "pre-petition" shopping sprees, hoping to skirt bankruptcy laws. These shopping sprees take advantage of the fact that only debts of $500 or more, for luxury goods or services, are deemed fraudulent in bankruptcies (Topolnicki and MacDonald Aug. 1993).
- Bust-out Schemes: "This is a scheme whereby a business and a good credit record is established, then extremely large orders of the business' product are purchased on credit. Once the large inventories are received, the goods are shipped "out the back door" to associates and the suppliers are left "holding the empty bag." Often records are destroyed, fires set and robberies are faked in an effort to hide or disguise what actually took place. The business files bankruptcy and the crime is complete (FBI 1989)."
- Multiple Bankruptcy Filings: Debtors may dodge paying their creditors by repeatedly filing for bankruptcy, thereby sticking credit cards and other businesses with unpaid bills (Topolnicki and MacDonald Aug. 1993).

Prevention: Lenders need to contractually prescribe allowable costs and conduct progress audits.

Check Fraud

Check fraud effects banks and their customers. Historically, if there is no gross negligence on the customer's part, the banks cover the losses from check fraud. However, late 1990s changes in banking laws require both the account holder and the bank to negotiate a settlement, so the customer is no longer held harmless. There were about 529,000 cases of check fraud in 1995 (Overstreet 5-9-97). In 1997 check frauds amounted to about $10 billion (Dow Jones Newswire Website 9-16-98). No matter if banks absorb the direct cost of individual check frauds, you can bet the consumer ultimately pays with higher bank fees.

There are four major classes of check fraud: i. check kiting, ii. counterfeit checks, iii. altered checks, and iv. stop payment fraud.

♦ <u>Check Kiting</u> "...exploits the float in the banking system, the day or so lag between the time you deposit a check in your bank and the time the check clears the bank it was written on...If the swindlers write fast enough and get their timing right, they can keep the cycle going for a while before the banks realize that one of them is short $50,000 (Smith 7-10-95)." There are four common check-kiting schemes:

▪ New Account Fraud: There are two common schemes: (1) "A criminal opens a new account using false information and incorrect addresses and telephone numbers. After conducting some small transactions or otherwise gaining information on the bank's procedures...[check posting, ATM transactions and identification requirements] the criminal deposits bogus or stolen checks into the account and [then] makes substantial withdrawals before the bank realizes it has been victimized." (2) "A criminal opens a corporate account using a fictitious company name and soon deposits a large amount in counterfeit checks into the account. After inflating the account with counterfeit checks over a short period, the criminal then asks the bank to prepare cashier's checks for a large proportion of the account balance (OCC Website)."

- Closed Account Fraud: Criminals can use checks drawn on closed accounts to make deposits into new accounts. If the float time between when the check clears exceeds that amount of time needed to cash a bad check, and the bad checks is in excess of the funds available in the current account, the criminal will be successful in cashing the bad check. This scheme often relies on criminals finding discarded checks from closed accounts. One variation of the scheme is the use of automatic teller machines to make the bad-check deposits (OCC Website).

- Fast Check Scheme: A simple scheme to steal checks, forge the endorsement, and utter the checks (USPIS Winter 1990-91).

- Unauthorized Use of Bank Account Float: Criminals can kite interest-free loans by trading bank drafts between various accounts to make it appear that an account has a larger than actual balance. In this case, the criminal gets an interest-free loan. If the kiter loses money that was borrowed, he or she may be unable to repay the loan because it had been predicated on an inflated account balance.

Prevention: Banks must closely monitor float times on clearing checks and investigate suspicious checks.

♦ Counterfeit Checks cause estimated annual losses in the $615 million per year range (Overstreet 5-9-97). Although not the predominant check fraud, counterfeiting is emerging as the fastest growing and most troublesome of all the check frauds (Overstreet 5-9-97). Here are some of the counterfeiting schemes:

- Refund Check Forgery: Criminals scan refund checks, or other corporate checks, into computers, print unauthorized checks, then write checks against the victim company's account (Information Plus 1994).

- Using false IDs and counterfeit payroll checks, organized crime members defraud banks. In some cases, the criminals call the targeted company's accounts receivable department, and using a pretext, obtain the company's bank account number (OCC Website). Overseas criminals may ask a business for help in transferring money into the US. The overseas criminals offer a large commission in exchange for the help, and, at the same time, ask for the company's bank account information for the transfer. The off shore-based criminals then use the account information to create counterfeit checks (OCC Website).

- Home Equity Coupon: A Denver man tried to cash a promotional coupon at a bank. The coupon was an advertising device, not a negotiable instrument (Lowe 6-13-98).

- Payroll Check Fraud: Criminals use desktop publishing programs on computers to make fake checks. The criminals create authentic looking checks by scanning company logos, obtaining the chief executive's signature from the annual report, and obtaining the account numbers by misrepresenting themselves, over the phone, to the company's accounts-receivable department (Holland 9-4-95).

- Demand Draft Fraud: "A demand draft resembles a personal check but carries no signature. In place of a signature, it has a notice that the account holder has given permission to have money withdrawn from his or her checking account to pay bills for goods and services." Criminals use a variety of techniques to obtain individual bank account numbers, and once they have them, they produce demand drafts to make withdrawals out of victim's accounts. The criminal may use fake telemarketing ploys, like promised prizes, or entice victims by promising credit cards once the victim supplies his or her bank account number (OCC Website). Alternatively, a criminal might trick a bank or business employee into giving up account numbers.

These tricks entail the criminal impersonating someone who had a legitimate right to the account information.

Prevention: Banks must develop and employ questioned-check and suspicious-check controls. Individuals, businesses and organizations should safeguard their bank account numbers and never give them out over the phone to persons who are not well known to the account holder.

♦ Altered Check Fraud

Criminals may alter checks in one of three ways to make unlawful gains: i. by altering the name on the payee line; ii. by altering the amount of the payment; and iii. by altering the payer's name. Unsophisticated alterations include erasures, strikeovers, or pen and ink corrections. More advanced alterations include bleaching or washing checks to allow for more believable alteration (USSS Website).

Prevention: Do not cash checks with alterations. See that the payee's name agrees with the identification of the person presenting the check. If someone presents a suspicious check, call the account holder named on the issuing check to verify the validity of the check. Study the payment amount to see if it is consistent with the check's purpose.

♦ Stop Payment Fraud

Victims of fraud, who paid by check, may attempt to stop payment, only to find that stop payments expire in six months and perpetrators may succeed in finding a bank that will cash the check after the stop payment expiration date (*Albuquerque Tribune* 8-13-95).

Prevention: Customers should try to get checks back that have stop payments on them. The issuer of the check may send a certified letter to the check recipient informing him or her that payment had been stopped and the payer has no intention of paying on the check.

FINANCIAL STATEMENT FRAUD

Introduction
Financial statements include any quantitative or descriptive information that has bearing on the financial status of a business, non-for-profit, individual, or government agency. "Statements that bank lenders use most often in making loans are the BALANCE SHEET (assets, liabilities, and net worth as of certain date); the INCOME STATEMENT summarizing income and expenses; and a corporation statement of retained earnings or partnership's statement of capital accounts (Fitch 1990)." Receiving a loan almost always depends upon a financial statement. Investment decisions such as choosing stocks, bonds, real estate, and private placements often rely on financial statements as well. Rating risks, like the risk inherent in bond issues, also rely heavily on financial statements. Finally, financial statements are critical tax collection and court adjudication tools—they serve in deciding tax payment schedules, divorce settlements, and bankruptcies. You can see that financial statements are at the heart of world lending, investing, government and personal finance.

To illustrate how financial statement fraud is instrumental in defrauding lenders, investors, tax authorities and courts, consider the following scenarios:

- To obtain a loan, a faltering car dealership falsifies its monthly revenues.
- To reduce a capital gain, a seller reduces a company's book value by inflating corporate liabilities. This discounted value is offset by the receipt of off-the-books kickbacks from the business buyer. Alternatively, a seller could enact the same scheme to defraud partners or shareholders. In this scenario, the part-

ners or shareholders net less in the legitimate sale, and the criminal nets more from the off-the-books payoff.

- A lawn mower manufacturer prematurely books earnings to inflate the appearance of its earnings growth .
- A party to a divorce hearing inflates his expenses in the hope that this would sway a judge into awarding a higher lump sum or maintenance payments.

With so much at stake, its easy to see why people falsify financial statements, and why detecting fraud in financial statements is critical to avoiding lending and securities fraud. Unfortunately, detecting fraud in financial statements is no mean feat. As a matter of fact, even the professionals in this field, auditors, seem to have a hard time detecting fraud (Greenberg 8-17-98).

There are three reasons why financial statement fraud often goes un-detected during audits: (1) Auditors are only required to make their reviews using GAAP (Generally Accepted Accounting Principal) criteria, and this allows auditors to limit the scope of their critique without creating a professional liability for themselves (Greenberg 8-17-98). (2) As contractors to the audited company, auditors have disincentives to either find wrongdoing or to make pointed comments. Often, if the audit is too critical, the auditor is fired (Greenberg 8-17-98). (3) Most frauds are found not by reviews of ledgers, but by an insider speaking up. The insider who has detailed knowledge of a business is in the best position to see wrongdoing, and he or she speaks up out of moral obligation or in response to work pressures.

In view of the failure of formal systems to find financial statement fraud, and absent a whistleblower, the average person or business is not going to be able to detect it. But understanding the systematics of financial statement fraud, as outlined below, and recognizing the importance of insiders in fraud busting gives the individual and the business-owner a hint of the difficulty of the task at hand.

No area of the borrowing-investing cycle is immune from financial statement fraud. It occurs throughout the borrowing-investing cycle, and in judicial determinations. Financial statement fraud occurs in: i. mis-stating financial background ii. mis-stating revenue, iii. mis-stating current expenses, iv. mis-represented assets and, v. mis-stating liabilities.

Mis-stated Financial Histories

An individual's, organization's, or business's financial history give financial statements the third dimension that better enables lender, investors, tax authorities, and courts the ability to judge the credit worthiness, investment potential, taxability, or potential to pay tort damages of an individual or of an organization. Financial statements may include falsification of any of the following information:

- The identity of the person or organization's principals.
- The individual's or organization's personal history.
- The entity's credit history.
- The entity's business track record.
- The entity's legal history.

An example of mis-stated financial history is the concealment of bankruptcies: Debtors may dodge paying their creditors by repeatedly filing for bankruptcy, thereby sticking credit cards and other businesses with unpaid bills (Topolnicki and MacDonald Aug. 1993).

Prevention: Conduct background and asset investigations.

Mis-stating Revenue
The amount, timing, and character of revenue all bear importantly on the financial status of an entity. Naturally, falsifying any one of these could deceive a lender, investor, tax authority, or court.

Revenue Amount and Timing Fraud
Altering the amount or timing of revenue payment can be achieved by: i. entering fictitious revenue, ii. deleting real revenue, iii. prematurely recording revenue (Schilit 1993), or iv. post-dating revenue (Schilit 1993).

There are two motivations to shift revenue to the present reporting period or to a future period. Shifting revenue to the present period may inflate the credit worthiness of a person or entity. Alternatively shifting revenue to a future reporting period may enhance the appearance of a company's earnings growth, and therefore its investment potential.

Three publicly traded companies illustrate the prevalence of mis-stated revenues:
- In 1998, critics charged the Sunbeam corporation with revenue shifting. Allegedly, the company orchestrated "early buy" and "bill and hold" sales promotions, aimed at getting retailers to purchase seasonal items such as barbecue grills early, with the agreement that they would be shipped when requested by the retailer (Brannigan 6-26-98). The effect of early sale-billings is to inflated present quarter earnings.
- Stock frauds like the 1980s ascent of ZZZZ Best (Sifakis 1993) and the 1997 climb of marketing company Cendant both relied on recording fictitious revenues. The Cendant debacle illustrates how sterling pedigrees are no shield against fraud—the company is New York Stock Exchange-listed and owns well-known brands like Ramada, Avis and Century 21 (Valdmanis 7-15-98).

Pending bankruptcy or divorce pose two other reasons to conceal revenue. In one case, by income shifting, a farmer tried to hide assets from a divorce proceeding to effect its outcome (Website, http://www. communinet.org/News_Journal/tax.html).

Prevention: Independent, competent audits.

Mis-Stated Revenue Character
Individuals or organizations may deceive by ignoring or manipulating accounting rules. One example is the failure to properly identify operating versus non-operating gains in a financial statement (Schilit 1993). A second example involves misrepresenting one-time gains as recurring gains (Schilit 1993).

Prevention: Audits.

Mis-stating Current Expenses
Individuals, businesses and organizations may mis-state their current expenses to make their current or future balance sheets look better (Schilit 1993). Mis-stating expenses, by falsely deleting, falsely creating, back-shifting, or forward-shifting, has nearly the same effect has mis-stating revenues. The primary difference is that mis-stated expenses do not effect gross revenue growth.

One example of expense concealment comes from bankruptcy cases: Some individuals have engaged in liberal "pre-petition" shopping sprees, hoping to skirt bankruptcy laws. These shopping sprees take advantage of the fact that only debts of $500 or more, for luxury goods or services, are deemed fraudulent in bankruptcies (Topolnicki and MacDonald Aug. 1993).

Prevention: Audits.

Mis-representing Assets

CHAPTER SIX'S Natural Resource Section describes what may be the most egregious of all cases of asset mis-representation, the Bre-X Mineral Company fraud of the 1990s. In this case, perpetrators claimed to have proven tens of millions of ounces of bankable gold in ore reserves at a remote Indonesian site. In fact, the site had no mineable reserves of ore.

Individuals or organization can mis-state their assets by: i. claiming fictitious assets, ii. failing to claim real assets, iii. inflating the value of assets, or iv. under-stating the value of assets.

Generally, people inflate assets to enhance their credit worthiness or, as in the Bre-X case, to artificially increase the investment appeal. In contrast, people diminish assets to reduce their exposure to a future liability.

The number of schemes available to manipulate assets is equal to the number of assets. Broadly, there are tangible and intangible assets. Tangible assets include buildings, machines, and raw materials. Intangibles include work forces, stocks, bonds, accounts receivable, and good will.

Here are a few examples of asset misrepresentation schemes:

- Asset Shifting: The fraudulent moving of assets onto or off of an organization's financial statement in order to enhance the appearance of the organization's financial health (Schilit 1993).
- Carrying Worthless Assets: The fraudulent failure to write-off non-performing assets as liabilities. This fraud is designed to artificially improve a business's balance sheet (Schilit 1993).
- Inflated Factoring: Businesses may inflate their accounts receivable to receive larger premiums from factoring companies that buy their debts (Jesilow, Pontell, and Geis 1993).

- Asset Manipulation Fraud: "A southern California contractor disclosed that the value of certain assets was improperly increased when the parent corporation acquired the company in a stock purchase transaction. While stepping-up certain assets, the corporation lowered the valuation of ...[other] assets for depreciation purposes and increased its values for other depreciable assets (DOD OIG 4-1-92 thru 9-30-92)."

- Asset Renting Fraud: An insurance company "rented" assets from others in order to deceive the State of Louisiana Department of Insurance into issuing an insurance license. "The indictment charges that the objectives of the conspiracy were to obtain a license...and to...continue in business although insolvent and unable to pay claims in a timely fashion (USPIS Winter 91/92)."

- Inflated Inventories: The fraudulent exaggeration of a business's inventories used to book extra sales or to receive undeserved loans or financing (Schilit 1993). In 1963, Allied Crude Vegetable Oil Refining CO defrauded investors of $175,000,000 in "The Great Salad Oil Swindle." This scheme involved representing water-filled tanks as oil filled and receiving investment financing based on the non-existent oil inventory (Schilit 1993).

Prevention: Audits with asset checks.

Mis-stating Liabilities

Individuals and organizations can mis-state their liabilities by: i. carrying fictitious liabilities, ii. not disclosing liabilities (Schilit 1993), iii. shifting liabilities forward, or iv. shifting liabilities backwards.

◆Fictitious Liabilities

An example of a fictitious liability would be a made-up lien against an asset, or a fraudulent debt. Someone who is subject to a pending judgment in a lawsuit might create fictitious liabilities to create the impression that they have a limited ability to pay damages.

◆Concealed Liabilities
A company that wanted to receive a loan might conceal liabilities. One possible concealment would be failing to disclose pollution at a property. Contamination is a liability because of regulation-mandated cleanup costs. Another hypothetical concealment involves making payoffs to a creditor to postpone the attachment of a lien.

◆Shifted Liabilities
Liabilities may be shifted forward by over-extending deprecations: A subtle tax and financial fraud where a business extends the write-off period of an asset over an unallowably long-time period in order to reduce the present-day cost of its liability. This fraud is designed to artificially improve a business's financial statement (Schilit 1993). Various forms of bribery could also be used to induce a creditor to temporarily re-schedule a debt.

Individuals or organizations may defraud by artificially shifting liabilities backwards for the same reasons that they create fictitious liabilities: To reduce payouts in: pending lawsuits, tax decisions, or other court actions. Shifting liabilities could also serve to fraudulently enhance the earnings growth of a business, and this might enhance the business's investment potential.

Prevention: Audits.

INSURANCE FRAUD

Introduction
The insurance industry estimates that as much as 30% of claims are fraudulent, costing an estimated $120 billion in 1995 (Bomer 1998). Between $30 billion and $100 billion of this fraud comes

from health care fraud (Bomer 1998). Somewhat unique, the insurance business is much like the government: Whereas the government creates a pool of funding from taxes, the insurance business creates a pool from premiums; whereas the government pays out entitlements to the eligible, the insurance companies pay out to policy holders and group beneficiaries. The only major difference between government and private insurance is that private insurers invest the money, known as float, during the time gap between when they take in premium money and when they pay it out as benefits. In contrast, the government just parks funds in bank accounts. As an aside, the absence of this investment step makes some people conclude that government retirement insurance, Social Security, is a Ponzi scheme, with no assurance to future beneficiaries.

Not only do insurers and government have similar finances, they also offer some of the same types of insurance: health, disability, worker's compensation and life insurance. And in the Medicare program, the US government manages the largest insurer in the world. Rather than splitting government insurance into the chapter on Government Fraud, the Handbook blends it here with the Insurance Chapter, because, frauds transcend the private insurance-government insurance boundary. Only the government insurance programs managed by the Social Security Administration are addressed in the Government Chapter.

So what makes government and insurance, and therefore, government-insurance, so rife with fraud? Well, by illustration, think about all of your household expenditures. On an on-going basis you pay for goods and services, and your knowledge of each good and service is detailed enough that you almost always know if you received the purchase and if the goods and services were of the promised quality. For example, if the heat did not work at your Chicago house during December, would you pay the gas bill? Of course not. If a fast-food hamburger came with a bun, lettuce, pickles, and mustard but no meat, would you pay for it? Of course not. But when someone says to their worker's compensation insurance carrier that their back pain prevents them from working, the insurance company has no direct knowledge of the worker's job, injury, or present condition, so each of these circumstances must be authenticated to make sure the claim is valid.

Imagine, then, that you are a large insurance company with thousands of claims to handle each day, and each claim contains a hundred items: You can begin to see the magnitude of the problem. Add to authenticating the bill the problem of authenticating the claimant— their identity and entitlement to benefits—and you can see that government insurance has nearly twice private insurance's authentication problem. To the criminal mind, insurance companies and government insurance look like unattended giant cookie jars—"TAKE SOME."

Perpetrators of Insurance Fraud

There are eight major lines of insurance: (1) health, (2) property, (3) liability, (4) worker's compensation, (5) vehicle, (6) life, (7) business and (7) disability. In addition, there are innumerable specialty lines of insurance. Some examples are garage keepers, liquor liability, and shipping. Companies like Lloyds of London will insure anything for a price, so you can see, insurance fraud could involve anything and any line of business. One interesting insurance niche is art insurance, covered in CHAPTER SIX, Investment fraud.

The forthcoming section is limited to fraud in the seven principal insurance lines. Consistent with the other sections of the Handbook, the structure of this section is by victim and perpetrator, rather than by business lines. This allows the reader to better identify the frauds than would an organization by insurance lines. For example, someone buying insurance could quickly thumb to the

Agent Fraud and Insurance Company Fraud sub-sections, and skip over the Customer Fraud sub-section.

Perpetrators of insurance fraud include customers (policyholders and group beneficiaries), individuals pretending to be customers (benefit converters), personal injury victims, property damage claimants, goods and services providers, insurance agents, insurance companies, and insurer employees.

Policyholder and Beneficiary Fraud occurs within three of the major operations of the insurance business: a. application, b. underwriting, and c. claims.

The insured may falsify any one of innumerable pieces of information required in application and for underwriting: a. medical histories, b. property ownership, c. pre-existing property damage, and d. claims history. They may also engage in conspiracies to defraud insurers.

Typical fraudulent claims include: a. exaggerating damages or injuries; b. making claims for fictitious or exaggerated injuries or diseases; c. making claims for items not owned or damaged; d. making claims for reimbursable services not rendered or goods not delivered; e. making exaggerated claims for reimbursable goods or services; f. making multiple claims for the same loss or injury; g. staging damage or injuries; and h. conspiring with non-policyholders or non-beneficiaries to make fraudulent claims. Here are some examples:

- Staged motor vehicle accidents, involving policyholders, medical providers, and adjusters, are one example of insurance fraud involving conspiracy (Adamson 2-24-98). Another type of staged damage is arson: The intentional destruction or damaging of property by means of fire.

- Medical Claim Conspiracy: A NASA "...contractor employee, the employee's spouse, and a friend engaged in a scheme to falsely bill costs to the health insurance program of the contractor..." by allowing the friend to submit about $26,000 in claims to the contractor employee's Federally-funded health insurance (NASA OIG 4-1-92 thru 9-30-92).
- Hospital Indemnity Policy Fraud: A couple defrauded insurance companies by purchasing indemnity policies (which pay for each day of hospitalization, even if the actual hospital expenses are paid by major medical policies) and then submitting fraudulent claims (USPIS Winter/Spring 1995).
- Hospital Invoices: A former hospital attorney submitted false invoices to his former employer, causing the hospital to pay for goods and services not provided (USPIS Spring 1990).

Benefit Conversion occurs when a policyholder or beneficiary allows a non-beneficiary to make a claim, or when a non-beneficiary falsely claims entitlement.

Since private insurance pools are much smaller than the US government's pools, private companies have a relatively small exposure to false identifications. In contrast, the US government has a very large pool of eligible beneficiaries. And by allowing Social Security Cards and driver's licenses to be used to apply for benefits, programs like Medicare or Medicaid are susceptible to those who submit altered or counterfeit identification.

Here are examples of conversion in life, property, and medical insurance policies:
- In Death Benefit Fraud a perpetrator buys a policy in the name of someone already dead, then produces the death certificate to make a claim. A grisly variation involved a doctor who killed a patient after he had the patient name the doctor as a beneficiary on a life insurance policy (Jesilow, Pontell, and Geis 1993).

- Property insurers look out for cases where an insured allows someone to falsely claim lost or damaged property on the insured's property or because of the insured's actions.
- Health insurance conversion occurs when an insured allows a friend to receive medication or treatment paid for by the insured's carrier.

Personal Injury Claimants are hurt by the actions, omissions, or property of another. When the claims are fictitious, exaggerated, or multiple, they may be fraudulent.

A typical fictitious injury could involve a staged accident where criminals steer an innocent vehicle owner into an accident, pretend to be injured, and then file a claim against the insured's insurer (Adamson 2-24-98). A staged slip-and-fall accident involves someone who pretends to be hurt during a fall at a business or at the residence of another person. After the fall, the faker files an insurance claim. A third type of false personal injury claim involves the genuinely injured who file multiple claims—a person injured in a slip and fall accident at a grocery who files both for reimbursement from their own insurer and from the grocery store's insurer.

A personal injury claim that results in permanent disability poses the greatest liability to insurers. If the claim is sustained, the insurer must make a large lump sum pay-off or lifetime payments to the personal injury claimant.

Personal Property Claimants may commit fraud by making claims for fictitious damage, by exaggerating claims, or by making multiple claims.

Just as frauds can make false claims for personal injuries, they can also stage accidents to make false claims for motor vehicle damage (*WSJ* 5-26-95). With faked vehicle damage, the criminal uses a ve-

hicle that has previous body damage, stages an accident with innocent parties or with co-conspirators, and files an insurance claim
for damage. In this case, the claim is not made against the claimant's policy. Instead, it is made against the unwitting victim's insurer.

Exaggerated claims also come from genuine theft and fire losses—
the insured falsely claims to have lost items or claims to have lost
items that he or she never had.

Disasters present one of the best opportunities for false and exaggerated property claims. Insurers try to quickly adjust claims to
avoid hardship, and some people take advantage of the expedited
response.

Prevention: Insurance companies have active anti-fraud programs,
so no comment is appropriate here.

Insurance Goods and Services Providers commit fraud when
they engage in staged accidents, submit bills for services not rendered, inflate bills, or use other deceptions to make claims. Health
care providers are notorious for fraudulent billings. Fraudulent
billing practices occur throughout the medical service cycle from
ambulance service, onto hospital care, and even in funeral services
(See Funeral Service Fraud in the CONSUMER CHAPTER).
Motor vehicle insurance is the other line of insurance with a high
susceptibility to fraudulent billings. Second to the staged accidents
described above, body shops are most likely to make the false
claims. Body shop fraud is described at the end of the following
section.

Health Provider Fraud
Ambulance services, doctors, nurses, clinics, hospitals, medical
device, and pharmaceutical manufacturers have all been charged
with making fraudulent insurance claims. The public appears to be

particularly fascinated by physicians committing fraud. Perhaps this is because physicians are held in high esteem and because they are highly compensated.

◆ Ambulance service fraud

Law enforcement agents catch <u>ambulance services</u> in a variety of schemes:

- Charging ambulance rates for transportation in vans and cars (FBI 1989).
- Charging for fictitious rides given to the dead or hospitalized (Jesilow, Pontell, and Geis 1993).
- Charging for the use of fully equipped ambulance, when less expensive transportation would have worked (DOD OIG 4-1-93 through 9-30-93).
- Charging for services not rendered during the ambulance ride such as oxygen administration (FBI 1994).
- Charging for inflated trip mileages: Ambulances usually charge one way, but may commit fraud by charging for both ways (FBI 1994).

Periodicals, Jesilow, Pontell, and Geis (1993) and law enforcement reports cite numerous examples of <u>doctor-clinic-hospital</u>-perpetrated frauds. These frauds fall into a number of broad categories: a. referral fraud, b. inflated billings, c. fictitious billings, d. billings for unauthorized, unnecessary or un-approved goods and services, e. billing for services converted to ineligible beneficiaries and providers, and f. non-competitive billing practices.

◆ Referral Fraud
Although it was a mainstay of medicine prior to the emergence of government-funded health insurance, the US government criminalized paying fees for referrals. Basically, the government views referral fees as kickbacks. The government maintains that referrals encourage price inflation by giving providers an incentive to refer

patients to the provider who charges the highest fee. Obviously, the person who makes a referral would expect a higher fee when referring a patient to a more expensive consultant (Jesilow, Pontell, and Geis 1993). Referral fees also encourage excessive care because the referring provider receives additional income from referrals without expending additional time or resources. Medical providers may pay referrals to attorneys in personal injury cases, to other doctors, to clinics, and, potentially to police or firefighters. The slang term for referring is "capping" (California Department of Insurance Website).

Unethical medical providers have used various schemes to conceal referrals. These schemes include joint ventures where doctors may conspire with medical service companies to set-up companies designed to receive referrals from the physicians. These joint ventures may circumvent US government anti-referral laws, and thereby can be a fraudulent scheme (HHS Website 12-19-94). Like other kickbacks, referral fees may be concealed as vacations or other goods or services.

◆ Fictitious Billings - Services Not Rendered
If you think about each of the goods and services a medical provider might provide, guessing the number to be over a million probably would not be an exaggeration. Obviously, a criminally-minded health-care provider could bill for any of these even though they were not delivered. Examples of fictitious billings are legion:

- A service provider forges a patient's signature on an authorization to obtain approval for a non-rendered service (Jesilow, Pontell, and Geis 1993).
- A provider takes a sample, such as urine or blood, from the patient, but fails to run the analysis. This is called Sink Test Fraud (FBI 1994).
- "A pharmacist continues billing an insurance company for maintenance prescriptions for a patient who has long since

moved into a nursing home that furnishes all her medications (Bomer 1998)."

- "A provider bills Medicare and an insurance company for services to a patient who has been dead for two years (Bomer 1998)."
- "Foreign doctors are bilking US insurance companies by submitting fake bills with the consent of the insured, or by inflating bills, according to the FBI..... In Pakistan and Bangladesh, huge bills have been submitted for emergency surgery allegedly performed on Americans (Blue Cross and Blue Shield Website 1998)."
- Home health-service providers have billed for visits that they never made (HHS OIG Website 12-19-94).

◆ Inflated Billings seem to be a favorite fraud in health care. Actually, smart procurement-fraud criminals prefer inflated billing to all other frauds because this type of fraud has a lot more wiggle room in a criminal defense than do fictitious billings. The wiggle room comes from the fact that when a perpetrator is questioned about inflated billings he can respond: a. the service was rendered; b. how can someone quibble over a few minutes one way or another; and c. these are mistakes. Inflated billings come in two categories, inflated goods and services charges and inflated time charges.

Here are six inflated goods and service schemes:

- Over-utilization of Medical Services: A scheme to always run the maximum number of test and procedures (Jesilow, Pontell, and Geis 1993).
- Non-credentialed Health Care: A scheme to render technician-level services charged as professional-level services. For instance, a doctor may pretend to have drawn a patient's blood, when, in fact, he had a phlebotomist do it. From the annals of government fraud, a psychiatrist, "... allowed noncredentialed employees to conduct psychiatric sessions [, he] then submitted

113

bills indicating he treated the patients (DOD OIG, 10-1-93 thru 3-31-93)."

- Upcoding: The fraudulent medical billing practice of "exaggerating the severity of a condition," in order to bill insurance companies for more money (Langreth 10-23-97).

- Prescription Splitting Scam: Health care providers have defrauded insurance companies and government insurance by splitting prescription into smaller orders to obtain extra dispensing fees (FBI 1994).

- Prescription Multiple Billing Fraud: Health care providers have defrauded insurance companies and government insurance by billing multiple times for the same prescription (FBI 1994).

- Prescription Manufacturer Kickbacks: Drug makers have given pharmacies incentives to persuade physicians to prescribe medicines. Manufacturers have also given doctors airline frequent flier mile credits for prescribing certain medicines. Another scheme involved drug manufacturers paying doctors to conduct research where the physicians are only required to keep minimal records. Each of these schemes may constitute violations of US government anti-kickback statutes (HHS Website 12-19-94).

- Foreshortened Medical Exams: One doctor was accused of charging Medicaid the full price for comprehensive exams, when he fact, he only rendered cursory ones (Jesilow, Pontell, and Geis 1993).

Here are two inflated-time-charge schemes: i. Concurrent Medical Billing: A scheme where a medical provider sees more than one patient at a time and then charges as though he or she saw each patient separately (*WSJ* 8-29-95); and ii. Up-billing: A scheme where time-based charged are always estimated to the next higher time charge. For example, a 31 minute examination may always be charged as a one hour examination (Langreth 10-23-97).

114

◆ <u>Unnecessary or Un-approved Goods and Services</u>, like inflated billings, come in great variety. One insidious aspect of unnecessary procedures is that these enhance the risk to patients. For example, no surgery comes without a mortality risk, so any un-needed surgery, in particular, places patient at un-due risk (Jesilow, Pontell, and Geis 1993):

- "A chiropractor continues treating an auto accident victim—and billing his insurance company—for years after treatment no longer is needed (Bomer 1998)."
- Blood Test Scheme: A doctor and co-conspirator were found guilty of submitting altered health care claims. They offered "free" blood tests at malls, later altering insurance claims, to meet the requirements for payment: medical necessity (USPIS Fall 1990).
- Medical Appearance Fee: One doctor was forced to make restitution after he charged Medicaid for attending, but not participating in surgeries (Jesilow, Pontell, and Geis 1993).
- A podiatrist ordered foot x-rays even when they were not needed (Jesilow, Pontell, and Geis 1993).
- Certificate of Medical Need Fraud: A federal grand jury indicted an owner and office manager of a medical products company for defrauding Medicare. "The companies allegedly used telemarketers to call elderly people across the country and urge them to accept medical equipment by stating they were entitled to it and that it was absolutely free....The companies mailed allegedly forged or altered "Certificates of Medical Necessity" to the respondents' doctors, implying that their patients had ordered the equipment from the companies....While the equipment was not charged to the elderly recipients, the Medicare program suffered millions of dollars in losses from the alleged fraud (USPIS Winter/Spring 1995)."
- Rolling Medical Labs: Two men over-billed health care providers of over $50 million during a ten year period. They used mobile diagnostic testing laboratories to order the "same bat-

tery of sophisticated and expensive tests for their patients, regardless of the patients' ages or medical conditions, and sometimes before the doctors had even examined them....Most of the patients were in normal physical health and had no need for the tests, and in fact had only come to the clinic to receive the "free" exams offered by telephone solicitors (USPIS Winter/Spring 1995)."

- Psychiatric Hospital Maximum Allowable Billing Scheme: Unscrupulous hospitals and health care professionals admit patients into psychiatric hospitals for treatment they do not need. The hospitals treat for the maximum payable days on an insurance policy, generally 28 days, then discharge the patient (FBI 1994).

- Medical Screening Fraud: "Operators of rolling labs advertise free medical testing and "screening" and often "screen" the patient for Medicare, Medicaid of [sic] private insurance companies. Once they obtain the information, they perform and bill for many unnecessary medical tests. It is common for these businessmen to perpetrate their frauds by paying kickbacks to the senior citizen home's manager or bill for phony services (FBI 1994)."

- Hospice Care Fraud: In violation of federal law, some hospice providers encourage ineligible people to apply for hospice care so that the provider can receive government payments (Franz 5-10-98).

- Sample Drug Sale: A doctor sold complementary drug samples and then billed Medicare for dispensing them (Nordenberg March-April 1998).

- Some medical providers dispensed expired drugs and then charged Medicare for them (Schatz 8-25-95).

- Home health care providers have billed both for visits to non-home-bound beneficiaries and for providing un-needed services to the homebound (HHS OIG Website 12-19-94).

- Medicare providers offer seniors grocery shopping or house-keeping services and then charge Medicare for these unallowable costs (HHS OIG Website 12-19-94).
- Some medical supply companies try to circumvent controls on billing for overhead supplies by charging the Medicare part B program for general supplies like tape, adhesive remover, skin creams, and syringes (HHS OIG Website 12-19-94).

A classic medical fraud is quackery: Falsely claiming health benefits for un-proved medications, devices, or treatments (Marvin Sept. 1994). Colloquially, a quack is an incompetent or impostor doctor. The number of un-approved procedures is nearly infinite, and here are a few:

- "An unlicensed person pretends to be a doctor, treats patients and collects from their insurance companies (Bomer 1998)."
- "A cancer clinic in Mexico collects $5,000 directly from a patient, then uses the name of a Texas clinic (which is usually only a mail drop) to bill his insurance company for a much larger amount (Bomer 1998)."
- Psychiatrist Sex Billing: Some psychiatrists charged Medicaid for time when they had sex with patients (Jesilow, Pontell, and Geis 1993).
- Wave Medical Therapy: "The treatment while relatively painless, is very expensive. A doctor simply "waves" his or her hand during routine rounds and later submits bills to the government program or insurance companies for $125 in individual therapy. Private insurers have provided allegations [*sic*] involving millions or dollars in fraudulent billings (FBI 1994)."
- Get-acquainted Coffees: One criminal enterprise charged US Medicare group therapy fees for hosting social hours (Website http://www.thonline.com/th/news/1996/th0514/stories/10738.htm).

- Unjustified Prescriptions: Some doctors write prescriptions without examining the patient—a fraudulent practice if billed to Medicare (Jesilow, Pontell, and Geis 1993).
- Health care providers may commit fraud by promising miracle, un-approved, treatments for serious diseases and then charging insurers for conventional, allowable treatments (Bomer 1998).

◆ Conversion to Ineligible Beneficiaries and Providers

Health care providers can defraud insurers by converting goods and services to people who are ineligible for benefits. Alternatively, doctors have been known to help their fallen brethren by converting charging eligibility to disbarred colleagues:

- Doctors may create Prescription Mills, businesses where they write prescriptions with the intent to feed street-supplies to drug dealers (FBI 1989).
- Doctors may knowingly or unknowingly write prescriptions for drugs that will be used by a non-beneficiary (Jesilow, Pontell, and Geis, 1993).
- Doctors may bill for services rendered by another health care provider who is not eligible to bill the insurer (Jesilow, Pontell, and Geis 1993).

In one egregious case, a clinic owner took advantage of special discounts on prescriptions. The owner resold the discounted prescriptions to wholesalers at significant mark-ups. The primary victims were insurers who underwrote the discount program (USPIS Summer 1998).

◆ Non-competitive Billings

Health care providers can engage in anti-competitive practices that conceal cost shifting or otherwise undercut competitors. Two examples involve waiving fees. In one case, the violator waives mandatory patient Medicare Part B copayments. This practice directly violates the law and serves to increase the number of marginal services provided (HHS Website 12-19-94). A second case involved a wealthy financier who paid large fines after "selling expensive blood tests to doctors at no great cost (or none) while charging Medicare a bundle... (MOJO WIE Website May 1995)."

Prevention: Anytime a claimant or beneficiary suspects health care fraud, he or she should report their suspicion to the government or private insurer that is providing the service.

Medical Device and Pharmaceutical Fraud

The US Food and Drug Administration (FDA) regulates the manufacturing, storage, handling, and use of medications, test kits and devices that have medical applications. The only exceptions are vitamins and other items sold without promised medical benefits. So if someone or some business touts a therapeutic benefit for a drug or device that has not been FDA-approved, the claim is fraudulent. If a business or individual makes an insurance claim for the un-approved device or medication, this is probably fraudulent too.

Examples of un-approved devices, medications, and test kits include:

- Useless AIDS and Hepatitis A test kits (NFIC Website Dec 1997).
- Repackaged Medical Devices: In a grisly deception, a perpetrator sold old, used pacemakers, some of which had originally been intended for animal use (MOJO WIE Website May 1995).
- Un-approved uses for approved medications.
- Un-approved drug manufacturing processes.
- Dietary supplements(Napier Mar 1994).
- Cellular therapy (Napier Mar 1994).
- Chaparral, an herb (Napier Mar 1994).
- Coenzyme Q-10, a synthetic enzyme touted as an aging retardant (Napier Mar 1994).

- Germanium, a natural element touted for Alzheimer's disease treatment (Napier Mar 1994).
- Gerovital-H3, a compound touted for a variety of illnesses (Napier Mar 1994).
- Herbal remedies (Napier Mar 1994).
- Low-intensity lasers touted for arthritis pain (Napier Mar 1994).
- Magnetism touted for arthritis (Napier Mar 1994).
- RIFE generators touted for medical diagnosis (Napier Mar 1994).
- Superoxide dismutase, a human-generated compound touted as an anti-aging and Alzheimer's treatment (Napier Mar 1994).
- Perpetrators illegally offer real and counterfeit steroid through the mail (USPIS Spring 1990).

In addition to un-proven claims for medical devices, product fraud, and procedure fraud, medical procedure fraud also includes instances when individuals disparage proven techniques. For example, one physician complained that angioplasty and bypass surgery do not work, when in fact clinical studies show that they are effective. The critic touted non-traditional and un-approved treatments (*NCAHF Newsletter* Nov-Dec 1997).

Prevention: Anytime a claimant or beneficiary suspects health care product, device, or treatment fraud, he or she should report the provider to the US Food and Drug Administration.

Agent Fraud
The most prevalent insurance agent fraud is embezzlement, both by agent impersonators (the unlicensed) and by registered agents. Agents can embezzle both from customers and from the insurers that they represent. There are other agent-perpetrated frauds: i. churning and ii. sliding coverage.

◆ Embezzling customer funds

- One example of agent impersonation involved title insurance. Perpetrators required prospective oil and gas lease investors to pay advanced fees for title searches. The victims received neither a title search nor the rights to any oil and gas leases (USPIS Spring 1990).

- Insurance agents defrauded independent truckers by collecting fees for the truckers' membership in an "association" which was supposed to insure the trucks. The fee did not provide insurance, and victims lost $1.3 million plus losses derived from uncovered accidents (DOT OIG 4-1-92 thru 9-30-92).

- Another embezzlement involved medical malpractice insurance: Two brothers operated a series of unlicensed insurance companies which offered high-risk doctors liability insurance at below-market rates. The brothers defrauded doctors of millions of dollars. When a malpractice claim was submitted against one of their insured doctors, the claim was defended only to the extent of the doctor's $5,000 deductible and a $5,000 "surcharge;" if the claim exceeded the deductible amount, the criminals denied coverage, delayed paying or simply dissolved the company and started again under another shell (USPIS Winter/Spring 1995).

◆ Embezzling from insurance companies

- Life Insurance Cash Value Fraud involves insurance agents who falsify requests for loans against policyholders' insurance policies. In one case, an agent made the requests to the parent insurance companies, then forged the checks when the companies mailed the loans (USPIS Spring 1991).

- Life Insurance Issuance Fraud: Dishonest life insurance salesmen submit fraudulent life insurance applications to insurers to receive an undue commission check (USPIS Summer 1990).

- One insurance adjuster diverted legitimate claim payments from policyholders to his friends (USPIS Summer 1998).

◆ Churning is the unethical reimbursement of one insurance policy for the primary purpose of buying another, similar policy. This is done at the agent's urging to generate extra commissions:

- Insurance Policy Churning: Federal courts sentenced an insurance salesman to 20 years in jail because he, "sold clients whole life insurance, individual retirement accounts and annuities in which he periodically would roll over policies from one company to another through misrepresentations and false pretenses (USPIS Winter 1990-91)." Annuity churning is particularly insidious, because agents may obtain multiple layers of commissions, sometimes amounting to many tens of percent, in annuity sales.
- One unique scheme involved licensed agents who defrauded insurers by churning policies annually. The twist was that each insurer offered a promotion—the first year at no charge, so by churning, the agent pocketed customer's premiums, but made no payments as they churned the policies from one insurer to another (Rivero 12-23-97).

◆ Policy Sliding is the undisclosed addition of coverages to existing policyholders. Unethical insurance agents do this to enhance their commissions. Vehicle insurance is especially susceptible (Bomer 1998).

Prevention: (1) Check with the state Insurance Commissioner to find out if the agent is registered and to find out his or her discipline record. (2) Never pay with cash or a money order for insurance. (3) Always insist on a binder from the agent, and make sure the binder is on the insurer's form or letterhead. (4) Make sure the policy arrives from the insurance company, not the agent, within 30 days. (5) If an agent repeatedly urges you to buy new policies for the same coverage, contact the underwriting insurance company, seek competitive bids from other agents, and consider contacting your state's insurance commissioner. (6) Report all suspicious activity to the state insurance commissioner.

Body Shops, or other vehicle repair businesses can defraud auto insurers by any number of schemes:

- Overestimating the cost of repairs.
- Falsifying the amount of damage.
- Staging exaggerated damage by replacing undamaged parts for damaged ones prior to adjusting. After the adjuster leaves, the shop replaces the original good parts (CBS 8-24-95).
- Entering into complex conspiracies with vehicle owners and others to stage accidents.

Prevention: Is mostly the responsibility of the insurer. Try to use shops that are pre-approved by your insurer. Take pictures of the damages prior to repair.

Insurance Company Fraud is committed against customers, agents, and/or against government regulators. Fraud against customers includes inflating premiums, false billings, bad-faith claims adjusting, and financial fraud.

Failing to deliver promised discounts is an example of insurer fraud targeting customers. In this scheme, the insurer promises to provide discounts to policy holders for safety measures such as air bags (Sifakis 1993) good driving records, smoke detectors in homes, or other fire safety equipment, but they never deliver the discount.

One major class of insurance company fraud is bad-faith adjusting: The deliberate denial of valid claims (Shernoff, Gage, and Levine 1995). A common example of this practice occurs with low-wage workers who file valid worker's compensation claims. Some insurers try to trick the claimant into technical violations, such as immaterial lies, in order to disqualify the claims. Some insurers may not even develop a pretext for denying claims—they simply deny most all claims. One example of bad-faith adjusting occurred in a property claim related to a disaster. In this case, a woman who switched property insurers prior to a natural disaster found herself fighting both her previous and current insurers over the disaster loss: The company that carried the insurance at the time of the loss claimed that the damage was pre-existing, and the prior insurer said that the losses occurred from the disaster. Both tried to deny paying the claim (Schmid 4-22-98).

The obvious example of insurers defrauding agents would be if a company failed to pay promised commissions or other benefits such as retirement benefits.

When a private insurer is a contractor to government, it could be involved in any number of contract frauds. For a detailed discussion, see CHAPTER SEVEN - Operations Fraud. One specific example involved a large insurance company that defrauded the Defense Department health insurance program when it converted government money, left over from the operation of a health insurance contract, to its own account (DOD OIG 10-1-92 thru 3-31-93).

Prevention: Report any suspicious activity to the state insurance commissioner. If you suspect bad-faith adjusting, consult with a private attorney who specializes in insurance claims.

Insurance Company Employees can be involved in any number frauds as detailed in CHAPTER SEVEN'S Employee, Customer, and Competitor Fraud section. Some frauds unique to insurance are:

- Bad Faith Adjusting: An insurance company employee may either falsely deny or endorse a false claim to reciprocate payoffs from the claimant.

- Embezzlement: An employee can cause automated payment systems to issue claim payments or premium reimbursements to the employee or one of his or her associates.
- Insurance Conspiracies: Twenty defendants allegedly defrauded insurance companies through a chain of falsified insurance claims. "The investigation revealed a pattern of fraud and corruption by public adjusters, who represented the insured parties; by independent and general adjusters, who are employed by insurance companies to process and settle claims; by salvers, who appraise damaged goods; and by homeowners and business owners. It was found that the public adjuster, policyholder and general or independent adjuster would work together to either greatly inflate the amount of the claim or stage a totally fictitious and false claim. Typically, half of the false claims paid would be kicked back to the public adjuster who would then split it with the company adjusters and other individuals who aided in the scheme (USPIS Winter/Spring 1993)."

Prevention: This is the job of the insurance company.

Whoever makes or presents to any person or official in the civil, military, or naval service of the United States, or to any department or agency there-of, any claim upon or against the United States, or any department or agency thereof, knowing such claim to be false, fictitious, or fraudulent, shall be imprisoned not more than five years and shall be subject to a fine in the amount provided in this title.

18 United States Code §287

CHAPTER FIVE - GOVERNMENT FRAUD

INTRODUCTION

Nearly half of the US economy is devoted to government spending. Stories of fraud against government are legion—the $200 Department of Defense toilet seats, welfare moms who claim 15 dependents, and Chicago aldermen who are forever receiving kickbacks. Why is government prone to fraud? Because some money is delegated to patronage rather than to the most cost-effective programs, and because the stewards of government funds have little incentive to manage wisely. As a matter of fact, government managers have incentives to waste. If they return money to a treasury at the end of a fiscal year, the public representatives will naturally conclude that the organization received more than it needed, so next year's appropriation must be smaller. If the saving trend continued, a fiscally responsible agency would conscientiously save its way out of existence—no cushy pensions for abolished agency workers.

As troubling as fraud in government is, waste is actually a much larger loss than fraud. Waste is rampant, because, as explained above, not only is there a lack of incentive to reign it in, there are actually dis-incentives. The lack of positive incentive comes from the fact that government workers seldom receive recognition for being under budget, and they certainly do not receive monetary rewards for doing so. One notable exception to the lack of incentives rule are the Offices of Inspector General, internal fraud investigative units attached to each federal government agency. They do audit, investigate and inspect, but they have no administrative authority, so agencies may ignore IG recommendations. But waste is not the target of this Handbook, so onto government, its programs, and the fraud in them.

This discussion will focus almost exclusively on federal funds, because, even if state and local governments implement programs, most fraud emanates from federally-funded programs. After tax collection, the executive branch of government fulfills two roles, the administration of entitlements and the implementation of services. Entitlements consist of those programs designed to redistribute wealth to specific segments of society. These include mostly social services: Social Security programs, welfare programs, public health programs, veterans programs and disability programs. Services include programs that benefit select groups and programs that have an overall societal benefit. Examples of programs benefiting select groups include transportation funding for specific cities, farm subsidies, basic research grants to universities, funding for local law enforcement and education supports for local school districts. Program funding that benefits all society includes defense spending, law enforcement, space research, public health research, and diplomacy.

Individual citizens are the target audience for this Chapter. Individuals may wish to read this for background information on program fraud or as cautionary tales designed to discourage readers who would-be criminals. Remarkably, there is one way for individuals to capitalize on fraud that they detect in federal programs—the False Claims Act has a *qui tam* provision that allows individuals to sue people who commit fraud and to collect a bounty if the suit is successful. While this might seem like an obscure road to riches, some former employees in the defense industry reaped handsome, multi-million dollar purses for their efforts, so don't scoff at the idea. If you detect major fraud against a government program, take your allegation to a private attorney who specializes in this area.

With its Inspectors General and 10,000 plus FBI agents, the federal government would derive little benefit from my suggestions for fraud prevention, so none are forthcoming.

ENTITLEMENT PROGRAMS

Education

The Department of Education provides grants and loans to students and educational institutions. They also fund education research. For schemes that abuse research funding, see CHAPTER NINE, Science Fraud. The following anecdotes detail common grant and loan schemes, which impact the Department of Education:

- Phantom Students: Criminals have used educational fronts, naming non-existent students as loan applicants, to defraud the US Department of Education of grant and loan money (DOE OIG Website).
- PLUS Loan Fraud: The US Department of Education offers Parent Loans for Undergraduate Students (Plus) to support students in colleges universities and graduate school. Seventy five individuals were indicted for falsifying PLUS Loan applications by submitting the names of non-existent children, citing non-existent references, employers, and financial aid officers, and using false Social Security numbers (USPIS Fall 1991).
- School Accreditation Fraud: A vocational school officer faced indictment for falsely stating the school was accredited, and therefore eligible for US Department of Education Pell Grants.

Students and the US Government both suffered (USPIS Fall 1990).

Food Stamps And Lunch Programs

The Department of Agriculture administers the Food Stamp and School Meal Programs. Prior to the Food Stamp reforms of the mid-1990's, the Food Stamp program was one of the most fraud-riddled of all. Food Stamp fraud primarily involves brokering the Stamps for money. The recipient would sell the Stamps at a discount to face value and use the gains for something other than food. Criminal groceries would launder the money by acting as brokerage houses for the illegally sold Stamps. The grocery laundering alone cost the Food Stamp program as much as $1 billion per year (Emshwiller 6-1-95). Other abuses of the Stamps included using them to buy non-approved items like alcohol and tobacco or inflating the price of approved items and then kicking back cash to the recipient (USPIS Winter/Spring 1994).

A major 1995 reform attempted to limit illegal Stamp sales. The change involved issuing debit cards— called EBTs. Unfortunately, instead of squelching food benefit fraud, the electronic system merely caused exploiters to shift their strategies. Instead of treating Stamps as cash, contemporary food benefit frauds ask groceries to: i. add fictitious charges to generate cash; ii. buy the whole card at a discount to its face value, or iii. (for grocers not enrolled in the system) to enlist the help of another, crooked, enrolled grocer to cash-out the card. In the last case, the grocer who is ineligible to receive EBT charges gives the EBT number to an enrolled grocer. The co-conspirator then makes charges on his account without actually selling anything. The three conspirators: the EBT beneficiary, the grocer at hand, and the grocer enrolled in the benefit system, split the illegal gain. The one advantage of the electronic system over the old Stamp system is that the computer-monitored EBT is much more easily controlled and investigated (Burks 3-2-95).

The primary fraud in school meal supports involves contractors overstating of the number of children who participate in school lunch programs. The overestimates lead to inflated food reimbursements (US Chamber of Commerce 1977).

Medicare And Medicaid

These two programs, administered by the Department of Health and Human Services, comprise the largest teamed costs in the federal budget. By and large, fraud in these programs is covered in the FINANCE CHAPTER'S Insurance Section.

Social Security Fraud

The US Social Security Administration is responsible for the Social Security Retirement Plan, Supplemental Social Security Insurance, and the administration of Social Security Numbers and Cards. As claimed benefits, the Retirement and Supplemental programs are magnets for fraud. In 1994 the Department of Health and Human Services' Inspector General estimated the annual cost of fraud in Social Security programs at $24 billion (Acello 11-3-94). The Social Security card is a *de facto* national identification in the United States. Nearly all benefits, financial transactions (including and especially loans), and ownership rights rely on the Social Security number. The importance of the card and number make the program the identifier most likely to be counterfeited in the United States. Obviously, the Social Security Administration has a lot on their hands.

Beyond being the target of fraud, critics target the Social Security Administration as the perpetrator of fraud. Because the Administration shuffles SS income into the general ledger of the United States, and uses the funds to buy debt rather than to invest, critics call the pension the worst Ponzi Scheme in history (Sloan 2-16-98).

Social Security Retirement Fraud

There are a variety of schemes criminals use to make false Social Security pension claims:

- falsifying the age of a recipient to pre-maturely receive benefits;
- assuming the identity of another to receive another person's benefits;
- making duplicate claims; and
- accepting, or continuing to collect benefits for a beneficiary who died.

One case of benefit-theft involved criminals who obtained the identities of widows, applied for their Social Security benefits, and diverted them from the widow to the criminal (Sifakis 1993).

A second identity fraud (see CHAPTER THREE'S Identity Fraud Section) involved a California man who "searched old newspapers for the names of children whose deaths were reported decades earlier. He obtained their birth certificates from State agencies, used these to obtain SSN's [Social Security Numbers], and then established medical histories under each of the false identities. With the identities in hand, he filed for Supplemental Security Income (HHS OIG 1989).

Social Security Supplemental Benefits Fraud

Supplementary Benefits are awarded to widows and dependents whose spouse or guardian dies or loses their ability to work. The benefits are also awarded to workers who become so disabled that they cannot work. Fraudulent schemes include: (1) claiming a false permanent disability, (2) claiming the loss of a fictitious wage-earner, and (3) continuing to claim benefits for a disabled wage earner who has died. The willfully and marginally disabled may also be engaged in Disability Benefits fraud: A *Wall Street Journal* (MacDonald 1-20-95) editorial accused the Social Security Administration and some claimants of defrauding taxpayers by allowing alcoholics, drug addicts, and parents who cause their children to misbehave or to fail in school, to claim disability even though the claimant's behavior is discretionary.

Social Security Number and Card Fraud

Criminals use Social Security Numbers in a great variety of schemes that rely on identity fraud (HHS OIG 1989):

- applying for unemployment benefits.
- applying for worker's compensation benefits.
- applying for various types of immigration status.
- applying for welfare benefits.
- avoiding creditors.
- making falsified loan or credit applications
- evading taxes.
- evading required reports on currency transaction.
- avoiding paying back student loans.

An individual commits Social Security number fraud when: (1) he or she uses a fictitious number, (2) assumes the number of another person, (3) manufactures a counterfeit card, or (4) alters the name or number on a valid card.

Social Security Officer Impersonation

Many variation of the traditional confidence game rely on impersonating government or business officials. Social Security officers are not immune from this ruse: Criminals convinced a pensioner that she had been overpaid by the Social Security Administration, and they defrauded her by insisting that she write a check to them immediately (Sifakis 1993).

Welfare

Prior to the Welfare Reform Act of 1996, public assistance fraud was one of the most insidious of all benefit frauds. By reducing the number of people on the welfare roles, the 1996 legislation greatly diminished the total amount of fraud. Welfare fraud employs nearly the same schemes as insurance benefit fraud, so for details see CHAPTER TWO's Insurance Section. Typical benefit schemes involve: i. applying for un-entitled benefits, ii. applying for multiple benefits, or iii. exaggerating the amount due to a beneficiary. A criminal may make false entitlement applications by falsifying their income, job status, household status, or number of dependents (US Chamber of Commerce 1977). A typical false application for multiple benefits would include using multiple addresses (Betts 4-18-94).

Veterans Affairs

By and large, the Veterans Administration handles medical and disability insurance and pensions, and fraud in these types of programs is covered above in the Social Security Section and in CHAPTER FOUR'S Insurance Section.

The VA also offers educational assistance. One school took advantage of these benefits. The low-budget school helped veterans receive government loans, but offered substandard classes and paid kickbacks to the veterans for their enrollment. The "classes" were actually meetings (USPIS Summer 1998).

SERVICE PROGRAMS

Customs

US Customs laws are designed to exclude prohibited imports, to control prohibited exports, to regulate trade agreements, and to implement other US trade policies. Although criminal statutes other than fraud statutes enforce most smuggling, diversion, and violation of specific laws, many of these trade violations involve a greater or lesser element of deception, and therefore fraud. The fraud is often tied to falsification of documents.

Three common categories of customs fraud are : i. import fraud, ii. trade support fraud, and iii. trade tax fraud.

Import Fraud
The most prevalent kinds of customs fraud are the falsification of import-export records to unlawfully facilitate trade and the importation of counterfeit goods.

One example of document falsification comes from the world of art museums and dealers. These art traders are known to falsify customs documents to move art into the US (Hoving 1996, Conklin 1994).

Sifakis (1993) describes an elaborate import fraud in which the perpetrator removes some critical element of a controlled item with the expectation that the items will be seized. Once customs seizes the items and discovers the flaw, the items are sold at auction. The original importer then buys back the items at an extreme discount. Finally, the items are then rehabilitated with the missing element, and sold at a profit.

CHAPTER SEVEN'S Competitor Fraud Section details the extent and impact of counterfeit goods.

Trade Support Fraud
The US government administers a number of customs laws designed to promote export of US goods. Lawbreakers circumvent these laws: They buy discounted goods that are intended for export, and then simply sell the goods in the US (Segal Oct 1995); or, they ship preferentially-bought goods and then return them to the US with false bills of lading. Once returned, the criminal sells the goods in the US market at prices that undercut the manufacturer's price. This scheme defrauds the US manufacturers and US Customs (Segal Oct 1995).

A second set of schemes relies on government insurance for exports. The European Union looses millions annually to food-product export fraud. One scheme takes advantage of insurance for food that has gone bad prior to delivery. In this scheme, the claimant states the food was of a higher grade than it actually was, thereby receiving higher compensated than their actual loss (*Economist* 7-30-94).

<u>Customs Tax Fraud</u>
International trading companies defraud the US Treasury by as much as $109 billion per year by artificially inflating the cost basis of imports and artificially deflating the price of exports. The price manipulations cause the net profits to be understated, thereby reducing the import-export taxes (DeGeorge 3-21-94).

Defense

The bulk of defense program fraud lies in procurements, and this is covered in the Handbook's CHAPTER SEVEN, Operations.

Disasters

The Federal Emergency Management Administration makes loans and grants after disasters like floods, fires, earthquakes, hurricanes, and tornadoes. These programs are subject to the same frauds as are financial institutions, so see CHAPTER TWO for details.

Farms

After the Great Depression, one of the mainstays of US agricultural policy was price supports and crop insurance. The US Department of Agriculture administers these programs. During the latter half of the 1990s these supports were diminished piecemeal, but crop insurance remains largely intact and serves as an on-going fraud magnet. The most common price support schemes involve farm families making multiple applications for the same crop. The classic example of this scheme is where a husband and wife apply for support under separate names (US Chamber of Commerce 1977).

In a more complex scheme, called a Mississippi Christmas Tree, perpetrators create a number of fictitious identities to make multiple claims for the same crop support (PBS 5-5-98).

Crop insurance was designed to protect farmers against catastrophic loss. A great variety of schemes abuse these insurance policies (Rose and Freivogel 1-15-95):

- by claiming crop losses that did not occur;
- by deliberately allowing crops to wither or spoil;
- by choosing crops that were likely to fail;
- by making multiple claims for the same failed crop;
- by falsely claiming hail damage;
- by planting on land that had been set aside from production;
- by being allowed to buy insurance after the crop failed;
- by claiming losses on more acres than were actually planted ;
- and by falsifying production records.

Law Enforcement

See the Corruption section in CHAPTER EIGHT, Public Interest Fraud.

Postal Fraud

Postal fraud includes both schemes to defraud the US Postal Service of revenue and use of the mail and mail systems to commit fraud. The latter will not be addressed here because nearly any scheme constitutes postal fraud when the crime involves use of the mail. For examples, see CHAPTER TWO'S Banking-Lending section, CHAPTER SEVEN'S Contract Fraud section, or CHAPTER SIX, Investment Fraud. Like any organization, the Postal Service also has instances of employee fraud. For a discussion of these schemes, see the Customer, Employee, and Competitor section of CHAPTER SEVEN, Operations Fraud. After the exclusions, there are three principal varieties of postal fraud: meter fraud, stamp fraud, and mail-volume fraud. By dollar value, meter fraud greatly overshadows the other two areas—the US General Accounting Office estimated annual meter fraud losses at $150 million (*LI Business News* 6-23-97).

Meter Fraud

Businesses defraud the US Postal Service of revenue by tampering with mechanical postal meters. The impact of these schemes is diminishing due to the increased use of electronic meters (*LI Business News* 6-23-97).

Mail Volume Fraud

Two former postal employees and a bulk mailer were charged in a scheme to defraud the Postal Service by understating the volume of bulk mail (USPIS Winter 1990-91).

Stamp Fraud

Criminals can literally wash cancelled stamps (USPIS Summer 1990), or potentially, print counterfeit stamps.

<u>Change of Address Fraud</u> deserves singular mention here because it has the potential to disastrously impact its victims. In this scheme, criminals use change of address cards to redirect postal customer mail to other locations. In one case, a man was indicted after he, "...took mail discarded into the post office lobby trash can by post office box holders, changed the address on the mail to his home address and ordered merchandise, charging that merchandise to the true boxholders' charge accounts (USPIS Fall 1990)."

Research

CHAPTER NINE, Science Fraud, addresses fraud in research programs.

Small Business Administration

The SBA is primarily a lender, so fraud in their programs is nearly identical to those described in CHAPTER FOUR'S Financial

Statements and Banking-Lending sections. The Real Estate section in CHAPTER SIX also addresses lending fraud.

The sure way to be cheated is to think one's self more cunning than others.

Duc François de La Rochefoucauld

CHAPTER SIX - INVESTMENT FRAUD

INTRODUCTION

For individuals, investments come in two major classes, ownership interests and debt interests. Investments are any expenditure of capital, assets, effort, or goodwill toward ownership or debt interest with the intention of bringing a return that exceeds the initial expense. There are two ownership-investment asset classes, intangible assets and tangible assets. Intangible assets, though found in a great variety, are generally paper investments like stocks, bonds, and certificates of deposits. Tangible assets consist of things like real estate, oil wells, gold mines, gems, coins, art, and other collectibles. Whereas ownership-interest investors generally expect their returns to come from asset appreciation, debt investors expect a fixed rate of return plus the scheduled return of their principal. Nearly innumerable schemes target buyers and holders of both tangible and intangible assets.

Universal investment frauds include i. selling an asset that does not exist or is not owned by the seller, ii. misrepresenting the character, value, or potential return of an asset, and iii. mismanaging an asset so as to deprive the rightful owner of its use or investment potential.

The following discussion reviews fraud in tangible assets: art, coins, gems, minerals, mines, oil and gas, and real estate; and in intangible assets: stocks, bonds and futures contracts.

ART FRAUD

Introduction

Hoving's *False Impressions* (1996) and Conklin's *Art Crime* (1994) paint a picture of an art world filled with fraud. In fact, Hoving (1996), the former director of the Metropolitan Museum of Art, estimates that fully 40% of all art is fraudulent. As discussed in the Handbook's Introduction, fake art dates back to antiquity. If the pervasiveness of art fraud is any indicator, it serves as an allegory for fraud in all walks of life.

No area of the art business is devoid of fraud. Artists, art restorers, art dealers, art auction houses, private collectors, and museums are each known to have engaged in art fraud. Common schemes include: i. counterfeiting art, ii. altering art, iii. lying about the provenance of a piece, iv. deceptive sales practices, v. art tax fraud, vi. art insurance fraud and, vii. art smuggling.

Counterfeiting Art

While second-rate imitators produce most fakes, this is not always the case. Masters are known to have counterfeited the work of other masters: Rubens copied the works of earlier masters (Hoving 1996). Some masters have even orchestrated the counterfeiting of their own works by directing their disciples. In this case the artist designs, partakes in, and/or oversees the completion of a work, but allows others to construct the whole or parts of it. This is only fraudulent if the artist fails to describe the production style (Hoving 1996). Koestler (in Schilit 1993) relates a story about Picasso in which, in jest or in truth, Picasso reportedly said "I often paint fakes."

Talented fakers go to great lengths to study their prey, refine their techniques, and choose their medium. One painting counterfeiter chose different elements from many different paintings of a master to create a "new" original of the grand master (Hoving 1996). Presumably, this prevented unfavorable comparisons of a work with the original. Other counterfeiters go to great lengths to obtain age-appropriate materials for their works. For example, creative art frauds can purchase antique paints or manufacture new paints with age-appropriate materials to make more credible fake paintings (Hoving 1996).

Hoving (1996) "gave awards" for the best of fakes—Best Medium for Counterfeit Art: Clay—it is easily aged to bolster its fake authenticity—Most Counterfeited Art: "The prize for the most prolifically faked item of the nineteenth century goes to the makers of thousands of pretty terra-cotta Greek fifth-to third-century-B.C. figurines...."

The *ignorati* buy mass-produced fakes of the best-known artists: Pablo Picasso, Marc Chagall, Joan Miró and Salvador Dali. Perpetrators offer counterfeit prints by phone and in art galleries. Sales pitches include money back guarantee offers and bogus "certificates of authenticity (FTC 1-92)."

Altering Art

Restoration is an accepted practice in the art world. However, there is a fine line between restoration and alteration. While the middle ground may be called overly-aggressive restoration, the extreme amounts to fraud when the restoration so alters a piece as to greatly enhance its value or to greatly change its appearance. Frauds use a variety of techniques to alter original art or to make fake art look more authentic.

◆ Altered Originals
- Over-restoration: the excessive embellishment of an original work (Hoving 1996).
- Criminals may shave, cut, or otherwise modify a damaged sculpture to make it appear intact or complete (Hoving 1996).

- In a highly dramatic fraud, a perpetrator may spilt masters—art works have been cut in half to create two masters when there was once one, thereby increasing the total market price for the work (Sifakis 1993).

◆ Aging
Those frauds that set out to give credibility to counterfeits mostly involve aging to create the false impression that a work of art or antiquity is of the appropriate age. Here are some of the techniques counterfeiters use to age art (Hoving 1996):
- dirtying with soil,
- baking,
- cutting,
- knicking,
- irradiating,
- braking and repairing,
- adding age appropriate substances like paint, clay, soil or lead;
- discoloring ivory pieces "...by wrapping them in the skins of rabbits and burying them until the pelts decayed."

Prevention: Obtain one or more appraisals from established, independent appraisers. For major purchases, conduct a background investigation on the seller. Ask for a warranty. Obtain a sales receipt or a sales contract.

Lying About the Provenance of a Piece
One of the methods used to authenticate artwork is to research and retell the work's creation and ownership history, its provenance. Here are a few examples of provenance fraud:

- An art dealer allegedly misrepresented the provenance of fine art by stating, in a sales brochure, that the art had been in the Smithsonian Institution (Smithsonian Institution OIG 4-1-93 thru 9-30-93).

- A man defrauded an insurance company of $410,000 by claiming that two pieces of art he owned were stolen from his home. In fact, the art works were property of the Vatican, and they had never left Rome. The perpetrator used two "amateurish photographs," to substantiate ownership (*Santa Fe New Mexican* 10-4-95).

Prevention: Obtain one or more appraisals from established, independent appraisers. For major purchases, conduct a background investigation on the seller. Ask for a warranty. Obtain a sales receipt or a sales contract.

Deceptive Sales Practices
Out-of-bounds sellers and auction houses manipulate and deceive art buyers with a variety of techniques: i. changing the context of a piece, ii. changing the artist's name, iii. manipulating auctions, iv. consignment theft, v. non-competitive sales, and vi. warrantless sales.

◆ Changing the Context of a Piece
- Art Association Fraud: Criminals may enhance the appearance of fraudulent art by adding a few pieces of authentic art to displays that were largely populated with fakes (Hoving 1996).
- Art Frame Fraud: Some dealers try to distract buyers by putting fabulous paintings in damaged frames and bad, or poorly-preserved works in immaculate frames (Hoving 1996). The calculation subliminally effects buyers' assessments of the core work.

◆ Changing the Artist's Name
Art dealers may misrender artists' names "...so they can't be held responsible for the authenticity (Dobrzynski 1-28-97)." For example, a work may be attributed to Monay, suggesting the work is a creation of grand master Claude Monet.

145

◆ Manipulating Auctions

Auction houses both misrepresent market conditions and manipulate auctions. The houses misrepresent and manipulate to foment the market and to pump-up sale prices:

- The auction houses have built-up buyer-impressions of the market by publishing total sales figures and turnover rates while at the same time failing to disclose the numbers or values of items that did not sell. This practice may lead customers to misjudge market trends (Burnham 1975 in Conkin 1994).

- Auction houses may use shills or they may fabricate bids to spur-on competitive bidding (Conklin 1994.) These questionable practices are known as "Bidding Off The Chandelier, Bidding off the Wall and Pulling Bids From the Air."

- Art buyers, or others, may collude in "auction rings" to under pay for auctioned items. By agreeing not to bid against one another, the sale price may be under market. After the sale, the conspirators pay each other off (Conklin 1994).

- Auction houses may be guilty of insider trading if the house, or its officials, secretly bid for items consigned to them (Conklin 1994).

- Some auction houses honor "secrete reserves"—the minimum price that a seller requires when he or she put an item up for auction. Some people believe "secrete reserves" constitute a fraudulent sales practice if the auction house fails to disclose that there is a minimum (Conklin 1994).

◆ Consignment Theft

Businesses that sell goods on consignment may defraud their customers by not paying the owner after his goods are sold (Consignment Fraud Website). Alternatively, the consignment shop may under-report the proceeds, thereby defrauding the owner of the actual sale price. Art consignors may be particularly susceptible to these schemes. One way to conceal the proceeds is for the consignee to ask the buyer for money and items in barter, and then to conceal the exchange of the bartered items (Conklin 1994).

◆ Non-competitive Sales

Underselling the Market: Dishonest brokers may avoid open market sales for items like fine art and make side deals to private buyers or other dealers, thereby defrauding the property owner of the best price (Conklin 1994).

◆ Warrantless Sales

Unscrupulous art dealers may sell non-authenticated art in an "as-is" condition, with no warranty of authenticity (Dobrzynski 1-28-97).

Prevention: In judging the authenticity of a piece, obtain one or more appraisals from established, independent appraisers. For major purchases, conduct a background investigation on the seller. Ask for a warranty. Obtain a sales receipt or a sales contract.

When buying at auction, be alert for fictitious or manipulated bids. Immediately confront the auction house if you detect questionable bids.

When selling works of significant value, insist the consignor allow you to contact the buyer, and take measures to insure brokers give works adequate exposure to the open market.

Art Tax and Insurance Fraud
◆ Tax Fraud

Some criminals use art in tax dodges by money laundering schemes (Conklin 1994) or by taking exaggerated tax deductions (Conklin 1994). In the money laundering schemes, criminals collude with sellers to concoct inflated sales prices for art. Under the veil of the inflated price, a portion of the reported transaction is siphoned to other accounts (Conklin 1994).

Inflated tax deductions come about by inflating the estimated value of a donated artwork. Donors can get inflated values by lying about the purchase price, altering a piece of art to enhance its value, or by paying-off an appraiser. In one complex scheme, a curator at Los Angeles's Getty Museum inflated appraisals on donated items by coordinating European dealers with donors. The dealers provided second-rate pieces with inflated appraisals, and the donors, sight-un-seen, claimed the donations. Some of the donations were made in the name of fictitious individuals (Conklin 1994).

◆ Art Insurance Fraud includes claims made for items not owned by the claimant, claims for items not lost, and exaggerated claims for legitimately owned and lost items. In one case a retired Alitalia employee made insurance claims for two pieces of art he said were stolen from his home. In fact the art was the property of the Vatican and had never left Italy (*Santa Fe New Mexican* 10-4-95).

Prevention: Use independent, credible appraisers. Beware of tax deduction deals that appear too good to be true and appraisals that appear out of line. As for insurance fraud, don't do it.

Art Import-Export Fraud
Traditionally, rogue dealers facilitated a portion of art trade by falsifying customs records (Hoving 1996, Conklin 1994). This is particularly true of antiquities where dealers would present falsified release papers from the originating country. Falsifications skirt laws designed to protect a country's cultural heritage.

COINS AND METAL INGOT FRAUD

Introduction
CHAPTER EIGHT'S Counterfeiting section addresses counterfeiting of contemporary currency. That discussion, however, does not review fraud in collectable currencies or ingots, so here is a short treatment of these investments.

Before reviewing the schemes, it is necessary to know something about rare coin and bill valuations. Without this information, it is hard to understand why anyone would go to the trouble described in the schemes. Five criteria govern collectable currency valuations: rarity, face value, aesthetics, origin, and metal content (for coins). Rarity is the attribute most falsified by those who commit collectable-currency. Rarity comes from: faulty production, short production runs, or a high loss rate. Losses increase over time, so, naturally, older coins tend to be rarer.

The proof of the identity of a coin mostly comes from authenticating its markings. Markings include artistic images, symbols, dates, and mint series. Each coin attribute is subject to counterfeiting and alteration. Examining markings, evaluating materials, and studying wear patterns all serve to authenticate currency.

One interesting aspect of currency (and stamp) collecting is that, in contrast to most other valuables, true production errors often make the coin or bill more, not less, valuable. This is so because genuine production errors are rare.

The most common collectable coin fraud is misgrading, the practice of inflating the quality of a collectable. Mail order sales are the most frequent source of these frauds (Lemke 1983). Beyond misgrading, there are three basic means to misrepresent collectable currencies: i. counterfeiting, ii. alteration, and iii. provenance fraud. In contrast, metals are elemental, so ingot fraud always involves misrepresenting the metal content of ingots. In addition to these misrepresentations, there are coin-based bait and switch and Advanced-fee schemes.

Currency Counterfeiting
Counterfeiting is the wholesale making of fake coins or bills. Most bill counterfeiters use a photo-mechanical or 'offset' method to

make a printing plate from a genuine note photograph. "Counterfeiters also use: (1) black and white, monochromatic, and color copiers, or (2) computer-driven, desk-top publishing systems with ink jet or laser printers (USSS Website)." If the counterfeit note poses for something old, the counterfeiter may use a variety of aging techniques to make the note age-appropriate: laundering, soiling, tearing, or knicking. Obviously, the more blemished the note, the less valuable, so too much fake-reality serves no purpose.

Counterfeiting collectable coins is a much more lucrative business than counterfeiting collectable notes. This is so because: coins date to antiquity; they endure the elements; and their numbers are so much greater than bills that they predominate the currency collecting field. While governments traditionally stamp coins, counterfeiters usually use the cast method (USSS Website). The stamp method involves centering a piece of metal and then stamping an impress onto it. In contrast, the cast method involves making a mold by taking a real coin and placing it in sand, wax, plastic, or soft metal; removing it; and then pouring liquid metal into the mold. Less frequently, counterfeiters use electrotype production; a method that relies on "dusting a mold with graphite to make it electroconductive, and electrodepositing on to a thin shell (as of copper) which is then backed up with lead and sometimes given an extra facing of a harder metal.... (Gove 1981)."

Currency Alteration
While both bills and coins may be altered, as in counterfeiting, the preferred alteration media are coins, not bills. Alterations disqualify currency for any collecting value and are almost always illegal (Herbert 1995). Frauds alter bills by erasures, by overprinting, and by gluing. To illustrate, an alterer may remove or add letters or serial numbers to a bill to turn an ordinary bill into a rare, more valuable one.

Some coin alterations cause rarities that are worthless at face value:
- coins that have a future date;
- "Wheat" pennies with the word "Cent" misspelled;
- coins that do not meet size specification (diameter and thickness) such as Texas Coins—enlarged by hammering; and dimes thinned by acid treatment;
- metal-plated coins such as pennies with gold-plating (Herbert 1995).

Perhaps the most notorious counterfeit coins are Nineteenth Century US gold coins, often minted in Mexico or Lebanon (Lemke 1983).

Coin alterations consist of changing the markings or artificially enhancing the grade. Here are some of the methods:
- restrikes;
- removal of markings by: tooling, heat treatment, or acid etching (Herbert 1995);
- adding markings by engraving tools or drilling and adding plugs (Herbert 1995);
- enameling, the addition of a superficial coat (Herbert 1995);
- altering existing marking, eg. changing a '2' to a '3' an '8' to a '3' or an 'S' to an 'O' (Cheung Websites no date);
- the appearance, or grade of coins may be enhanced by whizzing: buffing, cleaning, ultrasound, etching, wire brushing, or acid bathing. As in art restoration, there is a fine line between cleaning and enhancing, so these treatments are not always fraudulent.

Provenance Fraud
The source of a coin may effect its value. For example, if someone touted Roman coins as coming from a new-found Jerusalem cache, they may command a higher price than if their actual source were a hillside in Tuscany. In another hypothetical, gold doubloons from the foundered ship Atocha could command a higher value than

comparable ones from the Bank of Spain's vault. In both of these hypothetical examples, one can imagine enhanced value due to historical context and the temptation to falsify the origin of a coin.

Ingot Fraud
Metal ingots are precious metal bars or coins that are valued by weight, not face value. In contrast with coins, private manufacturers, not countries, issue ingots. Here are some of the frauds that misrepresent the value of ingots:

- The ingot may be underweight—a gold ingot could be sold as 2 ozs., when in fact it weighs 1.7 ozs.
- Base metal ingots could be covered with a precious metal plate, or even with gold or silver paint.
- A silver ingot may be sold as being platinum or as another platinum-group metal.
- Base-precious metal alloys may be sold as pure precious metal ingots.
- Counterfeit certification stamps may be placed on counterfeit ingots. For example, someone might put a fake Engelhard stamp on a precious-metal-covered lead bar.
- Criminals may drill holes and then insert precious-metal plugs into fake ingots so that when a buyer asks for an assay these plugs are offered as "drilled" samples (Nash 1976).
- Criminals misrepresent base-metal ingots with 0.999% silver as investment grade ingots with 99.9% silver—they say the bar is "triple nine" percent silver (Herbert 1995).
- Telemarketers sold the platinum group metal iridium as a precious metal with speculative investment value. In fact, it is not a precious metal (USPIS Summer 1998).

Bait and Switch and Advanced-fee Schemes
A coin bait and switch relies on deceitful advertising to attract victims. These schemes promise US $5 gold pieces at discount prices. When the buyer receives the coin, he or she finds a privately-

minted medal, devoid of collector or currency value. A common precious-metal advanced-fee fraud finds buyers who pay for their investment, but decline to take possession. Instead of taking delivery, the buyer pays a "storage fee." If the buyer ever asks for the coins, he or she finds them undeliverable because the company has gone out of business. Alternatively, the company wields a Ponzi Scheme, using new victims' money to buy coins for redemptions (Herbert 1995). As in all Ponzi Schemes, the perpetrators skim most of the invested money, so the vast majority of victims lose their entire investment.

Prevention: Buy from well-established dealers that offer money-back guarantees. Obtain independent appraisals from the American Numismatic Association. Avoid flea market and other non-traditional sources (Lemke 1983). Study the collecting literature prior to making purchases. Look at prospective buys with a hand lens; make note of any irregularities; confront the seller with the irregularities for an explanation. If buying many ingots, insist on random assays, and check the stamp certification numbers with the manufacturer's register.

GEM AND MINERAL FRAUD

Introduction
Gem and mineral collecting is another area, like mining, securities investments, and real estate, that are rife with fraud. This happens because each of these investments requires specialized knowledge or professional advice to make the best decisions. Gems and minerals make a mark of victims because they have enticing beauty and they elicit a greed-response from many. Greed encourages consumers and investors to rush into buying, and this hurry all-the-more increases the mutual attraction of criminals and victims.

As much as anything else, my experience as a victim of fraud by gem and mineral sellers convinced me of the need for an inexpensive handbook for fraud detection. I am trained in mineralogy and experienced in mineral collecting so I felt that, if in no other field, I should be immune from gem and mineral fraud. Unfortunately; I once paid an extraordinary mark-up for an aquamarine at a well-known retail gem seller; in Minas Gerais, Brazil, I paid $1,000 for a bag of worthless, reconstructed imperial topaz crystals; on the same trip I bought a glass, multi-colored tourmaline crystal; and in Mexico I once paid for some very beautiful amethyst crystals that had undisclosed color-enhancement, courtesy of a radiation or heat treatment—we could all benefit from a little fraud-awareness.

Gemstone Fraud
Gem fraud includes: (1) inflated pricing, (2) gem switching, (3) artificial stone substitution, (4) falsified grading, (5) undisclosed enhancement, (6) under carating and short weighting, (7) identification fraud (8) flaw concealment, and (9) appraisal fraud.

◆ Inflated Pricing
Dealers may entice buyers by promising wholesale or discount prices that are actually full-retail valuations. They may also received undeserved enrichment by misrepresenting the character of the stone.

In one phone-driven scheme, Canadian-based telemarketers defrauded investors of $22 million by inducing victims to buy gemstones for which the companies said it had overseas buyers. "The victims purchased additional gemstones to meet the conditions of the purported buyers, however there were no buyers, no sales on behalf of the victims, and the gemstones they were required to purchase were actually low-value stones they had bought at roughly 10 times their appraised value (USPIS Winter/Spring 1994)."

◆ Gem Switching
A dealer or jeweler may switch stones before a buyer comes back to pick up his or her newly-mounted purchase. Alternatively, dur-

ing the course of a repair or remounting, the jeweler may switch an original high-grade stone with an impostor of lesser value.

◆ Artificial Stone Substitution
The best-known artificial gem substitution is cubic zirconia for diamond, but there are many other diamond impostors:
- synthetic diamond (FTC 5-98),
- moissanite (FTC 5-98),
- strontium titanite,
- gadolinium gallium,
- yttrium aluminum garnet,
- synthetic rutile, sapphire, and spinel,
- natural zircon, and
- glass (Matlins and Bonanno 1995).

One sneaky scheme conceals glass posing for diamond by putting silver-foil-backing on the mounting bottom to enhance the refractivity of the glass (Matlins and Bonanno 1995).

Substitutions occur with other gemstones as well: Heat-treated natural topaz can be substituted for aquamarine, natural citron quartz for imperial topaz, and any variety of synthetic stones, including and especially synthetic rubies and sapphires, for their natural analogs. Although they are not minerals, pearls are gems, and dealers may misrepresent cultured or imitation pearls as the real thing, thereby defrauding consumers (FTC 5-98).

◆ Falsified Grading is the misrepresentation of a graded gemstone. The best and most universal illustration comes from diamond grading: Diamonds are graded by certified gemologists who evaluates: color, cut, clarity, and carats. Any one of these traits may be deliberately misrepresented to defraud a buyer.

◆ Undisclosed Enhancement in diamond sales represent the tip of gemstone enhancement fraud, but these schemes illustrate the scope of potential enhancement fraud. There are a variety of means by which diamond dealers may alter the appearance of a stone:

- Diamond Drilling Fraud involves diamonds that have been drilled with lasers to remove imperfections. After drilling, fillers can be added to conceal the hole or to fill-in natural cracks (Knight Website);
- Yellow Diamond Enhancing involves putting a thin, white film on yellow diamonds to make them appear white (Sifakis 1993);
- Sputtering involves painting a thin coat on diamonds to change their color (Matlins and Bonanno 1995);
- Sellers may enhance or change stones by a variety of wax, oil, heating, dye and radiation treatments;
- Sellers may fail to disclose known repairs or restorations of stones. Opaque gems like turquoise, opal or jade specimens are more susceptible to this type of fraud. One example of repair is plastic or glue impregnation. This is used on stones that are often fractured like turquoise and emerald.
- Sellers may dye pearls and fail to disclose the treatment to buyers (FTC 5-98).

◆ Under Carating, or for non-diamonds, under weighting, is simply the misrepresentation of the weight of one or more stones. One scheme misrepresents by falsely declaring the weight of the largest stone in a setting with many stones. The given value is often equal to the summary value of all of the stones. This violates FTC regulations (Matlins and Bonanno 1995).

◆ Misidentification
The deliberate misidentification of a gemstone is identification fraud. When most people think of gemstones their mind runs a list including diamonds, rubies, emeralds, sapphires, emeralds, topaz..., but as thoughts progress... nothing else comes to mind. In fact, there are more than 70 gemstones (Sinkankas 1959). Have you ever heard of tanzanite or alexandrite (both are rare colored gemstones)? If someone offered to sell you a tanzanite would you have

any way to distinguished the proffered stone from an irradiated-to-blue topaz? Probably not... so you can see how easy it would be to pass off an inexpensive stone for one of higher value.

◆ Jeweler-<u>Concealed Flaws</u> come about with carefully designed jewelry mounts or brackets (Matlins and Bonanno 1995) .

◆ <u>False Appraisal</u> is the deliberate false appraising of a gemstone or jewelry. These are some of the appraisal schemes:

- An appraiser might falsify an appraisal if he or she are paid a percentage of the appraised value—the higher the valuation of the stone, the higher his or her commission (Liu 7-27-97);
- An appraiser could be in collusion with a gem dealer, and mis-appraise a stone in return for a kickback from the dealer;
- An appraiser may also be in collusion with a gem owner in a plot to defraud insurers. In this scenario, the excessive appraisal is used to set the stage for a future fictitious loss-claim against an insurance company;
- Sellers could provide counterfeit certifications (Matlins and Bonanno 1995);
- Sellers could alter a valid, written appraisal (Matlins and Bonanno 1995).

Mineral Specimen Fraud

Mineral specimen fraud includes: (1) undisclosed repairs and restoration, (2) undisclosed alteration, (3) falsified provenance, (4) identity fraud, and (5) short flats.

◆ <u>Undisclosed Repairs and Restorations</u>

As is true in art, mineral specimens are often repaired or restored to reclaim their original appearance. These touch-ups commonly include gluing and plastic impregnation. The uncut specimens of commonly-fractured minerals such as emerald, turquoise, jade and (mineraloid) opal, are often impregnated with plastic or glue.

◆ Alterations, in contrast to repair and restoration, are changes someone makes to a mineral specimen to enhance its appearance and value beyond its original state. One example of alteration is Jade Fraud: In this scheme criminals inject liquid plastic into grade B jade to simulate grade A jade (Hamilton 11-21-94). A collector reportedly unveiled another example of jade fraud at the renowned Tucson Gem and Mineral Show where he purchased a large piece of jade that had a hollow, junk-filled interior (Kuehn 1997 Website).

◆ Falsified Provenance
As in art, the provenance of a mineral specimen, its source and ownership history, serves to authenticate its originality and, sometimes, to enhance its value. So if a seller lies about the source locality of a specimen, it could very likely change the asking price. For example, a 4" tall imperial topaz from the Thomas Mountains, Utah is likely to have a much greater value than the same-sized specimen from Ouro Prieto, Brazil, because the Utah specimen is much rarer.

◆ Identity Fraud
As with gemstones, dealers may misrepresent the species (type) of a mineral specimen in order to receive a higher price for it. For example, there are many exceedingly rare specimens that are invisible to the un-aided eye. These rarities do not form discrete crystals and are sometimes only found in non-descript clay or mineral mixtures. A sly dealer could pretend one of these minerals exists in some non-descript rock mixture, and the trusting buyer may be none-the-wiser if he or she does not subject a piece of the specimen to analysis.

◆ Short Flats
Mineral collectors buy bulk amounts of specimens in cardboard boxes called flats. Dealers may defraud a collector by showing one flat full of grade-A specimens, and then, upon delivery, drop off

the one grade-A flat along with others of much lower quality. Alternatively, the dealer, may "high-grade" the flats after the sale and before delivery, thereby taking out the one best specimen from each flat.

Prevention: Making valuations and authenticating gems and mineral specimens is too specialized an art for most buyers to handle by themselves. The only safeguards against fraudulent gems and minerals sales are to bone-up on the kind of material you are going to buy; to choose a reputable dealer, and to bring the gem or mineral to an independent expert for appraisal. Vetting dealers and appraisers involves obtaining background information. You can vet dealers by checking the local Better Business Bureau and you can vet appraisers by confirming their affiliations and choosing one who has Gemological Institute of America. Otherwise *caveat emptor*.

Two other measures are worth noting: One way to guard against gemstone switching is to have the stone plotted or mapped by an independent gemmologist. Plotting involves the measurement of the dimensions of the stone and the detailed description of its characteristics (Liu 7-27-97). The most current technology affords laser measurement of gemstones.

To avoid appraisal fraud: i. do not accept a referral for an appraiser from the seller; ii. choose a certified appraiser; and iii. pay a flat fee, not a sliding commission, for the appraisal. Independently finding an appraiser guards against collusion between the seller and the appraiser, choosing a certified appraiser makes it more likely the person knows what he or she are doing, and paying a flat fee guards against an inflated appraisal motivated by an inflated commission (Liu 7-27-97).

MINERAL AND ENERGY RESOURCE FRAUD

Introduction

Fraud occurs throughout the cycle of mineral and energy resource funding, exploration, development, production, and reclamation. By dollar value, most of the fraud occurs as securities (stock) fraud fronted to fund exploration, and as royalty fraud. Royalty fraud occurs when a commodity producer under-reports its production to reduce the royalty payments it owes to the commodity-owner.

Mineral and energy resource fraud differ from most frauds in that its victims are mostly the wealthy. When you consider that the wealthy alone have the money to risk, seeing them loose the most money is not so curious. Apparently, many successful entrepreneurs who win their prosperity by making or selling prosaic things like wheels, cloths, and office supplies, fancy the sign of real wealth is owning a gold mine or oil well. In one sense, the wealthy are correct: Uniquely rich mineral and energy resources pay phenomenal returns on investment. The only problem is that rich mineral and energy resources are hard to find, expensive to buy, and complex to develop. The novice's image of gold in nuggets and oil gushers is a fantasy in comparison to the actual diligent, intellectual, and costly steps needed to identify, prove, and develop a mineral and energy resource occurrence. Ironically, most new deposits now consist of minute quantities disseminated through large volumes of rock—no nuggets and no gushers.

The story of Bre-X Mineral Company is a dramatic, historic, and cautionary tale of the speculative frenzy engendered by the promise of giant mineral and energy resource strikes. Bre-X Minerals Ltd. began exploring for gold at Busang, Indonesia in 1993. During the ensuing three years, the company announced increasingly higher gold reserves for Busang (Heinzl 1997). The reports of growing reserves caused valuations for Bre-X to exceed $6 billion (Schreiner 1997). Even though a number of geologists and mineral exploration companies found reason to question the authenticity of the reported discovery, no one honed a critical pickaxe on the property until the Spring of 1997 when world-class gold producer Freeport McMoran demonstrated that there was no economic concentration of gold at the property and that the entire venture was a fraud (Waldman and Solomon 1997). The fraud financially crushed many small investors and heralded the end of the mid-1990s commodities boom—the price of gold crashed from $400 to under $300 soon thereafter.

Funding Fraud
Stock offerings, private placements, and self-funding provide the capital for mineral and energy resource projects. Fraud comes into play when promoters or business principals deceive investors as to how likely a discovery is to be made and what the likely returns on investment will be. Business principals may misrepresent any of the following parameters: a. their credentials, b. potential of a region, c. potential of a prospect, d. the presence of a certain commodity e. cost of exploration, f. cost of development, g. political expropriation risk, and h. environmental liability.

One example of fraud at the funding level would involve corporate officers who claim they are Ph.D.s with a history of important discoveries, when in fact they are former roustabouts with not a gallon of oil discovered. The false credentials can be used to disarm would-be investors.

A common low-budget fraud is the <u>Dirt Pile Scam</u>: A mining fraud in which an investor buys a specific amount of soil or "ore" which allegedly contains an economic quantity of metal. Dirt pile scams often work out of boiler rooms, using telemarketing techniques. In the scam, the dirt pile never has an economic metal value (New Mexico State Securities Division 1989).

Prevention: Obtain a background investigation of the project promoters. Hire an independent geologist or engineer to evaluate the property.

Exploration Fraud

It is almost impossible for the non-professional to know or confirm what field explorationists are doing or reporting on. This gulf of ignorance means explorationists can falsify most anything: a. the identity of the commodity at a property, b. assay results, c. field geology, d. drilling results, e. expenses, and f. property ownership.

A common exploration fraud involves claiming platinum in desert southwest sands. While there may be scattered southwestern US platinum occurrences, economic platinum placer deposits are as rare as hen's teeth.

Prevention: Hire an independent geologist or engineer to review the field operations and reports.

Development Fraud

Developing a mineral or energy resource often involves drilling, sampling, geostatistical analysis, laboratory work, engineering, and a detailed feasibility study. A criminal could falsify any one or all of these aspects of resource development. For example, perpetrators of mining scams may stage activities at mine sites to falsely impress an investor (New Mexico State Securities Division 1989).

The Bre-X fraud, described above, is the classic development fraud. The company claimed to have developed nearly 100 million ounces of gold, when in fact the property did not contain an ounce of economically recoverable gold.

Prevention: Hire an independent geologist or engineer to review the feasibility study.

Production Fraud
To diminish the risk to any one participant, most energy or mineral properties have two sets of participants; owners and operators. While in some cases the underlying owners act as operators, very often the commodity owner is under-funded, and it seeks a larger entity to conduct exploration and development. When the owners give up their development and/or production rights they are paid by the operator or producer on a variety of schedules: i. a lease, ii. an advanced royalty paid against future production, iii. a production royalty based on the amount of the commodity produced, or iv. a net profits royalty.

Production fraud occurs either by falsifying the amount of a commodity that is produced or by falsifying production costs. If a producer or distributor lie about the quantity of material produced from a property, this may well effect the amount of money paid to the royalty owners. Royalty owners can be the business or individuals who originally owned the commodity, or later participants who contributed funding to the property. One common way to defraud royalty owners occurs with net earnings royalties. These royalties are paid after the operator has paid off all of its expenses. If the operator pads or inflates its expenses, the property may never show a net profit, so no royalties will be paid. A real-life royalty scam involved perpetrators who sold a property based on misrepresented productivity of oil and gas leases: The seller guaranteed that each of four wells were productive. In fact, one had a producing well, a second had a non-productive well, and the other two never had exploration wells drilled on them (USPIS Summer 1990).

Oil and gas and coal royalty fraud against the US government and American Indian Tribes has a long history. In an oil and gas royalty fraud, the producer under-reports the volume of oil and gas produced in order to short change the royalty holder. Texaco admitted to doing just that when it paid the state of Louisiana $250 million in 1994 for missed revenue (McMahon 4-4-98). In some cases, the royalty thief may not simply falsify the production records. Instead they may perpetrate a more sophisticated fraud involving modifying gages to read under-estimated flow volumes.

One renowned geologist who specialized in Mexico work relayed a cautionary tale about absentee landlords and their missed royalties. A Chicago scion sent the geologist to Guanajuanto, MX to see why the family silver mine failed to produce a profit. Very quickly, the geologist saw that the mine was indeed highly profitable: It was just that the mine manager and his crew took all of the profit themselves by shipping the high grade ore to their own private mill—the managers were falsifying the mine production.

Prevention: Make sure the production contract allows for un-announced site visits and production audits and hire an engineer to periodically conduct the visits and audits.

Reclamation Fraud

If an investor signs on as a silent general partner, his or her companions may defraud him or her by leaving an environmental mess at the property. If the silent partner is the only solvent partner, he or she could unwittingly be saddled with the entire bankrupting bill. Galactic Resources, a Canadian Company, did nearly that, when they left a cyanide trail in Colorado's Summitville Gold District. To date, the only solvent, culpable party at Summitville has been the US taxpayers in the form of the US Environmental Protection Agency (ATSDR Website).

Prevention: Hire an independent engineer to assess the environmental liabilities prior to entering into a project. Consider buying environmental insurance. Insist that the investment contract allow for un-announced audits and site visits. Make sure the posted bond is sufficient to cover the potential liability.

REAL ESTATE AND MORTGAGE FRAUD

Introduction

Although there are considerable safeguards, checks, and balances, fraud is found at every stage of the real estate business. To date, the most egregious fraud has been in lending where as much as 60% of an estimated $500 billion Saving and Loan loss came from civil and criminal frauds committed during the 1980s real estate boom (Kerry Sept 1991). Taxpayers paid because the lending institutions, the Thrifts, were, and still are, insured by the US government.

On the microeconomic level, real estate fraud hurts individual homeowners and investors when they end up with mis-represented properties. By example, the fraud emblematic of the post World War II era was the swamp land or barren desert for sale to city dwellers. In this scheme, real estate broker-developers sliced up worthless land into small lots and sold the lots, sight-un-seen to unwitting individuals who dreamed of a vacation lot.

Real estate fraud effects all socio-economic levels and all sectors of the economy. After all, the first investment most people acquire is a house, and home ownership is a core American value. Repair frauds (see CHAPTER THREE'S Consumer Fraud section) target the working class; vacation home and concealed house defects target the middle class; lending fraud includes consumers as frauds, lenders as criminals, and the government as a victim.

Real estate fraud is perpetrated by sellers who misrepresent properties, by dishonest brokers, by buyers who falsify their suitability for loans, by mortgage brokers who falsify financial application materials, by lending institutions that falsify financial statements and ignore lending guidelines, and by title companies that falsify title information.

Builder Fraud

More than any other real estate professionals, builders sell dreams. They build model homes with artificial water ways, pack them with showroom quality furnishings, and show would-be buyers glossy drawings of all the available models. (Not-to mention the free Pepsi and pretzels.) In buying a home before it is built, the buyer feels more attached by adding their in-put. Builders have a chance to commit, allow or participate in the following frauds:

- The selling of land to which they have no title.
- The taking of and running-off-with advanced-fees paid as down payments.
- The misrepresentation of his or her track-record, contractor licensing and/or building credentials.
- The misrepresentation that he or she carry worker's compensation and liability insurance.
- The substitution of low-quality parts and materials for the promised high-quality ones.
- The falsification of building inspections.
- The failure to disclose the presence of swelling soils or other natural hazards like landslide.
- The failure to disclose soil or groundwater contamination.
- The selling of property without conveying title insurance.

Prevention: Buyers must undertake a due diligence study of any prospective purchase either by verifying and inspecting themselves, or by hiring qualified inspectors. Don't buy property without title insurance.

There are a number of schemes that take place after the contracting is complete:
- At the close of a fixed-price contract the contractor may confront the homeowner with additional fees. The contractor may say that some costs were outside of the agreed-to contract, that he or she made a mistake in bidding the fixed-price contract, or that cost over-runs force him or her to make additional charges.

- After a contractor is done-and-gone, he or she may fraudulently attach a lien to the property, hoping to extract further payments.
- Another post-completion fraud is called lien sharking: A scheme whereby unscrupulous general contractors fail to pay their subcontractors, thereby inducing the sub to file liens against a building owner. The desperate subcontractors may then sell the liens to a consolidator who colors the title to the property. To clear the title, the property owner is forced to pay-off the liens, in effect paying for the work a second time (Sifakis 1993).

Prevention: Make sure written contracts itemize each cost. Have an attorney review all construction contracts. Check to see that all subcontractors are paid-off. Consider buying extended-coverage title insurance to cover undisclosed liens or other encumbrances.

Seller Misrepresentation

As stated in this section's Introduction, the classic real estate fraud is the selling of worthless swamp or desert (USPIS Winter 1989-90) land to buyers who fail to visit the lot before closing on their purchase. However, there are many other aspects of property that may be misrepresented:

- Flaws in the title.
- In the case of out-of-state buyers, the character of a lot may be falsified. For example, a seller may lie and say a property is on the beach when in fact it is across the street from the beach (USPIS Winter/Spring 1994).
- The seller may not actually own the property (Wright 1996).
- The property may be described as flaw-free when in fact it has flaws.
- The presence of swelling soils or other natural hazards like landslide.
- The presence of soil or groundwater contamination.
- The presence of termites or other insect infestations.
- The fact that well water is insufficient or non-potable.

167

- The fact that a septic system has not been inspected, does not work, or has leaks.
- The potential capital appreciation, rentability, and resale market for time-share units (Institute of Certified Financial Planners 1994) or other real estate investments.

Prevention: Buyers must undertake a due diligence study of all properties either by verifying and inspecting themselves, or by hiring qualified inspectors. Don't buy property without title insurance.

Broker Fraud

Licensed and unlicensed brokers have engaged in frauds other than misrepresenting properties:

- Unlicensed businesses, posing as land liquidation companies, solicit time-share, raw land, and campground-membership owners, with promises to match them with potential buyers. To receive the buyers' names, the owner must pay an advanced-fee. Ultimately the victim is never put in touch with any buyers or prospective trading partners (Lehman June 1995).
- Time Share Prize Fraud: A couple plead guilty to bankruptcy fraud and money laundering for their involvement in a scheme to entice customers into sitting through time share sales promotions. Whereas the couple was responsible for giving the customers prizes for attending the sales pitches, they seldom delivered the promised prizes (USPIS Winter 1989-90).
- Realtors, or other sellers or real property, may defraud their customers when they sell a property listing to another broker or to one of their friends or acquaintances. In a rapidly appreciating market, the unscrupulous broker may buy a property, or have a friend or acquaintance buy one of their own customer's properties without giving the property clear access to the market. The broker or his shill then quickly turns around and re-sells the property. By analogy to securities markets, this is a non-competitive brokering practice because it denies the seller

access to competitive markets. In some circles, non-competitive sales are called "pocket listings."

- Career criminals, posing as property owners or brokers, may rent or lease a property, advertise it again for rent or sale, and then take down payments from various parties before skipping town (Wright 1996).
- A real estate sales agent defrauded his former employer and a customer by taking a property listing with him when he left one agency. To conceal the unethical taking, he sent a falsified letter to his former employer. The letter pretended to be from the owner of the property, and it informed the former employer that the listing was going with the resigned agent to the new broker (Stretch 6-2-98).
- A real estate salesmen defrauded about 70 investors by embezzling the proceeds from real estate contract sales which he had brokered (USPIS Spring 1990).

Prevention: (1) Do not pay an advanced-fee for brokerage services. (2) Do not allow brokers to side-step the open market—insist on a few days of multi-listing in an outstanding market. (3) If suspicious of landlords or sellers, call the county assessor to check for ownership of a rental or sale property. (4) If a listing changes brokers, call all involved parties to see that change was proper. (5) When selling real estate contracts or mortgages, call the county recorder to see if any liens or encumbrances have been recorded.

Loan Application Falsification

Lending generally involves four entities: (1) the borrower, (2) a mortgage broker, (3) a lending institution, and (4) the US government which either insures the lender that makes the loan, or directly loans the money. Any of the former three are known to engage in application fraud.

◆ Borrower Fraud

Borrowers can falsify any of dozens of criteria on a loan application to obtain a loan or more money than justified:

- Applicants may falsify tax, income, debt, credit, or employment information in their mortgage application. The tax information is generally altered to show income that is higher than the actual income. Employment information may be altered to show a steadier employment history, exaggerated salary, or inflated job position (DeBoth 1998). Euphemisms for altering credit histories are "credit cleaning" and "skin shedding" (Staples Website).
- Air Loan Scams: Perpetrators apply for loans on non-existent properties (Willette 8-10-95).
- Individuals may defraud lenders by converting escrow funds to non-approved uses.
- Borrowers may bribe appraisers, or otherwise falsify loan applications to obtain a more sizable loan than would have been available had the application been truthfully completed.
- Borrowers may engage in questionable, rapid sales of properties (particularly raw land), called Flip Sales that may undermine the ability of lenders to conduct appraisals (Asbury Park Press Website).
- A title company owner may obtain multiple loans on the same properties by falsifying mortgage releases, recording the releases at county recorders, and then repeatedly applying for loans (Ingersoll 6-21-98).
- A real estate developer was indicted for defrauding construction subcontractors of their fees. The developer used a complex scheme whereby he mortgaged construction projects to himself, through shell companies, hired contractors to build the homes, and failed to pay for the contracting. Then, after the contractors filed liens on the properties, the developer foreclosed on himself to regain title to the property without the lien encumbrances (USPIS Spring 1990). The fraud here lies in the developer taking advantage of foreclosure laws and in his failing to disclose that he was both the borrower and the lender. By making himself the mortgage lender, he stood first in line to re-

cover the property from bad debts. By failing to disclose his unique position as borrower and lender, he committed fraud.

- Investors, speculators, fee appraisers, real estate agents, and others have conspired to defraud federally-insured mortgage programs by fronting "straw buyers" to purchase properties for inflated prices, and then having the purchaser default on the loan, leaving the taxpayer holding the bag (FBI 1989).

- A Los Angeles man "identified unencumbered vacant land, obtained credit history reports of the true property owners, and then applied for loans against the properties assuming the identity of the true property owners (USPIS Winter/Spring 1990)."

- Criminals may use falsified documents to obtain loans against another person's or business's property (L.A. County Department of Consumer Affairs Website).

- A federal grand jury indicted a couple for inflating the price of real estate in order to get financial institutions to loan a larger amount than the property's true value (USPIS Spring 1993).

Prevention: Government regulators and in-house auditors are responsible for auditing lending institutions. In any case, don't falsify loan apps..

◆ Mortgage Broker Fraud

Two common mortgage broker frauds are falsifying loan applications (DeBoth 1998) and encouraging loan flipping. Mortgage application falsification may be done with the knowledge of the borrower or without. When the broker is involved, they do it to obtain a commission that they might not otherwise receive. Loan flipping is an unethical practice where the broker (or lender) encourages the borrower to repeatedly refinance, each time assuming a loan with higher origination points and/or a higher interest rate. Brokers do this to churn commissions, and lenders do this to increase their revenue (Heady 5-31-98).

Prevention: Government regulators and in-house auditors are responsible for auditing lending institutions. Don't allow mortgage brokers to falsify applications on your behalf—check the final application before it goes to the lender and keep a copy.

Lending Institution Fraud
There are four common types of lending institution fraud: (1) encouraging borrowers to take un-needed or inappropriate loans; (2) falsifying loan application information to deceive regulators; (3) charging inappropriate fees to accelerate mortgage payments and; (4) violating Federal Trade Commission regulations that govern high-rate, high fee loans.

◆ Inappropriate Lending
- Unscrupulous lenders prey on the old or uninformed, inducing the victim to borrow money under deceptive lending terms. In one case, a woman needed a $3,000 roof repair, but was deceived into borrowing $15,000 at 18.9% (Hudson Fall 1993).
- Equity Strippers are aggressive lenders who trick homeowners into borrowing more than they can afford. Some of these unscrupulous lenders do this so that they can foreclose on the property after the borrower stops making payments on the loan (Heady 5-31-98).
- Reverse mortgages are financial contracts designed to allow individuals to use home equity to fuel periodic cash flow. They are also the source of lending schemes. In one scheme, criminals defraud unwitting homeowners by pulling a bait and switch: They secretively swap title release documents for the promised reverse mortgage agreements. While the trusting homeowner, often a senior, believes they are going to receive periodic payments through a reverse mortgage, in fact, they just signed away their homes (*San Francisco Chronicle* 5-11-98).
- A second reverse mortgage fraud involves telemarketers who persuade equity-rich homeowners to take lump-sum reverse mortgages and then buy annuities. What the telemarketer fails to disclose is that the annuities come with extraordinary 8% to

10% commissions that may jeopardize federal retirement benefits (BBB Web site).

◆ Falsified Loan Applications
Bank or savings and loan officers may falsify loan information to avoid federal regulatory enforcement action.

◆ Inappropriate Processing Fees
Dishonest companies offer to "assist" in making accelerated mortgage payments. For an extra fee, the company sends the payments onto the mortgage company. The problem is that no assistance is necessary—a borrower can simply send the payment to the mortgage company themselves (NFIC Website).

◆ Federal Trade Commission Violations
- The FTC regulates loans with high interest rates and/or high origination fees.
- The regulations have complex disclosure requirements to prevent the lender from deceiving the borrower.
- The regulations also have highly technical payment schedule, refinance, default specifications that must be disclosed to the borrower and that must not be violated.
- One example involves Negative Amortizations: The illegal mortgage-lending practice where borrowers monthly payments do not go toward lowering the principal due. This type of mortgage payment prevents the borrower from ever paying off a debt (FTC 5-96).

Prevention: (1) Have an attorney or accountant review any second mortgages or above-market rate loans. Beware of lenders that solicit you. (2) Government regulators and in-house auditors are responsible for auditing lending institutions. (3) Do not use a processing company to accelerate mortgage payments. The mortgage company will handle this at no additional charge. Study Federal Trade Commission guidelines for high-rate, high-fee loans prior to agreeing to one.

Miscellaneous Real Estate Fraud

◆ Fraud by Government Officials

Lazy county assessors may bunch properties of highly varied valuations into one group, then assess all of the properties at one, inflated rate. This causes the owners of less expensive properties to pay the same square-footage appraisals as those who own highly refined properties.

Prevention: Review your annual tax assessment. Call the county assessor for an explanation of the basis for the assessment.

◆ Buyer Defrauding Seller

- A federal jury convicted five Seattle residents of purchasing distressed properties through quit claims, then selling or renting the properties without paying the underlying mortgages, thereby eventually causing financial hardship to both the original owner and the buyers. This is known as equity skimming (USPIS Fall 1990).
- Criminals defraud property owners by tendering worthless stock (Conklin 1994), counterfeit checks and money, and other counterfeit securities in payment for real property.

Prevention: Conduct background checks on anyone to whom you lend money, rent, or sell property.

◆ Moving Company Fraud

Dishonest movers entice victims into house-moving services, then ask for additional fees once the goods are moved (Goldberg 6-7-93).

Prevention: Sign fixed-price contracts, and pay upon completion of service, not before. Do not pay cash. Write on check, "paid in full."

◆ Partnership Fraud

"Partner-wanted positions are sometimes nothing but deceptive frauds to get your investment in a supposedly profitable business claiming the need for new funds (City of Denver 9-84)." Real estate businesses may engage in this partnership fraud.

Prevention: Conduct a due diligence study on all investments and a background check on all prospective partners.

◆ Real Estate Petty Mail Fraud

Criminals sent new Arizona homeowners notices that they must pay a $25 to secure their "homestead act rights." The notices pretended to be from the "State Recording Office," but in fact, homestead act protection against creditors is automatic, and no fee was required (Jensen 1-23-98).

Prevention: Call the county assessor or recorder to check the validity of a charge prior to paying any fees.

◆ Seller Defrauding Investors

▪ Two perpetrators defrauded investors by selling promissory notes based on fraudulent property valuations. The valuations were fraudulent because "straw buyers," in collusion with the sellers, gave inflated purchase prices to the seller. The perpetrators then sold investors value-inflated promissory notes secured by deeds of trust based on the manipulated appraisals (USPIS Summer 1991).

▪ A career criminal embezzled money from private investors. He asked to borrow money under the pretext of paying off a mortgage (Nash 1976).

Prevention: (1) Promissory note investors should conduct independent appraisals of the property that underlies a loan. (2) Private mortgage investors should convey their investments through a title company to obtain a deed for the property or a lien on the property.

◆ Sellers Defrauding Realtors in a convoluted scheme: A buyer says he desperately wants to buy a specific piece of property. The price he proposes to pay is inflated. The greedy Realtor goes to the property owner and offers to buy the property at a somewhat inflated price. The Realtor is willing to pay an inflated price because he is convinced he has a greater fool who will pay even more. After the Realtor buys the property, the straw buyer disappears, or says he is no longer interested in the property. In this scam, the straw buyer and the seller are accomplices who defrauded the Realtor by inducing him to pay an inflated price for the property (Sifakis 1993).

Prevention: No one should buy real property without first obtaining an independent appraisal of the property. Anyone offering an inflated price should be viewed with suspicion.

SECURITIES FRAUD

Introduction
A security is any "...note, stock, bond, evidence of debt, interest or participation in profit sharing agreement, investment contract, voting trust certificate, fractional undivided interest in oil, gas, or other mineral rights, or any warrant to subscribe to, or purchase, any of the foregoing or other similar instruments (NASAA 1986)." This Section focuses on stocks, bonds, and futures, the most prevalent securities.

By their essential nature, as paper assets, securities are prone to fraud. This is true because the buying and selling of paper does not necessitate any physical examination. Unlike tangible property transfers, which frequently entail physical inspections and due diligence steps, securities transfers are most often made by mail or instantaneously by phone, fax or Internet. The frequency of securities fraud is multiplied by the attraction criminals have to the opportunities as well as the ease of enacting the frauds.

Securities frauds are equal opportunity: Schemes target all of the market players: i. customers, ii. brokerage houses, and iii. the broader market. The most common of all securities frauds are sales by unregistered brokers and sales of unregistered securities. If all this makes securities fraud sound far too easy, take heart. As with other sectors of society that are highly susceptible to fraud, the risk in securities is mitigated by an array of regulatory and investigative agencies that specifically target securities fraud.

The US Securities and Exchange Commission has the broadest mandate and furthest reach of all US securities regulators. The SEC has a self-regulating, private parallel, the National Association of Securities Dealers. A variety of regulators focus on more specialized markets, such as the Commodities Futures Trading Commission, which regulates futures markets, and a number of agencies in the US Department of Treasury which oversee lending and banking. These various federal agencies freely enlist the FBI when they uncover signs of major fraud. Individual states also have securities and insurance divisions which license and oversee securities brokers. This phalanx of regulators makes for formidable deterrents against securities fraud. Unfortunately, while regulators and law enforcement protect markets, they do not routinely make whole the losses of individuals. To thwart these potential losses, the individual investors must be aware of securities-fraud schemes.

Stock Fraud

◆ Fraud Against Customers

Since brokerage houses and brokers are in positions of fiduciary trust, society expects them to behave. When they don't, their transgressions take on an exaggerated pall. Broker-fraud occurs throughout the investment cycle: a. in opening accounts, b. in managing account, c. in sales and d. in account trades.

✶ Account Openings afford a number of opportunities for fraud: a. Unlicensed brokers may try to sell their services; b. Licensed or unlicensed brokers may try to sell unlicensed securities; c. Licensed or unlicensed brokers may falsify their track records to make customers think the broker is outstanding; and d. Licensed or unlicensed brokers may falsely claim that there is no loss potential or say that he or she will reimburse any losses.

177

One scheme, here coined "Fifty-fifty Sales Pitch," is the cleverest sales fraud of all: A broker cold-calls ten potential customers. To the first five, he says, "Just give me one chance. I guarantee that XYZ company will go up during the next six months. If you buy it through an account with me, and it doesn't go up, I'll refund any loss and you can close your account." When he cold-calls the other five potential customers he says, "Just give me one chance. We will sell XYZ company short (borrow the stock from the brokerage house, sell it immediately, and then, ideally, pay back the stock with devalued shares bought on the open market at a later date). If the stock does not go down in the next six months, and you take a loss, I'll cover your loss and you can close the account." After six months, the broker reimburses those on the losing side of the trade, closes their accounts, and sends them down the road. For those five with the winning trades, the broker claims prescient genius, and secures their permission to make discretionary trades.

*Fraud in Managing Accounts
Once a broker has an account, he manages the funds in the account, recommends purchases and sales, and sees trades executed. Account management avails a number of opportunities for fraud:

- Fraudulent securities traders may conceal trading losses from customers in order to continue churning an account or to otherwise take advantage of a client (CFTC Website).
- A broker embezzled $1.1 million from a pension and tried to cover it up by pretending soured investments caused the loss (Rafi Aug 1998).
- Stock Account Transfer Fraud: An assistant manager for a major brokerage firm used a fictitious name to create a number of accounts, then transferred a number of the firm's customers' accounts into her account, then directed the redemption of the funds to herself (USPIS Fall 1991).

- Bucket Shop: "... The bucket shop operator accepted a client's money without ever actually buying or selling securities as the client ordered. Instead he held the money and gambled that the customer's [stock picks] were wrong. When too many customers were right, the bucket shop closed its doors and opened a new office (NASAA 1986)."
- Self-Dealing: A scheme where a banker, trustee, or other person in a position of trust allots preferred loans, contracts, or other intrusted things of value (to himself or others connected to him), thereby creating a conflict of interest.
- Annuity Embezzlement: An insurance agent urged some of his elderly customers to cash-in their annuities for re-investment. Instead of reinvesting, he converted the funds to his own use (USPIS Summer 1998).

*Fraudulent Sales

Brokers engage in sales fraud when: they sell investments that are inappropriate for the client, engage in commission gouging, or sell illegal securities. Marginal brokerage houses use dynamiters: "... salesman who utilizes high pressure tactics and deceit to sell stock. Usually used for the final sale in a series of sales just before the sales group drops the promotion [of an individual speculative stock] (NASAA 1986)."

■ Inappropriate Sales

Upon opening a new account, investors complete new account profiles which state their investment goals and describe their investment experience. The broker must stick to the investment objectives and make recommendations consistent with the investor's experience. For example, if the investor stated that he was inexperienced and wished to only buy conservative investments for short-term goals, broker sales of penny gold stocks would be highly inappropriate. [Penny stocks are: "inexpensive stocks issued for new ventures. At their best, legitimate penny stocks are extremely speculative; at their worst, their prices are easily manipulated by the company and broker-dealers, leaving the unsuspecting investors holding worthless paper (Institute of Certified Financial Planners 1994)." The most speculative of penny stocks is the "Blind Pool or Blank Check," a stock whose underline business has no known or specific business (USPIS Fall 1991).]

Although not stock frauds, to illustrate inappropriate sales, consider the landmark cases of two major brokerage firms that saw their customers file complaints resulting from the firms' misrepresentation of risk, exaggeration of performance, and falsification of key facts governing the sale of limited partnerships. Many of the partnerships were represented as "fixed-income" investments, but in fact, investors lost substantial portions of their principal (Maremont 4-25-94). "Prudential, a subsidiary of Prudential Insurance CO., defrauded its customers by selling them risky real estate, oil and natural gas limited partnerships and assuring them that their money was safe, according to the SEC complaint filed last year (Walsh 10-13-94)."

■ Commission Gouging
The primary means of inflating commission revenues is by churning, the practice of making excessive sales using the same principal in order to generate commissions for the broker. One particularly insidious churning practice involves annuities—annuities are insurance products, some of which are stock mutual funds, that shelter current profits from taxes. They fall under the insurance umbrella because they have a small insurance component which protects the principal from loss. Unethical insurance salesmen may encourage victims to buy annuities when they are inappropriate or to sell one annuity and buy another, thereby giving the agent a large commission.

A variation of annuity churning is selling annuities in a retirement plan: By using a tax-sheltered account to buy an annuity, the investor is paying twice for the same benefit—the tax shelter. When a broker encourages this sale, it can be for no reason other than to generate undue commissions for him or herself.

Forbes (Androshick and Eaton 2-24-97) implies that independent stock brokers are particularly prone to commission gouging: Some securities companies, particularly insurance annuity sellers, are known for licensing independent, loosely supervised brokers who often sell securities with commission schedules ranging up to 40%. Some brokers sell questionable services in their fee schedules such as "Market Timing Services." Market timing is presumably a synonym for monitoring an investor's account, something brokers are supposed to do as a matter of course.

One other gouging practice employs excessive stock spreads: Unethical brokers may make exorbitant mark-ups by selling retail customers "low or no commission" stocks that have extreme spreads between the bid and ask price. The size of the spread represents profits to the broker (Weiss 12-15-97).

■ Illegal Securities
Here are four types of illegal securities:

- Unregistered securities,
- Foreign Options,
- Limited Edition Treasury Securities: The Securities and Exchange Commission warned of criminals offering "limited edition" treasury securities, a fictitious financial instrument (SEC Website),
- Chop Stocks: Stocks illegally purchased from wholesale brokers at deeply discounted prices and then resold to retail customers. The sale is illegal because these stocks are restricted by Rule 144 of the Securities and Exchange Commission. Making "book" entries of the stocks into customer accounts as opposed to issuing certificates conceals the illegal nature of the sales.

The certificates are not issued because their restricted nature is noted on the paper (Weiss 12-15-97).

*Fraudulent Account Trades

Trade executions are invisible to most investors. What better area to defraud the customer? Here are some of the fraudulent trading schemes:

- Bucketing: A non-competitive, illegal, brokerage trading practice. "Directly or indirectly taking the opposite side of a customer's order into the handling broker's own account or into an account in which he had an interest, without execution on an exchange (NASAA 1986)."
- Interpositioning: A fraudulent securities-brokerage practice in which the broker-dealer deceives a customer by making undisclosed non-competitive trades. These trades are completed by using the broker-dealer's account to buy securities, then selling the securities from the broker-dealer account to the customer, in effect, charging the customer two sets of commissions. In contrast, the customary practice is to place a market order for the customer, or to directly fill the order from inventory held by the broker-dealer. These interpositioned commissions can amount to 5% to 12% of the transaction, and in one case ran to 40.9% (Goldberg 1978).
- Post-Dated Trades: Brokers may defraud customers who place high-volume stock trades by placing orders throughout the day, then post-dating the earlier trades to raise the average price of all of the trades to the price of the order with the highest purchase price (Weiss 12-15-97). [Conversely, in executing a sell order with the sales spread throughout the day, the dishonest broker may post-date the trades to show the average price as lower than the actual price received.]
- Trading Ahead: The illegal practice where securities brokers make trades in advance of customer trades, using the foreknowledge to benefit themselves (CFTC 1997)

- Wash Sales: Securities trades completed without the intent to complete a transaction. Wash sales may be completed by brokers as a method of churning (CFTC 1997).

Prevention: Conduct background checks on prospective brokers and brokerage houses by calling the National Association of Securities Dealers and the Securities and Exchange Commission. Ask the two regulators if complaints or sanctions have been filed against either the broker or the brokerage house. Do not give brokers discretionary trading privileges for your accounts. Closely monitor all account statements. Immediately question any suspicious charges. If there are questionable trades, insist that the broker provide a "time and trades" printout to trace your specific trades. Seek competitive bids from other brokers if you make large trades or if you trade a lot. Confront your broker if one of his or her recommendations seem inconsistent with your investment profile or with your investment objectives. Do not engage in any preferred trading practices and report these, and any other questionable broker practices, to the regulators.

◆ Fraud Against Brokerage Houses

Both employees and customers are capable of defrauding brokerage houses. For a general discussion of employee fraud, see the Handbook's OPERATIONS CHAPTER. The discussion here is limited to brokerage-industry-specific frauds. Brokers may: a. falsify their experience, b. engage in schemes to cheat on securities exams (*WSJ* 2-26-97), or c. engage in unauthorized, rogue trading activities (see the Rogue Trader discussions in the Bond and Futures sections below). These rogue trades have the potential to shame, hurt profits, and even bankrupt brokerage houses.

Customer frauds typically involve falsifying background or trading-suitability information. Upon opening a new account, a customer fills in a financial and experience profile statement which is used to determine what type of investing is suitable for the account. If customers falsify their trading experience or asset statement, it could cause brokerage houses to incur liability for unsuccessful trades or to incur un-collectable debt.

In one patently fraudulent scheme, called "free-riding," the investor falsifies his suitability for credit, then makes trades based on his bogus credit profile. The *Wall Street Journal* (9-29-95) describes a free-rider who kept the money for his profitable trades but refused to pay for trade losses he incurred.

One bold criminal tried to use a counterfeit $10 million certificate of deposit as collateral on a loan from broker Smith Barney. The Smith Barney office was prepared to fend off this fraud because they had previously detected two individuals' attempts to pass off $300 million in counterfeit municipal bonds as collateral on a margin account (Braga 3-8-96).

Prevention: The best way for brokerages houses to vet employees and customers is to conduct careful interviews and to complete background checks in response to important inconsistencies.

◆ Fraud Against Stock Markets
Brokerage firms, individuals brokers, and shareholders have used a variety of schemes to manipulate the overall market. These schemes give un-due profits or advantages to individuals, to public company insiders, and to brokers.

∗Preferred Individuals
In a questionable practice, some brokers try to curry favor with their better customers by offering special dispensation when the customer incurs a loss. Here are two schemes:

▪ Warrant Payoff: Some stockbrokers illegally compensate preferred customers for stock trading losses by issuing "winning" warrants to buy other stock. The warrants, or rights to buy stocks, have a high likelihood of profitably paying off in a short amount of time (Weiss 12-15-97).

- Initial Public Offering Fraud: Dishonest stock brokers may issue initial public offerings to favored clients to make up for other trading losses. When the brokerage house is the underwriter, the recipient is often assured the opening price will far exceed the issue price, so the client will feel that he has been compensated for his loss.

The effect of these payoffs is to proffer an implicit promise of immunity from loss, and doing so is illegal.

*Insider Stock Manipulation
Insiders, those with knowledge of information that is restricted to a few in a public company, and those with controlling interests of publicly-traded securities, can illegally benefit themselves by trading on their proprietary knowledge or by using their dominant stock holdings to manipulate the stock market.

■ Insider Information
The illegal securities-trading practice where a "...person based that trading on non-public material information. And the person had access to that information by virtue of a relationship of trust or fiduciary duty that was violated by the trading (Fleckenstein 6-26-98)."

■ Trading Manipulations
- Stock Repurchase Fraud: Public companies may manipulate stock prices by announcing stock repurchases and then failing to follow through with the actual buys (Kracher and. Johnson Nov 1997). This practice is not illegal.
- Turnaround Deal: "A manipulation whereby a promoter prearranges an underwriting sale to go to reliable or nominee buyers for a specified period of time in order to show that a public distribution has been made. What the public does not know is that the promoter has put up his own money with the nominee or had guaranteed the purchaser(s) that he will buy the stock

back at a small profit to enable his own dealings later. Another variation is the use of nominee companies to purchase the underwriting. The object is that the promoter ends up with all the stock hidden from the authorities and also controls the money that he has paid for the stock because it is now in the treasury of the company he controls. He can then get his money back by management fees, phony or inflated invoices for work not done, or by selling the company worthless assets at inflated prices. In the end he receives the stock at virtually no cost to himself. Offshore and overseas banks are often used to launder the turnaround and the securities are registered in street names, usually the underwriting broker's in order to avoid transferring registrations at the transfer agent and leaving a record of the turnaround (NASAA 1986)."

- Back Dooring: "Selling back into the market stock which a promoter thought had been safely laid away. Can be a double crossing technique at the considerable expense of the promoter (NASAA 1986)."
- Box Job: "A fraudulent device whereby a group of people control most or all of a company's stock by means of hidden ownership, and, through such control, artificially manipulate or hype the stock to their advantage, with the stock generally being sold to the public once the conspirators have moved the stock to the desired "target" price (USPIS Fall 1991)."
- Jiggle the Market: "To affect the market price of shares within a narrow range. The purpose is to encourage the public to sell their holdings and enable a stock promoter to accumulate relatively low priced stock in anticipation of future market promotion (NASAA 1986)."
- Nominee Stock Purchases: Executives deceived the Securities and Exchange Commission and public stock purchasers by "making fraudulent purchases of stock in the names of nominees," to permit the stock offerings to proceed publicly. Without the fraudulent purchases, the firm would not have had

enough shares publicly distributed to meet requirements for public offerings (USPIS Winter 1990-91).

- Pump and Dump Scheme: Stock manipulators artificially raise the price of a narrowly traded security, and when investors step in to a surging stock, the manipulators sell their shares at inflated prices (Barrett 7-10-95).
- Parking Securities Fraud: When an investor arranges to sell securities and to later repurchase them at no risk of loss, he is engaged in securities parking (*WSJ* 9-29-95).

✳ Broker Scheme

Penny stock executives plead guilty to multiple charges stemming from their violation of Securities and Exchange Commission regulations governing the mandatory disclosure of brokers' partnership in multiple securities firms. The multiple associations were set up to allow the brokers to escape to a second firm if they were shut down by the SEC for securities violations (USPIS Winter 1990-91).

Prevention: None—the regulators don't need outside advice.

Bond Frauds

Bonds are securities that represent debt interests in business or government ventures. Companies issue bonds to raise capital to payoff debts like capital investments. For example, Caterpillar Corporation might issue bonds if it wished to build a new tractor factory. Alternatively, a company may issue bonds to raise money for acquiring other companies. Governments can also issue bonds to cover obligations for things like highways, water projects, or education financing.

Bonds are susceptible to the same schemes that pervade stock sales (see above): churning, misrepresentation, illegal trading practices, and embezzlement. One area open to bond-sale fraud by brokers involves the sale of exotic bonds that are high risk. If brokers fail to disclose the risk to their customers, this too may be fraud. Junk bonds; high-yield, low-quality issues; and "stripped bonds," bonds issued without principal repayment, are two examples of high-risk bonds. In one case, brokerage houses sold "toxic waste bonds," a form of stripped bond: These are highly volatile mortgage securities issued by the Federal National Mortgage Association (Fannie Mae). The brokerages failed to disclose the volatility of the securities. Unwary investors lost millions investing in these "stripped" notes which they thought were secure. Even though the securities were, in part, guaranteed by the Federal Government, they were still very sensitive to interest rates because these "stripped" mortgage loans do not include any principal repayment. Without principal repayment, these notes are highly exposed to changes in interest rates, and when interest rates went down in early 1990's, investors lost a substantial portion of their investment (Knecht 12-20-94).

Notwithstanding high-risk bonds, generally, bonds are a more conservative asset class than are stocks, so they neither attract the promoter-salesmen nor the greedy-investor elements that are so drawn to stocks. So what kind of fraud is left for the bond markets—schemes that center on the lending and debt aspect of bonds issues. Here are the most common bond frauds: i. misrepresentation during underwriting, ii. bond rating falsification, iii. misappropriation of funds raised from bonds, iv. yield burning, and v. rogue trading. These types of schemes effect institutions more than individual investors:

◆ Misrepresentation During Underwriting
Underwriting is the stage at which a brokerage house or other financial institution evaluates a proposed bond issue. During underwriting, the underwriter determines how much debt can successfully be sold, the face value of the debt, the interest rate of the debt, and who will participate in selling the new issue. The borrower may defraud the underwriter by misrepresenting its credit history, the nature of the underlying asset, or the pending use of the funds.

In one case, executives made false assurances about the feasibility of a municipal project (USPIS Winter 1990-91). The most egregious bond misrepresentations came from a 1980s investment mavin who is known as the poster boy for fraudulent bond underwritings. He staged corporate mergers based on the issuance of bonds with borrowing rates so high that they were destined not to perform.

Alternatively, underwriters may defraud borrowers by charging excessive commissions and failing to disclose the excessive fees, or by embezzling investor funds at the outset of a bond issue.

◆ Bond Rating Falsification
Upon issuance of a bond, independent bond-rating companies evaluate the underlying asset used to secure the bond and the issuer's ability to pay back the debt. The bond-rater then ranks the issue, using a scale of investment to junk-grade. If the debt issuer falsifies aspects of its issue, it may receive a more favorable rating than is justified, and therefore, the bond will sell at a higher premium than justified.

Conceivably, a debt issuer could bribe a bond-rater to obtain a more favorable rating, but I did not find any examples of this crime.

◆ Misappropriation of Funds Raised From Bonds
Bond issuers can defraud investors by converting money raised in a debt issue for non-approved purposes. In effect, this is institutional embezzlement. In one case, an individual defrauded municipalities through the sale of municipal bonds. He and others persuaded various governmental municipalities to issue bonds to purchase nursing homes. Once the perpetrator received the funds from the bond issue, he embezzled them and induced the various municipalities to issue more bonds. Each subsequent bond issue went to cover the prior issue, in effect a "Ponzi" scheme (USPIS Winter/Spring 1993).

◆ <u>Yield Burning</u> "...occurs when investment banks slap excessive markups on bonds used to complete certain types of municipal issues...By marking up the bonds, and thus "burning" down their yields, underwriters pocket money that should have gone to the federal government, or sometimes, the municipality (Gasparino and Connor 8-17-98)."

◆ <u>Rogue Traders</u> are securities traders who trade in defiance of their sponsor's or market's guidelines. Rogues often cause huge losses and use deceptive methods to conceal their losses (Shirouza et al 9-20-96 and *Economist* 12-23-95). Rogue traders can operate within the borrower's operation or in brokerage houses. A number of major securities scandals in the 1990s involved rogue bond traders. Here are two examples, one from a municipal bond in-house manager and a second from a brokerage house rogue:

In a notorious example, the former Orange County Treasurer shifted bond-derived assets from various municipalities to avoid detection of massive losses he incurred by using risky Treasury Bill security trading strategies. The risky trades were made without the knowledge of the various municipalities that pooled their funds into the County fund (Emshwiller and Pasztor 3-31-95).

As an example of brokerage house malfeasance, the Securities and Exchange Commission accused Kidder Peabody of harboring an in-house rogue trader. The trader allegedly "...created $350 million in phony bond-trading profits from 1991 and 1994 to mask $80 million in losses (Lowry 7-22-98)."
Prevention: Since most bond fraud is institutional, it is up to in-house audits, management controls, and regulators to detect fraud.

Futures Fraud

A futures contract is a "...negotiable contract to make or take delivery of a standardized amount of commodity or financial instrument during a specific month... (Fitch 1990)." Designers of futures markets set out to allow commodity producers, like gold miners or farmers, to hedge their production. By fixing a present day price for a future delivery, a commodity producer could better control the risk in their business. The added control came from knowing in advance the sale price of their commodity. To assure market liquidity, the futures markets had to be open to any willing trader, so increasingly, the futures markets were driven by traders who neither produced commodities nor intended to deliver commodities. The traders devised complex trading strategies like "straddles" and "strangles" to reduce their risk exposure. In noting one more aspect of futures trading, the fact that futures expire on a specific date, it is easy to see that futures are vastly more volatile and risky than their brethren securities, stocks and bonds. To balance the risk, futures offer high potential returns.

The volatility of futures, the high potential return, and the vast array of complex trading strategies make the futures markets a fraud magnet. The complexity of futures trading puts it on par with the risks inherent in direct investments in natural resource development, gem-buying, and art investing: Each of these requires specialized knowledge and experience to intelligently invest. Instead of building the required knowledge and experience, many people are tempted to dismiss the complexity and simply plunge in. This naïve posture is an invitation to fraud.

Futures-trading fraud occurs in account sales and in trading. Here are the general categories of futures-trading fraud: i. misrepresented risk, ii. account mis-appropriation, iii concealed losses, iv. non-competitive trading, v. manipulative trading and vi. rogue trading.

◆ Misrepresented Risk

The simplest futures fraud involves brokers misrepresenting risk to entice unwitting investors. The broker's incentive is to open an account and then churn it until the entire principal has gone to commissions. Misrepresentation includes exaggerating the likelihood of profits and understating the inherent risk in futures trading (CFTC 7-10-92). Alternatively, the broker may exaggerate his or her track record in order to secure discretionary trading privileges with their customer's accounts (CFTC Website).

◆ Account Misappropriation

Brokers can misappropriate investor funds by: a. trading outside of prescribed guidelines, b. redirecting trade proceeds, and c. embezzlement.

Futures traders often manage pool accounts. These accounts blend a number of investor's funds into one trading account (CFTC 1997). Pools are especially susceptible to fraud when brokers have discretionary trading privileges and individuals in the pool are lax in their oversight. The lax oversight comes from the fact that many pool investors view their account as gambling or a lark investment: They had no firm investment goals in mind.

As can happen with any security, unethical brokers who trade multiple discretionary accounts may allocate winning and losing trades to, respectively, preferred and un-preferred clients. In one case, a Prudential Securities broker traded energy futures contracts and allotted the winning and losing trade after the fact, rather than assigning positions to different account before making the trades (Eichwald 6-20-95).

◆ Concealed Losses

Fraudulent securities traders may conceal trading losses from customers in order to continue churning an account or to otherwise take advantage of a client (CFTC Website).

◆ Non-competitive Trading most directly harms customers. Like any fraud, they also indirectly harm society at large, in this case the markets, by undermining people's confidence in the institution's integrity. Trades can be non-competitive because they have no reasonable chance of achieving a profit or because they deny the customer access to the true market.

*Unprofitable Trade

Brokers can take advantage of novice customers by executing deliberately unprofitable trades called alligator spreads: "Any options transaction in which commissions eat up all potential profit (NASAA 1986)."

*Limited Access Trading

Dishonest brokers have devised a variety of methods to side-step the futures markets and the CFTC regulations. These illegal trades unfairly enrich the trader by inflating his or her commission. Any scheme that circumvents the formal market is non-competitive (CFTC 1997):

- Accommodation Trading: A non-competitive securities trading practice whereby two brokers conspire to conduct non-pit trading, thereby depriving the customers access to the open market (CFTC 1997).
- Commodity Trading Profit Fraud: Two executives of a commodities trading company plead guilty to defrauding investors "by stealing trading profits and profitable investments opportunities from customers, and by transferring trading losses and unfavorable market risks to customers. These goals were achieved, in part, through the execution of unlawful noncompetitive trades on the COMEX, which trades were concealed, in part, by altering, destroying, and rewriting trade cards (USPIS Winter 91/92)."
- Ginzy Trading: non-competitive commodities trading practice where floor traders split large trades to manipulate the transaction price (CFTC 1997).

◆ Manipulative Trading

Manipulative trades can target either the markets or customers, as opposed to non-competitive trading which mostly hurts customers. Manipulative trades that harm customers do so by pitting the broker's interest against his or her customer. Trades that impact the market do so by taking advantage of weaknesses in the futures markets.

✱Trades Against Customers

- Trading Ahead: The illegal practice where securities brokers make trades in advance of customer trades, using their foreknowledge to benefit themselves (CFTC 1997).
- Interpositioning: A fraudulent securities-brokerage practice in which the broker-dealer deceives a customer by making undisclosed non-competitive trades. These trades are completed by using the broker-dealer's account to buy securities, then selling the securities from the broker-dealer account to the customer, in effect, charging the customer two sets of commissions. In contrast, the customary practice is to place a market order for the customer, or to directly fill the order from inventory held by the broker-dealer. Interpositioned commissions can amount to 5% to 12% of the transaction, and in one case ran to 40.9% (Goldberg 1978).
- Prearranged Commodities Trading Fraud: A commodities exchange executive defrauded customers through purchases of "30 gold futures contracts for his personal account at a price below the market price and resell[ing] them at a higher price, thereby realizing a profit that should have accrued to the customers (USPIS Winter 91/92)."

✱Trades Against the Market

Traders defrauded the Chicago Board of Trade by acting in concert to buy put options on T-Bonds prior to selling T-Bond futures, thereby realizing a $1.5 million gain by manipulating the market (CFTC 1-10-94).

◆ Rogue Trading

Rogue traders are securities traders who make trades in defiance of their sponsor's or market's guidelines. Rogue traders mostly trade brokerage house accounts, so their impact is mostly in-house. Rogues often cause huge losses and use deceptive methods to conceal their losses (Shirouza *et. al.* 9-20-96 and *Economist* 12-23-95). A number of high-profile rogue traders harmed trading firms and rocked 1990s futures markets:

- A trader at First Capital Strategists racked up a $128 million loss by engaging in "uncovered" index futures risk arbitrage. The trades involved borrowing stock from other financial companies and buying or selling index contracts to take advantage of the difference between the value of the underlying borrowed stock and present-day futures prices. Instead of balancing each futures position with an opposing position, called covering, the trader left the futures positions "uncovered," thereby incurring great risks. When the trades went awry, losses escalated (Wyatt 7-2-95).

- In a notorious example, the former Orange County California Treasurer used risky Treasury Bill security-trading strategies as part of a scheme to defy County investment rules. The risky trades were made without the knowledge of the various municipalities that pooled their funds into the County fund (Emshwiller and Pasztor 3-31-95).

- A metals market trader roiled the copper markets by trying to corner them. In a scheme that involved altering trade documents, collusion with other traders, and laying away copper inventories to squeeze the markets, Sumitomo's Yasua Hamanaka successfully kept copper prices at inflated prices for one year. The trading activity lead to losses in the $1.8 billion range. These manipulations may have been done with the complicity of Sumitomo management (Dwyer et al. 7-1-96).

- One rogue, Nicholas W. Leeson, will be forever known as the man who broke Barings PLC, an institution that had Rock of Gibraltar-like stature (It financed the US government's nineteenth century Louisiana Purchase). The rogue trader, with the complicity of negligent managers, lost $1 billion in futures trading. The losses mounted up from bad bets in currency futures positions. Like an undisciplined lender, Leeson and Barings left sour positions to go fallow and mount-up (Brauchli, Bray, and Sesit 3-6-95).

Prevention: Conduct background checks on prospective brokers and brokerage houses by calling the National Association of Securities Dealers and the Commodities Futures Trading Commission. Ask the two regulators if complaints or sanctions have been filed against either the broker or the brokerage house. Do not give brokers discretionary trading privileges for your accounts. Closely monitor all account statements. Immediately question any suspicious charges. Seek competitive bids from other brokers if you make large trades or if your trade a lot. Confront your broker if one of his or her recommendations seem inconsistent with your investment profile or with your investment objectives. Report any questionable practices to the regulators.

Of Wages and Profit in the different Employments of Labor and Stock

Adam Smith (1776)

CHAPTER SEVEN - OPERATIONS FRAUD

INTRODUCTION

Operations are the day-to-day activities of organizations. Operations are the lifeblood of government, business, and non-for-profits. There are two classes of operations, internal and external. Internal operations consists of managing employees and assets. External operations consists of bidding, contracting, and competing. Informal and formal bidding are the first steps in external operations, so they are the entrées to Operations Fraud.

BIDDING FRAUD

Introduction

Individuals and organizations all contract for goods and services. Goods and services contracts nearly all start out with formal or informal bidding. Most individuals ask for informal, verbal, bids prior to making major consumer or investments purchases. Many people even bid out every-day consumer items to capture small economies. Businesses and government all seek and offer bids for goods and services on a daily basis, so unfair and illegal bidding practices directly impact them, and impede the greater economy.

In an effort to create a level playing field for suppliers, the federal government has been the leader in designing competitive bidding forums. To match wits, the criminally-minded devise innumerable ways to rig bids. Most of the bidding schemes below are derived from the federal government's experience, but these same short-cuts can and do target state government, local government, and private entities.

Bid-rigging occurs throughout the bidding process: (1) pre-award, (2) award-phase, and (3) post-award (Model Procurement Code Project Staff 1984).

Pre-award Rigging comes in two varieties: i. bidder collusion, and ii. buyer corruption.

✶ Bidder Collusion
- Competitors declining to bid (McFarlane 1984);
- Competitors with an unwillingness to cross defined territories (McFarlane 1984);
- Patterned rotation of bid winners (McFarlane 1984);
- Partnering of competitors when either one could be effectively competing for the contract (McFarlane 1984).

✶ Buyer Corruption
- Excluding Qualified Bidders: Contract awards may be rigged if qualified bidders are excluded for insufficient reason (Listing, without definition, cited from Financial Crime Investigator Website).
- Leaking Bid Data: Information revealed to bidders for the purpose of influencing the award of one or more contracts (Listing, without definition, cited from Financial Crime Investigator Website).
- Pre-qualification of Bidders: A scheme whereby potentially competitive contractors are eliminated from bidding in order to manipulate contract awards (Model Procurement Code Project Staff 1984).
- Restricted Time Limitation: A form of bid-rigging where the award is fixed by setting an insufficient time period for competitors to draft bids (Dopp 1996).

- Rigged Specifications: The unjustified alteration of contract specifications undertaken to alter the awarding of contracts (Listing, without definition, cited from Financial Crime Investigator Website)
- Tailored Specifications: A type of bid-rigging where "specifications are deliberately and unnecessarily made so restrictive that only one supplier can meet them (Dopp 1996)."
- Un-approved Disclosure of Bidding Criteria: Bid-rigging may be facilitated by selectively providing information to various competing bidders or pre-award opening of bids (Model Procurement Code Project Staff 1984).
- Unbalanced Bidding: A complex fraud involving variable-quantity, variable item, procurement contracts. In this scheme, one bidder is given prior knowledge of specific quantities of items that are likely to be purchased over time. The foreknowledge allows the insider to both win the contract award and to make a higher profit on the sales (Model Procurement Code Project Staff 1984).
- Unnecessary Bonding: Contract bids may be rigged by setting up discriminatory pre-bid bonding requirements to eliminate otherwise qualified contractors (Model Procurement Code Project Staff 1984).

Award Phase Rigging comes in the same categories as pre-award rigging: bidder collusion and buyer corruption:

✶ <u>Bidder Collusion</u>
- Collusive Bidding: The coordinated effort by two or more contract bidders to effect the outcome of a competitive contract bid (Listing, without definition, cited from Financial Crime Investigator Website);
- Competitors declining to bid (McFarlane 1984);
- Competitors making anomalously low bids (McFarlane 1984);
- Identical line items on separate bids (McFarlane 1984);

- Partnering of competitors when either one could be effectively competing for the contract (McFarlane 1984).

* Buyer Corruption
- Waiver of Specification: Bidders are allowed to ignore certain bid criteria (Model Procurement Code Project Staff 1984).

Post-Award Rigging comes in three forms: i. bidder collusion, ii. buyer corruption, and iii. winner corruption.

* Bidder Collusion
- Subsequent to the rejection of all initial bids, the withdrawal from bidding by some of the initial competitors (McFarlane 1984).

* Buyer Corruption
- Late Bidding: Allowing one competitor to submit a bid after bid closing. This may be accompanied by leaked competitor bid information (Model Procurement Code Project Staff 1984).

* Winner Corruption transitions into contract performance fraud. The transition period lies after contract award and before delivery of the contracted goods and services.
- Contract Manipulation: After a contract award, contractors may deceive the customer in a variety of schemes: (1) The winner may refuse to deal with one or more or the losers; (2) The winner may require its subcontractors to buy materials at inflated prices; (3) The winner may require subcontractors to purchase materials exclusively from the contract winner; or (4) The winner may require subcontractors to buy materials from it for unrelated jobs (McFarlane 1984).
- Contract Mistake: Contractors may commit fraud by using a claim of "mistake" to alter the award or administration of a contract: (1) After winning a contract award, the winner may say its price was mistaken and raise it to a level just below the

next-best competitor's price; (2) Upon realizing the bid was non-competitive, and in violation of applicable contracting regulations, the bidder may withdraw its claim after winning; or (3) A losing bidder may claim that its bid was a mistake and ask that it be modified, thereby enabling it to win the contract (Model Procurement Code Project Staff 1984).

- Contract Price Modification: Contractors ask for price increases after winning competitive bids on fixed-price contracts (Model Procurement Code Project Staff 1984).
- Failure to Meet Contract Specifications: Contractors can gain un-due profits by failing to meet the contract criteria. The contractor may further the fraud by failing to disclose the deficiency (Listing, without definition, cited from Financial Crime Investigator Website).

Prevention: Maintaining the integrity of bidding is a complex chore. Standard safeguards include: establishing employee integrity, stern controls over bidding protocol, and post-bidding audits.

CONTRACT FRAUD

Introduction

Under common law theory, almost any transaction could be viewed as a contract, so, with few exceptioned topics, this whole Handbook could rightfully be "Contract Fraud." A Contract Fraud Handbook would be unwieldy, so instead, the Contract Fraud section focuses just on procurement-contract fraud. For procurement fraud in specialized industries like telecommunications, go to the respective Chapters.

The three most common procurement contracts are: i. fixed-price, ii. cost-plus, and iii. time and materials contracts. In a fixed-price contract, there is minor to no variability in the goods or services to be delivered or in the price to be paid. Contractors and customers generally use fixed-price contracts to deliver materials, but they can also be used to deliver buildings, airplanes, or long-term, stable services like security or janitorial services. Cost plus contracts are common for complex procurements like government defense contracts. These types of contracts assure that contractors who assume high risks on research and development projects will make a profit—the plus part is a percentage of the sale.

Time and materials are often used for services that have highly varied delivery costs. Examples of these are consulting services, legal services, and creative services like advertising.

There are five universal classes of contract fraud: (1) conversion, (2) failure to deliver, (3) pricing and mis-charging fraud, (4) failure to meet specifications, and (5) failure to disclose developments that are material to the contract.

Conversion is the contracting equivalent of employee embezzlement. Once a contractor takes funds, goods, or services that were entrusted to it, and converts to its own use or, to the use of another, it is illegal conversion, a form of theft. One case involved a major US Department of Energy contractor that converted a state-of-the-art piece of analytical equipment to its own use. The contractor asked the government for the money for the equipment, installed it, and immediately began using it for their private customers. When other government contractors asked to use it, the contractor kept explaining that the equipment was not available.

Failure to Deliver can be piecemeal or complete. If the failure is unintentional, then it is likely to be treated as an administrative or civil violation. If is intentional, or results from willful ignorance, then the victim may have a case for criminal remedies.

One example of intentional failure to deliver involved a US Air Force contractor that falsely certified progress payments. Although he claimed to have made full delivery, in fact, he only delivered 59 of 195 contracted units (USPIS Summer 1990).

Pricing and Mis-charging Fraud are mirrors of each other. Pricing fraud occurs when a contractor intentionally, or by willful ignorance, charges inflated or otherwise fraudulent prices. This may occur at the outset of a contract or during subsequent price modifications. Mis-charging occurs when the contractor ignores contract specifications, charging for un-allowable goods or services. Presumably, the contractor relies on the customer's lack of oversight for the charges to go through. If caught, he relies on the "mistake" defense.

＊ Pricing Fraud
- Cost Plus Contract Fraud: A CEO of a pipe supply company defrauded his clients by fraudulently and artificially inflating prices (USPIS Winter 1990-91).
- Defective Pricing: The federal Truth in Negotiations Act specifies that prices which are not current, accurate, and complete as of the date of the price agreement are defective and may be disallowed by the buyer in a contract (NASA OIG 10-1-92 thru 3-31-93). In one case, the government won a $5.1 million settlement from a company that "knowingly failed to disclose required costs and pricing data to the Air Force (DOD OIG 4-1-92 thru 9-30-92)."
- Labor Estimate Falsification: Raytheon Company paid the government $2.7 million because it "falsified labor cost estimates on 26 sole source contracts that caused the Navy to pay inflated prices (DOD OIG 4-1-92 thru 9-30-92)."
- Inflated Billings: Perpetrators misrepresent office supplies as being available at a discount, then, after the victim company begins to order the supplies, the criminal increases the billing prices by multiples of the original price, hoping the victim will pay the invoice without examining it. The criminal may also use bribes, in the forms of gifts sent to the company purchasing agent's home, in order to induce the purchasing agent into overlooking or furthering the scheme (USPIS Summer 1990).

- Inflated time charges: Unscrupulous lawyers over-bill clients, among other ways, by overestimating time spent on cases, and by charging for time they don't work (Stevens 1-13-95).

✶ Mis-charging Fraud - Things That Should Not Be Charged or Are Deceptively Charged

- Co-Mingling Contracts: The deliberate mixing together of two or more contracts, in either the bidding or execution stage, designed to deceptively effect the outcome of one or more of the contracts (Listing, without definition, cited from The Financial Crime Investigator Website). Also known as cross charging. In a major Defense Department case, the Boeing Company settled for $75 million after it, "...improperly charged millions of dollars in research and development costs to Government contracts, which Boeing had improperly characterized as overhead on its manufacturing and production efforts (DOD OIG 4-1-94 thru 9-30-94)."
- Double Billing: The criminal practice of deliberately billing twice for the same goods or services. In one scheme against the Department of Defense, a contractor double-billed follow-on contracts (DOD OIG). In another example, lawyers double bill clients by submitting work already completed, from prior clients, to new clients (Jacobs 9-18-95).
- Emergency Procurements: A contract fraud scheme where public officials ignore existing contracts or contracting procedures by repeatedly calling for exigent supplies or services. These emergency procurements may occur repeatedly over time, or in a rash of purchases. The scheme may involve kickbacks to the officials (Model Procurement Code Project Staff 1984).
- Rate-mixing: Charging a premium rate for work completed by lower-level employees. For example, charging a secretary's work at the rate of a law firm's full partner (Stevens 1-13-95).

- Split Purchases: The structured buying of goods or services to evade management or audit review (Listing, without definition, cited from The Financial Crime Investigator Website).
- Surcharges: Unethical lawyers subvert billing agreements with their clients by adding surcharges to service, such as photocopying, which had previously negotiated fixed prices (Stevens 1-13-95).
- Housekeeping Contract fraud: A Chicago businesswoman defrauded the City of Chicago by submitting inflated bills and fictitious information about her business (USPIS Winter/Spring 1995).
- Unallowable Costs: Some laws, regulations or contracts universally exclude specific items. Alcohol, tobacco, and illegal services like prostitution are typical exclusions. In one case, a company supplying maintenance, under an assistance program, for a foreign government, defrauded the US government by charging for unallowable foreign expenses [presumably entertainment and alcohol] (DOD OIG 4-1-92 thru 9-30-92). A number of highly publicized cases occurred in the early 1990's when the federal government accused Universities of mischarging unallowable cost. Allegedly, the Universities charged the government for items like yachts and flowers by spreading government funds into diverse "cost pools" which included the unallowable costs (Anderson 1-9-92 and Pool and Aldhous 8-8-91).
- Unnecessary Purchases: The buying of goods or services that are not needed by the parent organization but do benefit the contractor or its employee (Listing, without definition, cited from The Financial Crime Investigator Website).
- Unrendered Goods and Services: Contractor may charge for goods or services that were either undelivered or not-rendered.
- Work Break Fraud: "...Employees of the [NASA] contractor had improperly charged the time spent on breaks to overhead during a 7-year period (NASA OIG 4-1-94 thru 9-30-94)."

Failure to Meet Specifications can involve: i. product substitution, ii. weight and measurement fraud, iii. short orders, iv. missed delivery date, v. damage, vi. mis-represented re-sales, or vii. falsified bonds or insurance. As with mis-charging fraud, specification fraud can be hard to prove because of the latitude given to the "mistake" defense.

✳ Product Substitution
Just as there are counterfeit consumer goods, so there are counterfeit industrial supplies. The classic product substitution items are bolts. Bolts are used to build building, bridges, airplanes, and other infrastructures, so substituting a substandard bolt for one that meets specifications is no joke. This kind of fraud is closely allied to Weight and Measurement Fraud. One federal law, the Buy America Act, specifically requires government contractors to buy American products when possible. When a contractor substitutes a foreign part, it may violate the Act. For example, three manufacturing executives defrauded their clients by destroying required "country of origin" markings on drill and router bits and re-marking them with "Made in USA" stamps (USPIS Spring 1991).

✳ Weight or Measurement Fraud takes place when the provider delivers product under specified weight or out of measured specification. For example, a food vendor may deliver 6-oz. chicken when the contract called for chickens of not less than 8 ozs.. Here are some actual examples:

- Relay Switch False Claims: A NASA contractor pled guilty to "... preparing and submitting false statements regarding testing of electronic relays used in the aerospace industry...the company sold commercial-grade relay switches and certified that they met rigorous testing requirements (NASA OIG 4-1-94 thru 9-30-94)."
- Substandard Concrete: Former employees of a concrete-testing company alleged that their employer defrauded the City of

Denver by pouring substandard concrete at Denver International Airport and induced the testing company to falsify the tests. The company diminished the quality of the concrete by adding excess sand, and concealed the fraud by altering scale readings and core tests (Kilzer 11-13-94).

✷ <u>Short Orders</u> fail to meet the contract-specified amount of goods or services.

✷ <u>Missed Delivery Dates</u> are common in all segments of society and seldom treated as crimes. However, if they are significant, recurring, and involve use of customer funds, it can take on the effect of kiting—the contractor uses his customer's money as an interest-free loan.

✷ <u>Damage</u>
Contractors can make extra money by delivering already damaged goods or concealing damages that occur in transit to the customer.

✷ <u>Misrepresented Re-sales</u>
Some manufacturers place marketing or re-selling restrictions on their wholesales to protect territories, to shelter markets, to develop markets, or to provide charity. A buyer may commit fraud by ignoring these terms and re-selling into the restricted markets.

In one example, a perpetrator took advantage of a US manufacturers' favorable pricing. The buyer received large discounts by promising to export items, but he subsequently shipped the items overseas and then had them returned to the US. To facilitate the scheme, he made false bills of lading to avoid import fees. This scheme defrauded both the US manufacturers and US Customs (Segal, Oct 1995).

In a second example, Postal Inspectors arrested a man for defrauding three airlines of fees due for shipping. The scheme involved booking shipping space then reselling the space, at a discount, to shippers. The airlines lost because the perpetrator never paid them for the shipping space he sold (USPIS Spring 1992).

✶ Falsified Bonds or Insurance
Contracts routinely require workman's compensation, general liability, and product liability insurance. A contractor may save money by ignoring these contractual obligation. This most commonly occurs with general construction contractors or their subcontractors. The contractor may advance this fraud with falsified proof of insurance documents or simply by failing to produce any documents.

In a second example, an individual plead guilty after he "...filed an affidavit of individual surety to claim ownership of assets worth over $41 million that were, in fact, worthless in support of a performance bond on a construction contract (NASA OIG 4-1-94 thru 9-30-94)."

Failure to Disclose Developments That Are Material To The Contract
Contractors may engage in fraud if they defy specific provisions of the contract regarding price changes, or if they fail to disclose discoveries of financial or management irregularities:

- Cost Reduction False Statement: An aerospace company defrauded the government when it failed to disclose cost reductions for component parts it delivered [Presumably, the contract required it to make the disclosure] (DOD OIG, 10-1-92 thru 3-31-93).
- Kickbacks: The payment of money, or other things of value, to a government or business employee for the purpose of effecting: i. a contract award, or ii. the administration of a contract.

Prevention: Contract fraud is so highly varied that no protocol can successfully vet all cases. Contractors must be inspected and audited to ensure performance.

EMPLOYEE, CUSTOMER, AND COMPETITOR FRAUD

Introduction
Although they have relatively narrow impact, employees, customers, and competitors do commit fraud. In fact, some industries, like retailing and food service, are dramatically impacted by these types of fraud. Organizations tend to downplay the occurrence of employee fraud because it reflects badly on an organization. Presumably, organizations think that internal fraud casts a dim light because it reveals internal weaknesses (*DP* 8-12-98). Customer frauds, like false contamination claims, receive dramatic attention, presumably as a warning to other would-be extortionists and because companies are compelled to publicize alleged product contamination to avoid harm to other customers. Competitor fraud, often in the form of industrial espionage, is much like internal fraud in that it tends to be settled quietly so as not to reveal the soft underbelly of an organization.

Internal Fraud
Internal, or employee fraud, can occur at any time in the employment cycle, from hiring, through separation, and onto post-separation benefits. Prospective employees can and do commit pre-employment fraud by falsifying credentials, employment histories, and other aspect of their past. Upon hiring, the most notorious fraud is the covering-up of embezzlements. Other internal frauds include: colluding with others to cause unjustified payments, failure to disclose conflicts of interest or outside income, and failure to disclose the release of company trade secrets. After leaving an organization, an employee may engage in fraud by claiming and receiving un-entitled benefits or by disregarding non-compete or employment contracts.

* <u>Pre-employment Fraud</u>
- Falsification of medical history: Prospective employees may lie about previous medical conditions, later causing employer loss by excessive leave, high insurance, or poor productivity (The Second Opinion Website).
- Falsification of employment history.
- Falsification of education.
- Falsification of training.
- Falsification of salary history.
- Providing rigged references.

* <u>Employment Fraud - Embezzlement</u>
- Concealment of embezzlement by falsifying records:
  * Embezzlement concealed as raises (Cyphert 3-20-98).
  * Embezzlement concealed has cash advances.
  * Embezzlement concealed as payments to others. Employees may setup fictitious companies to bill businesses or organizations for goods or services that have not been rendered (Cyphert 3-20-98).
  * Embezzlement concealed by "Lapping": "A fraud technique involving the misappropriation of customers' payments and failure to record the receipt of such funds. To cover the situation, subsequent payments are recorded as for the first customer's account rather than the accounts to which they should be credited. A form of "robbing Peter to pay Paul [Ponzi Scheme] (NASAA 1986)."
- Embezzlement by collusion with shoplifters or collusion with other types of outside theft.
- Embezzlement by prepaying hotels, checking out early, and pocketing the money returned from the hotel (Schmit 2-14-95).
- Embezzlement by downgrading from first class to coach on an airline and pocketing the difference (Schmit 2-14-95).
- Embezzlement by inflated travel statements.

- Embezzlement by cashing-in pre-paid airline tickets and not reimbursing the employer.
- Embezzlement by salami slicing accounts—a clerk defrauded her employer by adding overtime to employees' payroll then diverting the overtime payments to herself (Judson 1994).
- Embezzlement by Check Inclusion: A bookkeeper embezzled from his employer "...by including checks made out to himself in stacks of legitimate business checks prepared for the owner's signature. The bookkeeper took the checks for signature at times when the owner was busy (*WSJ* 10-2-95)."
- Embezzlement by purchases for personal use: The buying, renting or leasing of goods or services for personal rather than business, government, or organization use (Listing, without definition, taken from The Financial Crime Investigator Website).
- Embezzlement by computer-time theft: A NASA contract employee used a government telecommunications computer for his outside business (NASA OIG 4-1-94 thru 9-30-94).
- Embezzlement by interest diversion: Orange County Treasurer may have diverted interest earned in one municipality's account to other accounts in order to conceal trade losses (*WSJ* 1-23-95).

✳ Fraud by Collusion With Others
- Concealment of kickbacks from suppliers.
- Concealment of kickbacks from competitors

✳ Time and Attendance Fraud
- Fraud by claiming un-due overtime.
- Fraud by failing to work charged normal hours.
- Medical Excuse Fraud: A Smithsonian Institution employee lost his job after he "photocopied previously submitted medical excuse forms and altered the dates prior to submitting them to management on seven different occasions (Smithsonian Institution OIG 10-1-92 thru 3-31-93)."

- Family Leave and Disability Act Fraud: Employees may falsify their parental, dependency, or disability status to obtain undeserved time-off.

✷ Failure to Disclose Conflicts of Interest
- Such as when an employee has an interest in competing venture.
- Such as when a close relative of an employee works for a competing venture.
- Such as when an employee works for a competing or related interest during his or her off-hours.

✷ Failure to Disclose Material Facts
- Illegal Commitments: A well-intentioned employee may violate government laws or regulations, conceal the violation, and wrongly think that they have aided the company by reducing near-term costs (Cyphert 3-20-98).

✷ The Release of Trade Secrets
- Failure to disclose the intentional or inadvertent release or sale of trade secrets.

✷ Post Employment Fraud
- Undisclosed violation of non-compete contracts.
- Undisclosed and unauthorized release of trade secrets.
- Unjustified claiming of health, unemployment, or other benefits.

Prevention: Background checks, payroll and financial audits, information controls, employment and non-compete contracts comprise basic safeguards against employee fraud.

Customer Fraud
So much media attention goes to consumer rights and the impact of illegal and unfair organization and business practices that it is easy

to lose sight of the fact that consumers defraud businesses too. There are six classes of customer fraud: (1) shoplifting and returned item fraud, (2) fast change schemes, (3) presentation of fraudulent identifications or falsified documents to buy regulated items, (4) claims of false injury, (5) false contamination claims, (6) false entitlement claims. CHAPTER TWO - Confidence games and CHAPTER THREE - Consumer Fraud, detail other, less common, consumer frauds.

✴ Shoplifting and Returned Item Fraud

- Shoplifters may steal items then try to return them while pretending he or she had purchased them (Wright 1996).
- Customers may buy an item, use it, them return it to the seller while claiming it had not been used. Also known as "return churn," "return fraud," and "boom-a-rang-buying" (Newborn 6-3-96).
- Sophisticated New Orleans-based criminals purchased a large amount of items from a Wal-Mart, tore off the bar code pricing, then returned them with new, counterfeit bar codes. Prior to being caught, the fraud netted the criminals $250,000 (Russell 3-17-97).

✴ Fast Change Schemes

- Criminals have a variety of fast-money schemes used to short-change cashiers. Most of these involve slight of hand and/or repeatedly asking for different change configurations (Sifakis 1993).

✴ Presentation of Fraudulent Identifications or Falsified Documents to Buy Regulated Items

- A customer may use counterfeit or altered identification to buy controlled substances, thereby causing the business to violate the law. Minors buying beer is an example. A more egregious example has minors buying a gun.

- A customer with a felony record may present falsified documents to facilitate purchasing a firearm.

* Claims of False Injury
- A customer may falsely claim to have been injured at a property or by a product.

* False Damages Claims
- A customer may fabricate contamination in a beverage or food. In a number of high-profile cases, individuals have tried to defraud food vendors by placing contaminants in the items and claiming the manufacturers sold contaminated food. These frauds include a rat-tail in McDonald's food, a syringe in soda cans (Koerner 4-14-97), and infamous cyanide scares.
- Fictitious Consumer Complaints: Two individuals defrauded consumer product companies of over $30,000 by filing false complaints about the companies' products. The two complained the products were "spoiled, inadequate, or otherwise defective (USPIS Spring 1991)."
- Damaged Luggage Fraud: Perpetrators "...mass mailed letters to thousands of hotels such as Hyatt, Holiday Inn, and the Marriott, falsely representing that hotel employees had caused damage to luggage and purses incident to nonexistent stays at hotels. In order not to raise any suspicions, the claims were less than $30 (USPIS Fall 1990)."
- Dry Cleaning False Billing: Hotels (and presumably, restaurants) receive billings for dry cleaning items that were purportedly stained at their business, but the charges are not preapproved or sustainable (Western 11-19-95).

* False Entitlement Claims
- A federal grand jury indicted seven individuals who manipulated a frequent flier award program. The manipulations were done to fraudulently gain free tickets from Pan American Airways, Inc. (USPIS 1990-91).

- A customer may falsify documents to sustain a false claim in a sweepstakes or contest.
- Coupon Redemption Schemes: Perpetrators collect or purchase, at a deep discount, store coupons, then ask, without purchasing the items, manufacturers to redeem the coupons (USPIS Summer 1990). In a more sophisticated scheme, a couple counterfeited cash register receipts and then submitted them for rebates (USPIS Summer 1998).
- A woman was found guilty of using computers to create fictitious receipts so she could obtain money from manufacturers' redemption programs. She was found with over 200,000 receipts, coupons and miscellenea related to the scheme (USPIS Winter 1989-90).
- Three men rigged radio station contests by: blocking the station's phone lines during promotional contests; calling-in answers to contest questions; and winning numerous prizes (Viles 5-3-93).

A variation of retail customer fraud is wholesale customer fraud. One way wholesale customers defraud vendors is by abusing incentive programs: These schemes take advantage of incentive and marketing development programs which are inducements wholesalers create to encourage promotion of their products. These promotions include "product displays, circulars, product discounts, [and] coupons..." In some cases, retailer have submitted false claims to their vendors for non-rendered promotions (Hyten 12-23-94).

Prevention: An effective loss control program includes: employee training, investigation of all product liability and injured customer claims, surveillance cameras, and audits of reward, coupon, and entitlement programs.

Competitor Fraud

Business competitors may engage in any number of unethical, non-competitive, or illegal acts to gain an advantage. Most of these do not involve deception, but some do. The most significant of this fraud is product counterfeiting. To understand the scale of counterfeiting fraud consider the following:

- The annual cost of product counterfeiting to US companies ranges from a $200 billion estimate (Green and Bruce 8-11-97) to $250 billion in the US alone (Hyten 8-9-96).
- One source states that 99% of the computer software used in some countries is counterfeit (Stipp 5-22-96).
- The same source estimates 70% of all medication sold overseas is counterfeit (Stipp 5-22-96).

Counterfeiters use a variety of schemes, some overt, some sneaky:

- Counterfeiters openly smuggle products into the US.
- Counterfeiters legally import un-branded products, then slap on designer labels once the product crosses the border (Green and Bruce 8-11-97).
- Counterfeiters "clone" product with a name similar to a well-know brand to piggyback another company's brand recognition. For example, a cloned phone may carry the name "Panasoic," which sound like Panasonic (NBC 8-2-95).

Here are two other competitor frauds:
- Competitors may disingenuously negotiate or confer with a business to gain trade secrets.
- A competitor may stage a crime or purposely commit slander or libel to harm another business.

Prevention: Competitor and market surveillance, aggressive trademark, patent, and copyright enforcement, and non-compete agreements in prospective joint-ventures and mergers .

Power tends to corrupt and
absolute power corrupts absolutely.
John Emerich Edward Dalberg-Acton

CHAPTER EIGHT - PUBLIC INTEREST FRAUD

INTRODUCTION

Public interest frauds involve people, systems, and institutions that serve the widest public audience. These include charities, public officials, currencies, elections, and tax fraud. Entitlements are another category with wide public interest. For these, see the CHAPTER FIVE - Government Fraud.

CHARITY FRAUD

"In 1990... total annual revenues of American charities reached $406 billion, more than 7% of that year's gross domestic product." About one quarter of these revenues came from donations. Surprisingly, there is very little oversight of charities because charities pay no taxes, and the IRS focuses its efforts on potential tax revenues. The lack of oversight leaves charities ripe for fraud (Kimelman 9-1-94).

The vast majority of charity fraud involves embezzling funds that were destined for the charitable beneficiary. As stated in the Handbook's introduction, embezzlement itself is not strictly fraud, but concealing the act is fraud. The runner-up for high impact charity fraud is telemarketing charity fraud. Charity Fraud occurs: (1) during solicitation, (2) in distributing funds, (3) in elections, (4) as a form of tax fraud, and (5) against matching donors.

Solicitation Fraud

Charities may commit solicitation fraud when:

- they misrepresent the percentage of donations that go to beneficiaries (as opposed to the portion used for overhead);
- they deceive donors into believing that there are matching donors;
- they misrepresent who the beneficiaries will be; or
- they misrepresent the tax benefits of a donation.

Charity telemarketing fraud is the top mechanism for solicitation frauds. Perpetrators pretend to represent charities, asking the victim to buy tickets for benefit shows, or to make a donation for handicapped children, or purchase light bulbs, or other household items at inflated prices. One example of solicitation fraud involved an AIDS Charity Scheme where two people defrauded donors by claiming they were collecting for an AIDS charity. Their promotional brochure falsely represented that the organization had affiliates in many major cities. The perpetrators also misrepresented the identities of the charity board. "Finally, the many public services and medical services claimed to be performed by ASAP had never been performed (USPIS Winter/Spring 1993)."

Badge-related charity fraud is an emerging charity fraud niche: "Raising money for police unions and associations under the guise of charity (Shaffer 6-20-93)," or pretending to have police affinities to defraud donors.

Distribution Fraud

After receiving donations, charities may commit distribution fraud against donors by:

- embezzling funds and concealing the embezzlement;
- changing the designated beneficiary without notifying donors;
- failing to reveal to donors other post-donation changes effecting the management or distribution of funds; and

- self-enrichment of charity officials, also known as inurement (Kimelman 9-1-94).

Note well, federal law does not require charities to distribute any set percentage of funds to beneficiaries. In fact, a charity may spend nearly all of its income on fund-raising and administrative costs. The only distribution requirement pertains to charitable trusts: These charities must annually disburse 5% of their assets for charitable purposes (Kimelman 9-1-94).

Election Campaign Fraud
Candidates or their election committees may defraud donors by deceiving them into believing that political contributions can be deducted as charitable contributions. This deception may be one-sided, with misrepresentations just made to donors, or two-sided, with misrepresentations also made to the IRS (Frankel 4-13-97).

Tax Fraud
Charitable contributions may be fraudulent tax deductions if:

- Non-cash items, such as art or cars, are donated and the donor claims an inflated value for the contribution. The inflated value may be arrived at in collusion with the charity, or by misrepresenting the value of the item to the charity.
- The contribution is actually a political contribution, payment for services, gratuity or kickback rather than a legitimate charitable contribution.
- The donor falsifies the size of an actual cash donation.
- The donor sets up abusive trusts (IRS CID 1997a Website) such as a revocable trust that is represented as in irrevocable trust, thereby denying the beneficiary the assured receipt of funds and disqualifying the tax deduction.
- The charity fails to pay taxes on money-generating activities that are not related to its charitable charter. For tax purposes, these are called "unrelated businesses (Kimelman 9-1-94)."

Matching Donor Fraud

Matching donors may be defrauded if a charity cites phantom seed donors to get undeserved matches or if a seed donor claims a single donation to multiple donors, thereby inflating the matching funds awarded to the seed donation (Knecht and Taylor 5-19-95). Alternatively, charities can defraud seed donors by inducing them to donate money under the false promise that matching donors will greatly enhance the magnitude of a donation. The New Era charity scam, a major fraud revealed in 1995, involved promises of matching funds (Knecht and Taylor 5-19-95).

Prevention: The front-line steps to prevent donor fraud are : (1) request a copy of the charity's IRS Form 990 and to have an accountant review it. If entries are missing, suspend giving until all of the information is provided by the charity; (2) contact the Philanthropy Advisory Service, Council of Better Business Bureaus, 4200 Wilson Blvd., Arlington, VA 22203 for background information; and (3) contact the National Charities Information Bureau, 19 Union Square West, New York, NY 10003 for background information (USPIS Website).

Post-donation checking may include: (1) requiring donation receipts from the charity; (2) confirming receipt of matching fund from the matching organization; (3) confirming distribution of funds or services to beneficiaries; and (4) requesting the charity's next-year IRS Form 990 when it is available.

CORRUPTION

Corruption is an area of white-collar crime with minor or accessory fraud. Most corruption of public officials involves bribery, and only in so far as the bribery is concealed by deception does it include fraud. One example of bribery and accessory fraud would involve a public official who received payoffs through a shell company or through an enterprise titled in another person's name. In addition to bribery, public officials perpetrate other fraudulent schemes. One notable area is election fraud, discussed in the forthcoming section. Also, the Handbook's CHAPTER SEVEN (Operations) reviews public employee fraud in bid-rigging and embezzlement cover-ups. Remaining for discussion here are a number of less common frauds that involve corruption of public employees: i. law enforcement falsification, ii. politicized policy, iii. fraudulent intervention, and iv. negligent falsification.

Law Enforcement Falsification
Of all fraud, law enforcement falsification probably is the most fearsome. Law enforcement is entrusted with special state powers, so the abuse of these powers is all the more egregious. Law enforcement officials are in a position to falsify testimony, to create fictitious evidence, to alter evidence, to withhold exculpatory evidence and to make false arrests. Caving into public pressure to solve high profile crimes, desire to enhance one's reputation, and kickbacks are some of the motivations for law enforcement corruption. As paranoid as these categories of fraud sound, there are dramatic examples:

- FBI Special Agent Frederick Whitehurst alleged that the Bureau's crime lab falsified some critical findings to bias trials (National Whistleblower Website 1997)
- Prosecutors and policemen have found themselves on the other side of the bench when they were accused of ignoring exculpatory evidence and prosecuting otherwise innocent parties. In the federal courts, the Jenks Act requires disclosure of exculpatory information.
- Alabama courts set free a death row convict after learning that prosecutors had withheld favorable evidence and three witnesses had recanted their testimony (Hansen June 1993).
- A wide-reaching 1996 investigation of Philadelphia police found some policemen would steal money from citizens and

then concoct evidence used to make a drug conviction (*Economist* 5-11-96).

- Senior officials have been found guilty of obstruction of justice for their role in destroying documents. The destruction sometimes takes place to conceal law enforcement misconduct.

Prevention: When arrested or detained by law enforcement, adhere to your Fifth Amendment Right to remain silent. Retain counsel immediately upon learning that you are the subject of an investigation. If you become a defendant, take an active role in learning about criminal defense and the rules of evidence.

Politicized Policy

Some editorials allege that government officials falsify studies and other evidence to achieve their political agendas. Alston Chase, a newspaper columnist, alleged that various US government agencies, including the EPA and National Park Service, try to alter public opinion and policy by altering and suppressing scientific research (Chase 6-19-98). Chase cites one investigation that found EPA "...doing analysis to justify a decision only after it has been made, then backdating documents and lying in court to cover it up." A second example of EPA abuse cites a federal court finding. The court took EPA to task for falsifying the results of passive smoke studies (*IBD* 7-29-98). A third editorial questioned the propriety of the US government's global warming policy. The editorial specifically alleged that government officials try to squelch open debate about global warming (Milloy and Gough 8-7-98).

Prevention: Scrutinize public science policy. Lobby representatives to encourage fact-based policy.

Fraudulent Intervention

Where some corrupt government employees can alter or fabricate evidence and testimony to unfairly implicate someone in a crime, others have abused their privileged access to falsely exonerate or unduly enrich individuals. In a 1990s IRS scandal, officials admitted that 1300 IRS employees had been investigated for snooping in tax records. Some had altered files to generate refunds for friends (Davis Aug 1995).

Prevention: Promptly respond to all government inquiries. Retain counsel or an accountant for any inquiries except the trivial. Question refunds or other correspondence that seem undue.

Negligent Falsification

Not all fraud by public officials is wanton and serious. Officials may negligently falsify information out of indifference or laziness. Although not criminal, this might fall under the rubric of civil fraud. One example involves lazy tax assessors who bunch properties of highly varied valuations into one group, then assess all of the properties at one, inflated rate. This bunching causes property owners with lower values properties to pay inflated real estate taxes.

Another example, often considered but seldom proved, comes from parking citations. Anyone who has gotten one after a short stop suspects some parking enforcement officers of jumping the gun in writing their tickets.

Prevention: Annually review your property assessments. Contest them if they seem high.

COUNTERFEITING

Counterfeiting is the manufacturing of fraudulent or unauthorized checks, birth certificates, currency, coins, property titles, stock certificates, bond certificates, and identifications (among many things). One survey of fraud examiners puts the annual business loss to all counterfeiting at an astonishing $400 billion per year (Waldsmith 5-28-98). No matter what the actual cost, the general phenomena of counterfeiting clearly fits in the Public Interest category because its negative effects transcend all aspects of society— it causes businesses, personal, and government losses and it undermines people's faith in public institutions.

CHAPTER THREE addresses counterfeit credit cards in the Credit Card section and counterfeit auto titles in the Auto section. CHAPTER FOUR'S Check Fraud section discusses counterfeit checks, and CHAPTER FIVE'S Social Security section discusses counterfeit Social Security cards. CHAPTER SIX explores both counterfeit art and counterfeit collectable coins and metal ingots. CHAPTER SEVEN's Competitor Fraud section describes counterfeit consumer products. These sections leave contemporary currency as the most significant un-addressed counterfeit, so here is a synopsis.

"Most counterfeiters use a photo-mechanical or 'offset' method to make a printing plate from a photograph of a genuine note." Counterfeiters also use: (1) black and white, monochromatic, and color copiers, or (2) computer-driven, desk-top publishing systems with ink jet or laser printers. Less sophisticated currency counterfeiting includes raising currency note denominations by gluing "...numerals from higher denomination notes to the corners of lower denomination notes (USSS Website)."

Although of minor impact, counterfeiters also duplicate coins. "Genuine coins are struck (stamped out) by special machinery. Most counterfeited coins are made by pouring liquid metal into molds or dies (USSS Website)."

Prevention: The detection of fraudulent documents is the province of professional document examiners. If you question the authenticity of a document, the easiest way to authenticate it by yourself is to contact the organization that issued it. The issuer should know whether or not the questioned document is original.

As for US currency and coins: Check the US Secret Service Website for a description of portrait, seal, border, serial number, watermark, color-shifting, microprinting, security thread, and paper characteristics of currency. With coins, look for mold or die imperfections like cracks or metal pimples on the coin's surface. For coins with values of ten cents and up, look at the outer edges, called reeding (USSS Website). If the reeding is uneven, crooked, or missing, the coin may be counterfeit. Alternatively, if you think bills or coins are counterfeit, call the US Secret Service.

ELECTION FRAUD

Election fraud is the use of deceit or misrepresentation to effect the outcome of an election. Election fraud does not have the financial impact of telecommunications fraud, or the human drama of medical fraud, but it has a corrosive effect on democracy, so an awareness of the many permutations of election fraud can reduce it, and thereby better society.

Election fraud is found throughout the election process:
- in the pre-election campaign financing stage;
- during voter registration;
- during absentee voting;
- at the polling place;
- during vote counting; and
- in contested elections.

While many people think of election fraud as a relict of a bygone society, anecdotes from 1990s journalists suggest fraudulent election practices are still widespread (Armbrister 1995, Hirezy 1996, Sabato and Simpson 1996, Mehlman and Mele 1997). These authors, and permutations on their anecdotes, illustrate 29 fraudulent election schemes:

◆ <u>Campaign Finance Fraud</u> occurs when donors try to circumvent funding laws. Common schemes include: a. Businesses that launder money to make illegal donations to federal election candidates (Kuntz 8-1-95). One way to do this is to give business employees or business associates money so that they can act as "Straw Men," donating for the business; b. Foreign contributors that launder to conceal their source; or c. Candidates who set-up questionable non-for-profit charities to funnel money into their campaigns.
Prevention: Audit election contributions.

◆ <u>Voter Registration Fraud</u> occurs when political parties, individuals, or government employees use a variety of techniques to bias the electorate pool:
- Individuals may induce ineligible, non-citizens, to register (Mehlman and Mele 1997).
- Individuals may lie about their residency in order to corrupt elections by voting in precincts where they have no jurisdiction (Mehlman and Mele 1997).
- Officials may use their own residences or government addresses for registrants' permanent address listing (Sabato and Simpson 1996).
- Officials may register the dead or other fictitious names.
- Individuals may register in more than one precinct by lying about their residency.
- County officials may throw-away or falsify valid registrations (Hirezy 1996).
- Election officials may violate election laws by allowing citizens to register after the voter registration deadline (Armbrister 1995).
- Convicted felons may illegally register and then cast ballots (Sabato and Simpson 1996).
- Campaign workers may register psychiatric patients who are ineligible to vote.

Prevention: Audit and surveillance of voter registration records.

◆ <u>Absentee Voter Fraud</u> takes advantage of the privilege to vote prior to elections for those who cannot cast a ballot on election day:

- Tuscalusa Alabama election committees allegedly coerced otherwise non-voting citizens to submit absentee ballots, presumably voting for the committee's candidate (*ABC* 10-24-95);
- Voters may cast two ballots by voting both in the pre-election absentee forum and at polling places on the day of election (Sabato and Simpson 1996);
- Campaign workers may pre-punch absentee ballots and have a voter sign them (Sabato and Simpson 1996);
- Campaign workers may induce voters to sign an absentee ballot and then take the un-filled ballot away for later completion (Sabato and Simpson 1996) and;
- Campaign workers may trick absentee voters into casting "straight party" tickets (Sabato and Simpson 1996).

Prevention: Audit absentee ballots and investigate questionable ballots.

◆ <u>Polling Fraud</u> occurs while bringing people to vote and during vote casting:

- Voter Herding: The gathering of otherwise non-voting citizens, particularly the aged and infirm, to induce them into voting (Armbrister 1995);
- Voter Intimidation: The threatening of citizens in order to sway their votes. In one example, voters living in public housing were told that they would lose their residences if they did not vote for one candidate (Armbrister 1995);
- Imposition of poll taxes: The illegal charging of fees designed to prevent a segment of a populace from voting;
- Individuals may vote more than once at the same location by presenting falsified identifications;
- Individuals may vote more than once by going to different polling stations;

- Unregistered or otherwise ineligible people may cast votes (Sabato and Simpson 1996);
- Campaign workers may instruct people as to how to vote (Sabato and Simpson 1996);
- Individuals may payoff voters with money or gratuities to influence their votes (Sabato and Simpson 1996) and;
- Campaign workers may trick voters into cast "straight party" tickets when that was not their intention (Sabato and Simpson 1996).

Prevention: Survey elections, require unique voter identification cards (Sabato and Simpson 1996), and audit votes.

◆ Vote-Counting Fraud occurs after votes have been cast and while the votes are being tallied:
- Election officials may simply falsify the tally (FBI 1989);
- officials may cast away or destroy some ballots or;
- theoretically, election officials could mechanically or electronically alter voting machines.

One probable sign of election fraud is when the number of cast votes exceeds the number of registered voters (Sabato and Simpson 1996).

Prevention: Survey vote tallies and audit results.

◆ Contested Election Fraud occurs when state legislatures, charged with the responsibility of deciding unclear election results, make extraordinarily biased interpretations of election laws to sway the outcome (Armbrister 1995).

Prevention: Citizen and judicial oversight of legislative decisions.

MALADMINISTRATION

While most fraud is committed to enrich the perpetrator, this is not always true. Scientists (See CHAPTER NINE), for one, are in a position to doctor research just for the sake of obtaining a predisposed result. Likewise, government employees may doctor procurements or program funding not to enrich themselves, but rather, just to fulfill their personal agendas. Here are two examples:

- Off-loading: The practice of one federal agency or federal contractor awarding contracts to another branch of government for the sole purpose of avoiding procurement regulations. Under some circumstances, specified by the Economy Act, off-loading is legal, but when used simply to avoid procurement regulations, while deceiving government regulators, it is not (DOD OIG 10-1-93 thru 3-31-93).
- The federal Anti-deficiency Act forbids government employees or contractors from spending more than Congress appropriated. So if a National Lab decides to juggle funds because it thinks proton gun research lacks merit while electron gun research warrants spending, it is committing fraud by misappropriating the funds.

TAX FRAUD

By dollar value, the largest single category of fraud against the government is tax fraud. A 1998 estimate puts the annual cost at $100 billion (*IBD* 7-30-98). One liberal estimate puts the value of the total shadow economy (off-book work and illegal transactions) at $600 to $1,200 billion per year (Ayres July/Aug 1996). With this estimate, the total lost revenue would range between $200 and $400 billion annually. Clearly the much-maligned IRS has its work cut out for itself.

Correlating to the estimate of unpaid taxes, fully one third of households underpay their taxes (*IBD* 7-30-98). Since so many are involved in tax evasion, maybe this is one section of the Handbook that need not be dwelled upon. For the curious 67% of society who want to know what their brethren are doing, the major categories of tax fraud are: i. unreported income, ii. underestimated income, iii. exaggerated and false tax deductions, iv. fraudulent exemptions v.

tax credit fraud, vii. false benefit claims, viii. tax refund fraud, ix. property tax fraud, x. sales tax fraud, xi. excise tax fraud, and xii. customs tax fraud.

Given the size of the tax code, some 5.5 million words (Troester 3-2-98), and the great range of taxes [one Website lists some 83 (http://rs7.loc.gov/cgi-bin/lex1.script)] it is obvious that a detail of all possible tax frauds is beyond the scope of this Handbook. Here are a few to illustrate the range:

Unreported Income
Income from illegal activities, such as narcotic sales, comprise the largest percentage of unreported income. Criminals use a variety of money laundering techniques to conceal these illegal gains. The second leading source of unreported income is money laundering. The third largest source is probably from small cash businesses that simply work off of the books. Lesser sources are bartering (Women's Connection Online Inc. 1997) and unreported capital gains, such as from the sales of unregistered property like collectibles.

Here are some examples of other unreported income:

- Income Shifting: Generating income then causing the money to be paid to another is fraudulent when used to deceive the US IRS (IRS CID 1997 Website).
- Soft Dollar Tax Fraud: The unreported receipt of goods or services as favors or gifts. In one example, a partner in a stock brokerage received gratuities from a stock trader, but failed to report the income to the IRS (Abrams 9-27-97).
- Withholding Tax Fraud: Educational institutions may defraud the IRS by not withholding taxes for foreign student scholarships or salaries (Lederman 5-24-97). Any employer may be engaged in tax fraud by failing to make adequate tax withholdings.

- Unreported Compensation: Perks like the use of a company car, frequent flier miles, or vacations, must be reported as income. Note also, embezzlers (see CHAPTER SEVEN's embezzlement section) must report their illicit gains.

Underestimated Income
This may be the most widespread fraud among otherwise law-abiding people. Those in cash businesses, especially the self-employed with small businesses, are in the best positions to underestimate income. Construction contractors may, for example, take partial payment for a job in a check, which is reported, and from cash, which is not.

Exaggerated and False Tax Deductions
Tax deduction fraud is mostly the domain of wealthier tax-payers and businesses, because they have the assets to deduct and the sophistication to do it. The Congress, IRS and sneaky tax-payers have an on-going tag and dodge over aggressive tax deductions ever since the 1970's when people used aggressive limited partnerships to create large losses. Every time Congress tightens up one area rife with deduction fraud, creative accountants find another un-scrutinized deduction. There are three classes of deduction frauds: i. false deductions, ii. inflated charity deductions, and iii. unallowable investment deductions:

◆ <u>False Deductions</u>
Taxpayers can falsify any number of allowable deductions:
- by taking the same deduction multiple times (Stecklow and Rebello 5-24-95);
- by claiming fictitious charitable contributions;
- by claiming fictitious pension contributions;
- by claiming fictitious casualty losses;
- by claiming fictitious capital losses.

Here are two examples of creative fake deductions:

231

- Double Depreciation Tax Fraud: Five individuals defrauded the IRS and investors by claiming double depreciation on real estate investments (USPIS Winter 1990-91).
- Pay Yourself Mortgage Scam: Taxpayers who own their home free and clear set up a shell corporation to which they pay a mortgage. When they count the payment as a tax deduction, the whole deal is a fraud (Packer 3-9-95).

◆ Inflated Charity Deductions

Taxpayers are allowed to deduct charitable contributions, but the rub comes from inflated appraisals. Favorite inflated appraisals are vehicles and art (Conklin 1994). Benefiting organizations may facilitate the tax fraud by signing-off on the inflated appraisal out of the goodness of their hearts or in response to bribes.

A taxpayer may obtain an inflated deduction by donating a junker vehicle and then taking a middle *Blue Book* value for the contribution.

◆ Unallowable Investment Deductions

One subtle tax fraud involves accelerated depreciation of assets to increase current deductions. A second class of unallowable deductions comes from limited partnerships that are not IRS-qualified. By example, an Oregon cattleman defrauded more than 1,000 investors by promising exceptional tax deductions from a cattle-based tax shelter. The IRS disallowed the shelter after many years, and investors were stuck with huge tax bills. The government sought indictments against the cattle operation (Grabner 3-27-98).

Fraudulent Exemptions

Exemptions are a complex area of the US tax code (as though there are any simple provisions). There are personal and dependent exemptions on the individual tax return, business exemptions for their contractors' tax liability, exemptions for some out-of-country status, and trust exemptions. Each of these areas are the subject of abuse:

◆ Personal and Dependent Exemption
Below specific income ceilings, taxpayers are allowed fixed exemptions for each individual in a family or for each dependent. In a form of identity fraud, wayward taxpayers assume a Social Security number for a phantom dependent (most often a child), file a false tax return, and thereafter receive undue exemptions.

There are also a number of patently fraudulent personal exemptions which rely on twisting the US Constitution. One, called a "private sovereign entity status" purports to exempt individuals from paying taxes. The tax dodge is based on the false assumption that an individual can declare themselves sovereigns, independent of the US. In another twist, individuals declare their allegiance to a state but but disavow the country (NFIC Web site 3-27-96).

◆ Business Exemptions for Contractors
In a well-known tax dodge, companies falsely declare employees to be independent contractors to avoid submitting withholding, Social Security, and Medicare taxes (Bryant-Friedland 2-16-98).

◆ Off-Shore Exemptions
Analogous to the "private sovereign entity status" describe above, there are a variety of tax dodges which misguidedly rely on people or assets residing offshore. These are often sold as "tax haven accounts," sold by mis-informed or unethical bankers or brokers who claim off-shore bank accounts are exempt from taxation—but they are not. In some cases, they are not even beyond the reach of US IRS scrutiny (NFIC 5-22-96).

Notwithstanding the fake identities, there are legitimate personal off-shore exemptions—the US tax code conditionally allows individuals to exempt a certain amount of out-of-county income. How-

233

ever, Social Security and Medicare taxes are not exempt. Not paying tax on amounts above the exempt level is tax fraud.

◆ Trust Exemptions

Abusive Trusts: "...typically involve the creation of one or more trusts into which the taxpayer transfers his or her personal and/or business assets and to which the taxpayers assigns his or her income. Establishing a foreign or domestic trust for the purpose of hiding income and assets from taxation is illegal (IRS CID 1997 Website)."

Tax Credit Fraud

The tax code allows for various credits to encourage developing sectors of the economy. These credits include credits for developing low-income housing, alternative energy credits, and enterprise zone credits to develop economically depressed sectors. A business or individual can commit fraud by falsely claiming credits. In one multi-armed fraud, a manufacturer deceived investors into believing that they were eligible for alternative energy tax credits. The perpetrator "...represented the solar power modules as being capable of producing electrical and thermal power...The investors were led to believe the solar power modules would pay for themselves through the sale of their power to utility companies and through tax credits (USPIS Fall 1991)."

False Benefit Claims

The states and federal government hold out various benefits to encourage low-income families to participate in the competitive economy. The largest of these programs are credits for paid childcare and earned income credits which are designed to bring the working-poor up to a living wage. Individuals can and do defraud the government by falsely claiming credit for childcare that was not rendered and by falsely claiming eligibility for the earned income credit (Sberna 10-23-95). There are two ways to falsify eligibility for the earned income credit: a. under-reporting income to go below the maximum income threshold, and b. falsely claiming dependents to increase the earned-income subsidy.

Tax Refund Fraud

Anytime someone holds out a flag saying they have a pot of money that is open to claims, people will step forward, rightfully or not, to make a claim. The tax refund system is such a pot and here are some of the refund frauds:

- A tax preparer filed fraudulent amended tax returns in the names of his clients to receive money from the IRS (USPIS Summer 1991).
- Criminals have defrauded the US government and tax filing services by filing false returns with false Social Security numbers to obtain loans from the filing service (Sberna 10-23-95).
- The government indicted an individual for submitting 266 fraudulent tax returns. The fraudulent returns caused the government to mistakenly refund millions of dollars (USPIS Fall 1990).
- Criminals file fictitious electronic tax returns to receive unentitled reimbursements (Information Plus 1994).

Property Tax Fraud

Property owners commit tax fraud when they fail to disclose the ownership of taxable property or when they undervalue taxable property. One common property tax fraud is for a homeowner to make off-the-books improvements, like finishing home basements, without telling the local tax authority. There are a variety of clever schemes involving motor vehicle taxes: a. An individual can pour money into a junker car to restore it, and then continue to carry its minimal value on the books. b. Residents of high-vehicle tax states like Washington try to register their vehicles in low-vehicle tax states like neighboring Oregon. c. Individuals or businesses can defraud states by failing to renew license plates, failing to transfer registrations from one state to another, or by switching valid plates onto vehicles that had expired registrations (KUSA News Denver 6-8-98).

Sales Tax Fraud

States and other local entities use sales taxes as a major revenue source. Businesses can defraud states by failing to collect and/or failing to pay the taxes. In one clever scheme, some New York City retailers help customers avoid city tax by boxing items and pretending to mail the purchases to out-of-city addresses so that the customer can avoid city tax. The retailer makes a record of the mailing, but lets the customer walk out the door with the item (Benke 6-15-98). Consumers avoid sales tax by traveling from their high-tax state to low or no tax states in order to shop. Residents of Washington State are known to do this on their weekend trips to neighboring Oregon.

An individual's largest single property tax is often the motor vehicle tax, and residents go to lengths to avoid or underpay this:

- Alabama-based Travelers (see CHAPTER THREE'S Home Repair Section) took advantage of a state law allowing them low-cost car registrations for vehicles older than 1974—they claimed late-model cars as pre-1974. This was a way to gain a title without paying the appropriate sales tax (Wright 1996)
- Vehicle buyers may request a receipt that states the sale price was less than the actual price in order to reduce their excise tax. Alternatively, the buyer may alter the sales receipt to reduce the tax.
- Titles may be counterfeit or altered to avoid paying sales tax (Wright 1996) thereby defrauding the state of revenue and the buyer of a clean title.
- Some Travelers defrauded state government by under-reporting the value of trailer homes, often saying that they were damaged and so not worth their book value (Wright 1996).

Excise Tax Fraud

Excise taxes are levied by the federal and state government on specific goods or commodities. In some cases, as for alcohol and tobacco, the excise tax is equivalent to a sin tax. These taxes are often so high that they present strong incentives for smuggling or off-the-book sales. In fact, organized crime has had an enduring hand in fuel tax frauds. In describing the magnitude of the frauds, the US Department of Transportation identified fuel tax schemes as a major loss of revenue to government treasuries. "Daisy chains [a string of companies designed to confuse] among bulk traders, bootlegging across state borders, misrepresentation of diesel fuel as home heating oil, and false refund claims are just some of the schemes that have been uncovered. Gasoline blenders are another source of potential evasion because gasoline purchased for blending with alcohol is taxed at a lower rate than gasoline designated for retail (DOT OIG 4-1-93 thru 9-30-93)."

Another fuel tax scheme involves organized criminals who "...used valid wholesaler permits of other oil companies to purchases millions of gallons of diesel fuel without payment of the tax. The fuel was subsequently sold at retail stations (Securities Division Washington State Department of Financial Institutions Website no date)."

Tobacco excise tax fraud is more often achieved through smuggling: Criminals transport tobacco products across international and state borders to avoids high excise taxes (IBD 6-10-98).

Customs Tax Fraud

The US government uses a variety of taxes and export incentives to bolster certain US industries and to protect others from unfair or unwelcome foreign competitors. Some businesses evade or manipulate these laws by falsifying customs documents. One scheme has exporters pretending to import goods for later export. By claiming the imports are for export, the firm is exempt from import taxes. If, instead, the importer sells the products within the US, it commits customs fraud by avoiding the import tax (Segal Oct 1995).

Sophisticated companies evade taxes by engaging in a form of import-export arbitrage: They defraud the US Treasury by as much as $109 billion per year by artificially inflating the cost basis of imports and artificially deflating the price of exports. The price manipulations cause the net profits to be understated, thereby reducing the import-export taxes (DeGeorge 3-21-94).

Prevention: It's the IRS's (and US Customs's) job. They have 100,000+ employees to collect taxes and ferret-out fraud (Troester 3-2-98).

What did these scientists have in common?
They had an outstanding intellect, they were
all informed in their research field and
recognized the missing links that if solved
would represent a breakthrough.

Efraim Racker(5-1-89), in profiling 'professional' science frauds.

CHAPTER NINE - SCIENCE FRAUD

INTRODUCTION

Purpose of Chapter
The Handbook includes a Science Fraud Chapter to lend breadth to an otherwise commercial emphasis and to serve the scientific community. The breadth is important to illustrate that not all fraud is financially motivated and that no corner of society is immune from fraud. The Handbook serves the scientific community by giving a readily available, concise synopsis of scientific fraud so scientists will know it when they see it and how to avoid it when it tempts them.

Science fraud encompasses criminal, civil and ethical fraud. Criminal fraud includes: making false claims, false reporting, and mischarging. To be prosecutable, the fraud either has to involve a significant amount of money, or cause substantial harm to individuals or organizations. To win a criminal conviction, the government must also prove that the perpetrator knowingly committed the act—no small feat. Civil fraud is nearly identical to criminal fraud. Notable differences include the fact that any party, not just the government, can make a civil fraud charge, and the burden of proof is lower—the plaintiff merely has to show that the defendant committed the act negligently (should have known). Ethical fraud is basically lying about something of importance. It differs from criminal and civil fraud in that it usually involves things of no apparent monetary value. For example, when a scientists fails to include a co-author on a paper, the act qualifies as ethical fraud because the omission is made to deceive the journal and peers by making it look like the named author is responsible for all of research. Ethical frauds are usually judged administratively or by peers. They rarely see the inside of a courtroom.

Organizing the discussion of science fraud with this hierarchy well serves the Chapter's likely readers, scientists. By studying this Chapter, the scientist will be in a good position to judge the severity of the transgression at hand: Could it be a violation of criminal law? Is it likely to spark a lawsuit? Will it attract administrative action, like sanctions, from the sponsoring organization? Will it pass unnoticed? Or will it simply inspire heated debate?

Motivations for Science Fraud

There are five reasons why scientists commit fraud: i. for financial or career gain, ii. to show their cleverness, iii. in response to competitive pressure, iv. out of malevolence or jealousy, and v. in haste, laziness or indifference.

■ Financial Gain: Scientists enrich themselves when they receive funding after falsifying contract or grant applications. Falsifying information in publications also potentially enriches a scientist when he or she is rewarded with promotions or pay raises on the strength of their publication history.

■ Cleverness: Apparently, some of the cleverest are never satisfied with the attention they receive. This may be akin to the computer-hacker syndrome—the cases of the precocious computer hand who breaks into secured systems just to show that he or she can do it. Racker (1989) makes the case that the most serious science frauds that came to his attention all involved outstanding scientists with promising careers.

■ Pressure: Goodstein (Website) identifies career pressure as one of the primary motivations behind science fraud. Presumably, the intense pressure in science careers supresses some people's ethics.

■ Malevolence or Jealousy: In reading about publications misconduct (see below), it is hard not to see that many of the battles over who should or should not be included as an author involve ill-will or jealousy.

■ Haste, Laziness, or Indifference: Lets face it, as glamorous as science seems from the outside looking in, much of it is in fact tedious. Goodstein (Website) opines that a large percentage of science fraud comes from researchers who "knew, or thought they knew what the answer would turn out to be if they went to all the trouble of doing the work properly..." Marsa (June 1992) describes the work of patriarchal scientists, Galileo, Kepler, Newton, Dalton, and Mendel, who may have fudged their results to accommodate their predispostions.

Enforcement Action Targeting Scientists
Prosecutors first targeted science fraud in the 1980s (Anderson 9-29-88) when federal officials started to successfully apply the federal False Claim Act (see below) to falsified grant applications. Since then, more and more scientists find themselves in court, both as defendants and as complaints or plaintiffs. Notwithstanding the growth in criminal and civil adjudications of alleged science fraud, the vast majority of the cases fall in the less severe realm of misconduct, also called ethical fraud—deviations from the norms of scientific standards, procedures and conduct that are not so grave as to be judged by a court.

Quirk in Science Fraud
Another quirk in science is that it is standard operating procedure to omit negative or indeterminate results—scientists usually publish only compelling observations and experimental findings. This

same approach in many other aspects of life, such as in the procurement of goods or services, would be viewed as fraud.

To illustrate, consider parallel examples in geological research and concrete aggregate procurement: A NSF-funded petrologist studying granite melts may run thousands of quench experiments—the controlled melting and freezing of silicate blends. To only reported the small fraction of the experiments that showed a pattern would be standard operating practice. In contrast, if a US Department of Defense construction contractor changed the moisture content of delivered concrete aggregate, he could well be charged with contract fraud. Of course, the different outcomes in the two examples mostly reflect the relative consequence of the omissions. Nonetheless, the accepted scientific practice of omitting data arguably creates a predisposition toward fraud in the scientific community.

CRIMINAL SCIENCE FRAUD

Spurred on by US Representative David Dingall's (D-MI) hearings in the mid-1990s, federal officials have taken a more aggressive approach to ferret out fraud in government-sponsored research. Investigators from the Office of Inspector Generals at the National Science Foundation, Department Health and Human Services, Department of Energy, NASA, the Department of Defense, the FBI, and other sundry agencies are charged with investigating alleged fraud in government contracts and grant research programs. Four major types of fraud emerged from these criminal investigations:

(1) False claims in grant and research applications. Scientists who knowingly include false information in contract or grant applications may be in violation of the Civil War era False Claims Act. The Act makes it felony to submit false claims to the government. If a scientist makes the false claim in collusion with another or others, they all may be charged with a second felony, Conspiracy. If the contract or grant is part of a larger project amounting to

242

$1,000,000 or more, the false claim could be prosecuted under the Major Fraud Act. Most False Claim prosecutions are pursued for services that are not rendered or for services that were rendered in ways materially different from the contract specifications. For example, if a physicist claims he built a new laser costing $500,000, when it actually cost $450,000, he is making a false claim. The scientists who claims to have worked 600 hours on a project when he actually only worked 250 is also making a false claim.

In one case, the National Science Foundation Inspector General investigated "...evidence that the owner of a small, high-technology business repeatedly submitted duplicate proposals to and received duplicate funding from, NSF, NASA, and various DOD agencies without informing the agencies as required by agency solicitations.... (NSF 10-1-93 thru 3-31-94)."

(2) False statements in reported research. Fabricating, altering, or withholding research results may violate the federal False Statements Act. False statements corrupt science and can have disastrous effects on the public. The French government indicted and, in 1992, convicted the head of the National Centre for Blood Transfusion for his role in failing to inform and protect the public against the threat the HIV virus posed through blood transfusions (Butlet 6-15-95). The scientist could have adopted existing HIV tests from Abbott Laboratories, a US company, but instead forestalled adopted the company's test until France could develop a comparable one (Stone 2-18-94). One author estimated the delay caused as many as 1,200 cases of AIDS (Maddox 6-10-93). This case illustrates how not just the commission, but also the omission of information, can also be treated as a criminal false statement.

In a second false statements case, a federal jury found a psychologist guilty of making false statements to the government after he falsified research on the treatment of hyperactivity in mentally retarded children. This marks the first conviction of scientists for fraud by federal courts (Anderson 9-29-88).

A less severe case of alleged false claims sullied the career of a Nobel Laureate. One of the Laureate's subordinates allegedly falsified work that went into a paper published by the journal *Cell*. An in-depth, eight year investigation ultimately exonerated both the subordinate and the principal investigator. Notwithstanding the exoneration, this case illustrates how an investigation can disrupt and tarnish even the most distinguished career (Anderson and Watson 7-16-92).

(3) Indirect cost mischarging. During the early 1990s federal investigators targeted a number universities, including Stanford, Harvard, and MIT for allegedly using government funds to cover unallowable costs like yachts and vacations (Pool and Aldhuos 8-8-9 and *Nature* 5-23-91). Administrators misappropriated the funds when they used overhead charges to spread tax dollars into diverse cost pools that included luxury items. Although using research dollars for specifically excluded costs can be criminally prosecuted, none of these investigations culminated in indictments. Nonetheless, these cases show that the ties between contract administration and scientists can draw scientists into criminal cases.

(4) Direct Misappropriation of research funds. Researchers are accustomed to using the budgets of well-endowed projects to cover less well-supported projects. Scientists also use existing funding to bridge the gap to start up new projects. These misappropriations, known as contract co-mingling or cross-charging, may be prosecuted under a variety of federal fraud statutes, including the Anti-Deficiency Act, a law that reinforces the House of Representatives as the only authority that can appropriate funds to projects.

In contrast to ethical fraud described below in the Misconduct section, the above acts are prosecuted because they most directly involve the allocation and use of significant amounts of taxpayer money. The dollar amount figures into a prosecution decision because when the prosecutor can show a significant monetary loss it is much easier to "sell" the case to a jury. Prosecutors decline misconduct cases because they often involve little to no money and therefore lack jury appeal.

Criminal Fraud Prevention: Research organization should require their staff and students to attend fraud-education seminars. The government is responsible for detection, but for the preliminary exposure of alleged fraud, each institution should develop a protocol for handling fraud investigations.

CIVIL SCIENCE FRAUD

If investigators cannot prove someone's fraudulent acts were intentional, but they can prove that the government lost money through deceit, the government is more likely to sue, than to prosecute. While governments alone have the power to press criminal charges, any potentially damaged party can sue. Accordingly, a variety of plaintiffs may press civil fraud suits: institutions against individuals, individuals against institutions, individuals against individuals, government against institutions or government against individuals. The following illustrate the role of civil proceedings in scientific disputes:

Individuals Sue Institutions both to remedy alleged fraud on the part of the institution or to counter allegations of fraud directed at the scientist:

A graduate student allegedly falsified mineralogical data which was submitted to the University as part of his M.S. Thesis. The University determined the data had been falsified, rescinded his degree, and was later sued by the student on the basis of the fact that he was denied due process. The student prevailed in his lawsuit against the University (Wilson W. Crook, III v. Board of Regents of the University of Michigan, et al. 9-17-85).

Various state and federal laws protect whistleblowers, individuals who bring forth allegations of wrong doing by their employers. These laws are designed to protect the public's interest in areas like fraud prevention and environmental protection. In one case, Mobil Oil dismissed a company scientist after he allegedly "...misused company assets such as postage and copying facilities...." The scientist won a lawsuit in which he countered that the fraud allegations were a rouse to punish him for exposing the company's environmental violations at its Chiba, Japan refinery (Holden 4-29-94).

Scientists Sue Scientists
One epidemiologist won a judgment of $2.1 million against another epidemiologist for the defendant's unauthorized taking of a questionnaire (Swinbanks 12-23-93).

A doctor filed suit against co-researchers, charging them with fraud and corruption for their role in blackballing her from meaningful research and for putting her name on a (tainted) paper without her permission (Cotton 2-12-92).

Government Sues Scientists
If the US government cannot sustain a criminal fraud allegation beyond a reasonable doubt, it has a number of other legal remedies, including: filing a Civil False Claims suit; using the Program Fraud Civil Remedies Act (PFRCA); or enjoining in a *qui tam* suit filed by a third party. A Civil False Claims suit does not allow for criminal sanction like incarceration, but it does allow for steep fines on the order of $10,000 per false claims plus treble damages. In a civil case, the government need not prove the perpetrator had foreknowledge of the crime, just that the perpetrator made or caused the false claim to be made. PFRCA is enforced by administrative

judges within the various Departments of the Executive Branch, and it allows for specific fines and recoveries.

A *qui tam* suit allows someone outside of government to sue for the government. The government may enjoin the suit, or allow the third party to pursue it on behalf of the government. A co-worker, subordinate, or knowledgeable competitor could file a *qui tam* suit against a scientist, scientists, or an institution. If the plaintiff prevails, he or she stands to receive substantial payment for their trouble—some *qui tam* plaintiffs won tens of millions of dollars.

In one *qui tam* lawsuit, an epidemiologist took the unusual step of using the civil False Claims Act to sue her co-workers, after they allegedly stole her research into infection rates during pregnancy. A Federal judge ruled in her favor, awarding her $1.9 million from the University of Alabama and four scientists (Hight 5-19-95). The first time the False Claims Act was used in a science dispute was in a 1989 against the University of Utah and its researcher John Ninnemann. J. Thomas Condie, a former technician in Ninnemann's lab, alleged that Ninnemann falsified data on the human immune response to burns (Taubes 2-4-94).

Civil Fraud Prevention: Research organization should require their staff and students to attend fraud-education seminars. Each institution should adopt a protocol for handling civil fraud allegations.

SCIENTIFIC MISCONDUCT

The introduction of this Handbook establishes that fraud is a form of misconduct. Whereas misconduct includes any deviation from conventional behavior, including white collar crime, scientists have informally come to use the word "misconduct" in a specialized way, as any deviation from generally accepted scientific practices. The National Science Foundation specifically defines misconduct more broadly, with two major aspects: "(1) Fabrication, falsification, plagiarism, or other serious deviation from accepted practices in proposing, carrying out, or reporting results from activities by NSF; or (2) Retaliation of any kind against a person who reported or provided information about suspected of alleged misconduct and who has not acted in bad faith (45 CFR Ch VI (10-1-91-Edition) Part 689.1.)"

To make further distinctions in scientific misconduct, the term ethical fraud is used to describe the least damaging instances of fraud in science. Administrative-science fraud is also an apt description since these instances of misconduct are handled administratively, but this term is somewhat misleading in that it suggests fraud by science administrators. Consequently, ethical science fraud is the best term to describe those scientific deceptions that are not serious enough to warrant judicial action. Ethical science fraud roughly correlates to part (1) of NSF's definition, except that the acts encompassed by the term are not sufficiently severe enough to warrant judicial action.

The body of the text below includes thirty three examples of ethical science fraud that came to light from administrative or peer reviews. These examples illustrate misconduct most likely to impact scientists and their sponsors. They fall into three major categories: experimental misconduct, publication of data misconduct, and publication attribution misconduct. There are a couple of types of misconduct that are outliers from the three major categories: conflicts of interests and curricula vitae falsification. (It should surprise no one in science that there are more examples of science misconduct involving publications than in any other category.)

Ethical fraud in science spans the continuum of scientific activities from: falsifying resumes when applying for a position; to falsifying experimental protocol; to concealing the use of unorthodox protocols; to falsely reporting experimental results; to giving undo credit to some co-workers or no credit to worthy co-workers; to failing to disclose conflicts of interests:

Experimental Misconduct includes:
- intentionally faulty experimental design;
- discarding of appropriate experimental controls;
- manipulation of experimental or observational outcomes;
- failure to retain pertinent data, and;
- failure to repeat inconclusive experiments.

＊ Intentional Faulty Design
There are no ready examples of intentional faulty experimental design, but one can imagine someone biasing results by knowingly excluding significant factors. For example, an ecologist might bias a bird study by intentionally limiting observations to snowy days, knowing that doing so will profoundly bias the results.

＊ Discarded Controls
Scientists can manipulate the outcome of research by discarding controls that are inconsistent with the (unethically) pre-determined outcome of an experiment [cited but not elaborated] (Deichmann and Muller-Hill 1998).

＊ Manipulation of Observations
A paleontologist was accused of reusing the same fossils at different locations and of taking fossils from one locale and placing them, out of context, at another locale (de Wit 3-1-94).

＊ Failure to Retain Supporting Data
Two investigators reviewed the bibliography of a researcher who allegedly engaged in widespread and long-term scientific misconduct. The investigators found seven papers where the subject and co-authors failed to retain data, thereby preventing others from authenticating the results (Stewart and Feder 1-15-87).

* Failure To Repeat An Experiment
In furtherance of a scientific fraud, a biochemist questioned the propriety of repeating an experiment. His reluctance undermined the doctrine of repeatability (Deichmann and Muller-Hill 1998).

Publication Misconduct
There are numerous examples of publication misconduct. The great number of examples presumably result from the efficacy of peer and reader review. Publication misconduct spans:
- falsification of data,
- falsification of methods,
- phantom experiments,
- withholding material data, and
- re-manufacturing data:

* Data Falsification
Data falsification exists both in the life and physical sciences. Here are three examples in the life sciences:
- One researcher fabricated an entire genre of research around a fictitious group of proteases which purportedly allowed ready detection of a variety of diseases and pregnancy (Deichmann and Muller-Hill 1998)
- A second researcher falsified a child's immunization records (Feder, Johnson, and Nicklin 1992).
- In a notorious biomedical fraud, John Darsee falsified heart research data that went into more than 100 publications in the 1980s (Marsa June 1992).

Examples of data falsification in the physical sciences come from a variety of fields:

- Author Howard Plotkin (1993) presented evidence of fraud in the physical science of meteoritics: A Nineteenth Century contract explorer for the US misrepresented the provenance of a meteorite by stating it was from Oregon, when in fact, it was a piece of the Chilean Imilac meteorites that had been purchased and fraudulently misrepresented.

- Manufacturing fictitious fossils or leaking fossils into the geologic record seems to be a favorite scheme of the fringe scientific community: Sikafis (1993) describes a variety of historic frauds involving fossils: (1). Nineteenth century miners deceived California State Geologist James D. Whitney into believing the skull of an early man had been found in Calaveras County, CA. (2). A non-scientist manufactured the figure of a giant man out of gypsum and toured the statue around the country, proclaiming it evidence of giants formerly inhabiting the earth. The statue was called the Cardiff Giant. (3). In 1912 Englishman Charles Dawson claimed to have dug up the skull of a prehistoric man in a gravel pit near Piltdown Common in England. The skull was later proved to be a fabrication.

- John Dalton, seminal Nineteenth Century chemist, reportedly published results that have never been replicated (Marsa June 1992).

Omission of material data or biased data selection are other aspects of data falsification—a commentary in *Nature* (10-1-87) suggests some researchers engage in misconduct by only presenting the data which supports their thesis and withholding contrary data from other researcher's scrutiny. Marsa (June 1992) reported charges that Nobel Lauriate Robert Millikan withheld experimental results that were unfavorable to his research biases.

✳ Methods Falsification

The reproducibility and, therefore, authenticity of experimental results rely on complete and accurate methods descriptions. Inadequate methods descriptions, therefore, may serve as fraud indicators. In one example of methods falsification, a doctor alleged that her superior falsified the "methods" section of a paper by asserting psychology patients received diagnostic tests but in fact, these tests were not undertaken (Cotton 2-12-92).

∗ Phantom Experiments
A commentary in *Nature* (10-1-87) suggests some researchers engage in misconduct by citing experiments that were never conducted to fill-in inadequate data or to compensate for gaps in control data.

∗ Withheld Data
A Michigan State University panel found one of its pathology graduate students guilty of misconduct after the student published an article without giving her co-authors a chance to see the data that supported the article. She also failed to obtain her advisor's permission to publish the paper (Maddox 1-28-93).

In something of a hedge on withholding data, some scientists appear to write deliberately ambiguous papers to side-step scrutiny (Stewart and Feder 1-15-87).

∗ Falsified Authorships
The questionable act of awarding "honorary authorship" (*Nature* 6-15-95) to senior scientists or to principal investigators who do not materially participate in a project is, perhaps, the most commonplace misconduct in modern science. Two other forms of authorship misconduct are faked co-authors and un-approved attribution. The following are examples of each:

- One researcher listed fictitious co-authors in a paper (Goodstein Autumn 1991).
- A doctor alleges her name was placed on a paper even though, "... she was never informed that her name would appear on the paper, disagrees with its conclusions and methods, and was unaware its existence until after its publication (Cotton 2-12-92)."
- Goodstein (Autumn 1991) found one instance where a researcher placed fictitious entries in a publication bibliography.

✶ Attribution Falsification
Just as inappropriate inclusion of authors can be misconduct, so too can inappropriate omission of deserving contributors (Niggs and Radulescu 7-13-94). In one case a doctor alleged that her superior gave her research ideas to male researchers without her permission and without crediting her (Cotton 2-12-92).

✶ Multiple Publication Misconduct
Scientists feel intense pressure to develop prodigious bibliographies, and some fall prey to misconduct in their desire to puff-up their biographies:

- Duplicate Publications: Some researchers publish the same research in more than one place. This is also called self-plagiarism (Niggs and Radulescu 7-13-94).
- Paper Recycling: Synonymous with plagiarism and may also be used to describe reuse of the same data by the same author (*Nature* 3-15-90).
- Salami Publications: Some researchers slice-up coherent bodies of research into too-small articles to bloat their bibliographies (Niggs and Radulescu 7-13-94).
- Simultaneous Duplicate Publications: The National Institute of Health wrestled with a quarrel between two researches who simultaneously submitted the same data describing the efficacy of an antibiotic. The data was identical, but the interpretations were different. One of the concerns focused on a subordinate's desire to freely publish data generated with public funds (McGourty 8-31-89).
- Unacknowledged Re-publication: Two science integrity investigators found a number of instances where the authors of scientific papers failed to state that data presented in a paper had been previously published (Stewart and Feder 1-15-87).

In something of a hybrid falsification-duplicate publication scheme, researchers guilty of duplicate publications may try to conceal their duplication by re-manufacturing data (Niggs and Radulescu 7-13-94).

Conflicts of Interest
Undisclosed conflicts of interests may amount to ethical fraud. For example, a National Science Foundation reviewer could be in conflict if he or she fails to reveal affiliations with someone whose proposal they are reviewing.

Here are two real-life examples of undisclosed conflicts of interest in science:

- A cardiologist deceived his sponsor by failing to disclose outside research income (Holden 11-26-93).
- A research psychologist won damages against two parties; another scientist who allegedly stole her work and the scientists who lead a panel of investigators. The plaintiff won under provisions of the Michigan Whistle-blower's Protection Act. The judge ruled in plaintiff's favor because the panel head choose panelists who participated with the defendant in grants, thereby putting the panelists in a conflict of interest (Anderson 10-1-93).

One conflict was so egregious as to be criminal: A university professor defrauded the NSF by hiring his relatives to work on an NSF grant without informing the sponsoring university; by having his relatives submit falsified payroll certifications; and by receiving kickbacks from his family (NSF OIG 4-1-1991 thru 9-30-1991).

Curricula Vitae Falsification
The scientific community heavily relies on resumes in admitting students; awarding scholarships and assistantships; awarding grants, contracts, and awards; and in hiring and promoting. Clearly, falsifying information in a resume undermines the integrity of the scientific community. In one case, the chairman of a university

ethics committee uncovered resume falsification of a senior scientist. The senior scientist also appeared to inflate his reputation by filling his publication bibliography with review or invited papers which qualify as "soft" publications (Rossiter 6-11-92).

The flip side of resume falsification is intentional defamation of a peer's resume: In un-attributable letters sent to *Nature*, to a London teaching hospital, and to the Wellcome Trust, someone falsely accused a British medical scientist of "fraudulently obtaining his medical degree," dismissal from a Ph.D. course, and unethical behavior. An investigation demonstrated the allegations were false (Webb 9-28-89).

Misconduct Prevention: Research organization should require their staff and students to attend misconduct-education seminars. All final candidates for hire should have their backgrounds checked against their resumes. As for vetting experiments and papers, the scientific community has been highly successful—the meaningless falsifications fall into obscurity and the meaningful fall to peer review and further investigation. Even so, "...technicians, students, and postdoctoral fellows..." should all be carefully supervised (Racker 5-11-89). Finally, the scientific community needs to educate its members about conflicts of interests: Those in positions of authority should sign conflict-of-interest acknowledgments to pin them down to specific standards.

It is double pleasure to deceive the deceiver.
Jean de La Fontaine

CHAPTER TEN - SUMMARY - CONCLUSION

SUMMARY AND SYNTHESIS

Without some analysis to lend perspective, it is easy to feel over-whelmed by the pervasiveness of fraud. Using published losses and some conjecture, the following list displays the relative impact of fraud in American society:

1. Tax Fraud and Counterfeit Goods Fraud tie for first place with annual losses for each in the $200 to $400 billion range.
2. Insurance Fraud and International Trade Fraud tie for second place with annual losses for each in the $100 billion range.
3. Fraud in the Social Security Programs, Medicare and Medicaid programs, Telemarketing, Auto Repair, and Securities Fraud tie for third place with guestimated annual losses for each in the $50 billion range.
4. Check and Lending Fraud take fourth place with annual losses for each in the $10 billion range.
5. Credit Card and Telephone Card losses vie for fifth place with annual losses for each in the $10 to $7 billion range.
6. Travel Fraud against customers and Retail Fraud against busi-nesses, each cost an estimated $5 billion annually.
7. Food Stamp, Welfare Fraud, and Cellular Phone Service fraud each cost $2 to $1 billion annually.

All told, fraud consumes 11% to 16% of the $8 trillion dollar an-nual US economy. Based on the estimates here is a synthesis of fraud's effects on the US economy:

- Tax Fraud has the single greatest fraud impact on government.
- Counterfeit goods have the greatest fraud impacts on manufacturers and property right holders.
- International Trade Fraud has the second highest impact on both business and government.
- The insurance business is the service-finance industry with the highest fraud liability.
- There are four tiers of fraud that directly impact individuals:
  a. Telemarketing-Auto Repair-Securities Fraud.
  b. Credit Card-Telephone-Check Fraud.
  c. Travel and Retail Fraud.
  d. All other consumer frauds.

The analysis shows that society would most benefit from better tax compliance and stronger enforcement of patents, trademarks, and copyrights. Individual consumer-investors would most benefit from:

* heightened awareness and policing of telemarketer, auto repair shop, securities business fraud and;
* safeguarding their credit cards, telephone cards and personal checks.

USING THE HANDBOOK TO OFFSET FRAUD

It is obvious that nothing written here will impact fraud prevention in government or major industries—those entities already have active prevention. So, as stated in the Preface, this book is directed at individual consumers, individual investors, those new to a job or an industry, to small businesses, and to professionals. If the reader matches a pending life experience with a scheme in the Handbook, it is fairly easy for him or her to take a cautious posture and avoid the trap. Unfortunately, some schemes will fall outside of the descriptions in the Handbook.

What then do you do if you cannot match frauds that are familiar to you to the situation at hand then? Prior to seeing the outcome unravel, you must think through the likely course of events before carrying forward. How do you model the course of a situation? By conducting thought experiments and/or by conducting due diligence studies for yourself. A thought experiment is the least expensive route, and it works for the vast majority of situations.

In a thought experiment the thinker imagines the natural course of events. A pen and paper help. For example, if a painting contractor knocks on your door and announces that your house needs new paint, you need to ask yourself what would have prompted you to seek a painting contractor and what steps would you have taken to award the contract. Naturally, you would inspect the house to see if it genuinely needed painting; you would make phone calls to various painters; seek competitive bids; and check the references of the one who is likely to win the contract.

The painter knocking on the door is in marked contrast to the model bidding—he approached you and you had not yet noticed the need for a paint job. In proceeding, you must decide whether or not to ignore the fraud indicator and use the solicitor anyway; to take further steps to determine if the soliciting painter is legitimate; or to develop evidence that the contractor is a fraud. If further investigation finds no evidence of fraud, the indicator was misguided, and it is safe to go ahead. If further inquiry supports the indicator, you might refer your information to law enforcement and avoid awarding the contract to the solicitor.

While thought experiments are sufficient to offset petty fraud and short cons, complex decisions, like making an investment or buying a house, require background, or due diligence studies. When the pending situation is outside of your depth, this information-gathering step is necessary as a predecessor to conducting a thought experiment. This added step entails researching the protocol for making the impending decision, or hiring a professional to assist you in the decision-making process. For example, most people use licensed real estate brokers to buy their homes. People use brokers because they lack knowledge of the detailed house-buying steps. Be forewarned, if you embrace the due diligence process but skip the thought experiment process, you may be trading exposure to one fraud, in this case schemes related to the house purchase, for exposure to another source of fraud, the potentially unethical real estate broker. For pending complex transactions, you need to complete both the due diligence study and the thought experiment.

MODEL FRAUD IDENTIFICATION

Identifying fraud is the key to preventing it. To guard against the frauds that are neither known to you nor are intuitively obvious to you, consider using the following paradigm:

➢ Think through the course of events prior to negotiating or soliciting for something of value. If your negotiation involves something unfamiliar to you, conduct background research or enlist someone's help. If someone unknown to you initiates a transaction on his or her own, be leery, step back, and employ this protocol as though you had initiated the contact.

➢ Upon discussing the proposal with the other party, be alert for aspects of the interaction that are inconsistent with your expectations. Make note of the inconsistencies.

➢ Decide if the inconsistencies are immaterial, serve as important fraud indicators, or merely cast an unfavorable shadow on the other party without destroying your interest in the proposal.

➤ If the inconsistencies are immaterial or not fatal, go ahead with your transaction. If the inconsistencies suggest a material fraud, withdraw from the transaction, or investigate to substantiate or negate the fraud indicator.

➤ If you, or someone serving as your professional assistant, substantiate the fraud indicator, consider referring the interaction to a law enforcement agency and don't carry forward the transaction.

While some readers may find this outline painfully obvious, I insist it bears mentioning. In my judgment, the vast majority of fraud can be avoided by employing the knowledge base in the Handbook and by dutifully observing the paradigm. Good luck.

Appendix

ABBREVIATIONS

ATSDR	Agency for Toxic Substances and Disease Registry
BBB	Better Business Bureau
CFTC	Commodity Futures Trading Commission
CID	Criminal Investigations Division
DOD	Department of Defense
DOE	Department of Education
DOT	Department of Transportation
DP	*Denver Post*
EPA	Environmental Protection Agency
FBI	Federal Bureau of Investigation
FDA	Food and Drug Administration
FTC	Federal Trade Commission
GAAP	Generally Accepted Accounting Principals
HHS	Health and Human Services Administration
HUD	Housing and Urban Development
IBD	*The Investors Business Daily*
IG	Inspector General
IRS	Internal Revenue Service
NSF	National Science Foundation
NASAA	North American Securities Administrators Association Inc.
NASD	National Association of Security Dealers
NFIC	National Fraud Information Center
NYT	*The New York Times*
OCC	The Office of the Comptroller of the Currency
OIG	The Office of Inspector General
PFCRA	Program Fraud Civil Remedies Act
SAR	Semiannual Report
SBA	Small Business Administration
SEC	Securities and Exchange Commission
USPIS	US Postal Inspection Service
USSS	US Secret Service
WSJ	*The Wall Street Journal*

RESOURCES

The following is a listing of private information resources and government enforcement agencies which pertain to each of the eight major fraud categories detailed in the Handbook. These contacts may give you advice as to how to remedy a fraud loss; they may open an investigation; or they may refer you to another organization which is better able to help you.

1. Confidence Games
- Local police.
- State police.
- FTC, Consumer Response Center, Washington, DC 20580, Phone (202) 382-4357. [When a retailer or service provider fails to deliver as promised.]
- FBI, consult blue pages in phone book [for serious fraud]. HQ contact at J. Edgar Hoover Bldg., 935 Pennsylvania Ave.,Washington, D.C. 20535-0001, phone (202) 324-3000.

2. Consumer Fraud
- Autosistance/Top Rip Off's Web site http://home. earth-link.net/~autosisttance/ripoff.html
- National Fraud Information Center, @ National Consumers League, 1701 K Street, N.W., Suite 1200,Washington, D.C.200061(800) 876-7060, Website http:www.fraud. org.htm.
- The Better Business Bureau, consult you local phone book for contact phone.
- Local police.
- State police.
- US Secrete Service, consult local phone book blue pages for contact number [For cellular phone theft].

3. Financial
- A FBI, consult blue pages in phone book. HQ contact at J. Edgar Hoover Bldg.; 935 Pennsylvania Ave., Washington, D.C.20535-0001, phone (202) 324-3000.
- Your State Attorney General, see local phone book blue pages.
- Your State Insurance Commissioner, see local phonebook blue pages [insurance fraud-insurance consumer complaints].

- US Department of Health and Human Service Office of Inspector General, 330 Independence Ave., SW, Washington, D.C. 20201, phone (800) 447-8477 [Medicare and Medicaid].

4. Government Fraud
- Offices of Inspector General for individual, federal Departments, Agencies, and Commissions—consult blue pages in phone book.
- FBI, consult blue pages in phone book. HQ contact at J. Edgar Hoover Bldg., 935 Pennsylvania Ave., Washington, D.C. 20535-0001, phone (202) 324-3000.
- Local or State Police.

5. Investment Fraud
- SEC, 450 Fifth St, NW, Washington, DC 20549 Phone (202) 948-7040
- NASD, (800) 289-9999. [Self-regulator for securities.]
- CFTC, 1155 21st St., N.W., Washington, D.C. 20581, (202) 418-000
- Your State Real Estate Commission, see local phonebook blue pages.
- Your State Securities Division, see local phone book blue pages.
- American Numismatic Association, 818 N. Cascade, Colorado Springs, CO 80903-3279, phone (719) 632-2646.
- Gemological Institute of America, 5345 Armada Dr., Carlsbad, CA 92008, phone (800) 421-7250.

6. Operations
- Local police.
- State police.
- FBI consult blue pages in phone book. HQ contact at J. Edgar Hoover Bldg., 935 Pennsylvania Ave., Washington, D.C. 20535- phone (202) 324-3000.

7. Public Interest Fraud
- FBI, consult local phone book blue pages. HQ contact at J. Edgar Hoover Bldg.,935Pennsylvania Ave., Washington, D.C. 20535-0001, phone (202) 324-3000.
- U.S. Secrete Service, consult local phone book blue pages for contact number [For counterfeiting and credit card fraud].
- Your State Attorney General, see local phone book blue pages.
- US Internal Revenue Service, consult local phone book blue pages or call (800) 829-2872.
- Your State Tax Collection Agency, see the local phone book for a Revenue or Tax Office Listing.

8. Science Fraud

- NSF OIG, 4201 Wilson Blvd., Arlington, VA 22230
- phone (703) 306-2001.
- US Department of Health and Human Service Office of Inspector General, 330 Independence Ave., SW, Washington, D.C. 20201, phone (800) 447-8477 [Medicare, Medicaid, and NIH program fraud].

FRAUD GLOSSARY

Abusive Trusts: "...typically involve the creation of one or more trusts into which the taxpayer transfers his or her personal and/or business assets and to which the taxpayers assigns his or her income." "Establishing a <u>foreign or domestic trust</u> for the purpose of hiding income and assets from taxation is illegal (IRS CID Website 1997)."

Accommodation Trading: A non-competitive securities trading practice whereby two brokers conspire to conduct non-pit trading, thereby depriving the customers access to the open market (CFTC 1997).

Advanced-fee Schemes: One of the most common frauds perpetrated against consumers and businesses. Perpetrators, often telemarketers, falsely promise "gifts," discount items or services will be delivered after the purchaser pays a small "Advanced-fee." In this scheme, the promised good or service is never delivered. Often the perpetrator covers his tracks by using shell companies or "bust-out" tactics that have him leaving town before anyone can catch up to him.

Affinity Fraud: Perpetrators defraud victims by claiming to have a similar background and then using the commonground to ask for Advanced-fees or to entice the victim into other fraudulent schemes, like investment frauds [cited but not described] (Securities Division, Washington State Department of Financial Institutions Website).

Aging Documents: A technique whereby the criminal washes, rubs, grinds, or otherwise increases the aged appearance of false documents to increase their credibility [cited but not fully described] (DOT 1978).

Alligator Spread: "Any options transaction in which commissions eat up all potential profit [May be used to defraud naive options investors.] (NASAA 1986)."

Altered Identification: "A genuine [identification] document that has some identification elements changed to match the bearer. Most often the name, photograph, age, and physical description are changed (DOT 1978)."

Arson: The destruction or damaging of property through fire is fraudulent when the intention is to make a false insurance claim and to conceal another crime, like murder.

Asset Renting Fraud: An insurance company "rented" assets from others in order to deceive the State of Louisiana Department of Insurance into issuing an insurance license. "The indictment charges that the objectives of the conspiracy were to obtain a license...and to...continue in business although insolvent and unable to pay claims in a timely fashion (USPIS Winter 91/92)."

Asset Shifting: The fraudulent moving of assets onto or off of an organization's financial statement in order to enhance the appearance of the organization's financial health (Schilit 1993).

Back Dooring: "Selling back into the market stock which a promoter thought had been safely laid away. Can be a double crossing technique at the considerable expense of the promoter (NASAA 1986)."

Bait and Switch: "A type of misleading advertising technique. A potential customer is lured by an apparently outstanding bargain ("the bait") but the would-be seller discourages (and sometimes refuses to make) the sale and instead promotes another, higher priced, product ("the switch") (NASAA 1986)."

Bid Rigging: Collusion by two or more contractors to influence the outcome of a contract award. Collusion may be achieved by any number of means: (1). Competitors making anomalously low bids. (2). Competitors declining to bid. (3). Competitors with an unwillingness to cross defined territories. (4). Patterned rotation of bid winners. (5). Identical line items on separate bids. (6). Partnering of competitors when either one could be effectively competing for the contract. (7). The rejection of an initial bid, with the subsequent decline to bid by some of the initial competitors (McFarlane 1984).

Big Store: Nash (1976) wrote that major frauds, requiring extended planning and finances, are called "The Big Store." These scenes are often elaborate stages with all present, except the victim, playing a carefully orchestrated role to defraud. The victims are people of substantial wealth.

Blind Pool: A stock whose underlying business has no known or specific business. A favored vehicle of penny stock frauds, also known as a "blank check" (USPIS Fall 1991).

Blue Box: A device that duplicates phone switching equipments' 2600-hertz tone so the user can receive long distance phone service without paying for it (Judson 1994).

Boiler Room: "A [telemarketing fraud] setting filled with desks, telephones, and salespeople who spend their days calling hundreds of prospects all over the country." "Typical investments sold by fraudulent operators have included coins, gemstones, art, oil and gas leases, interests in oil wells, application services related to cellular telephone licenses, precious metals such as gold and silver, or strategic metals such as chromium...Fraudulent companies often choose to sell investments that may fluctuate substantially in response to world events...The fraudulent seller's goal is to make it difficult for consumers to scrutinize their overinflated value claims (FTC May 1992)."

Box Job: "A fraudulent device whereby a group of people control most or all of a company's stock by means of hidden ownership, and, through such control, artificially manipulate or hype the stock to their advantage, with the stock generally being sold to the public once the conspirators have moved the stock to the desired "target" price (USPIS Fall 1991)."

Bucket Shop: "An illegal operation now almost extinct. The bucket shop operator accepted a client's money without ever actually buying or selling securities as the client ordered. Instead he held the money and gambled that the customers were wrong. When too many customers were right, the bucket shop closed its doors and opened a new office (NASAA 1986)."

Bucketing: A non-competitive, illegal, brokerage trading practice. "Directly or indirectly taking the opposite side of a customer's order into the handling broker's own account or into an account in which he had an interest, without execution on an exchange (NASAA 1986)."

Bunco: A colloquial word used to describe fraudulent schemes. Derived from pedjurations of the word "Banco," "Buncombe," or "Bunkum:" A rigged dice game dating from the nineteenth century (Nash, 1976). US Police Departments often have named their fraud investigation units Bunco Divisions.

Bust-out Schemes: "This is a scheme whereby a business and a good credit record is established, then extremely large orders of the business' product are purchased on credit. Once the large inventories are received, the goods are shipped "out the back door" to associates and the suppliers are left "holding the empty bag." Often records are destroyed, fires set and robberies are faked in an effort to hide or disguise what actually took place. The business files bankruptcy and the crime is complete (FBI 1989)." In one example of a bust-out scheme a perpetrator "created fictitious computer companies and then ordered computer parts and accessories from several legitimate computer companies throughout the United States. The subject paid for the merchandise with non-sufficient funds checks, sold it, then left town and started over again in another state (USPIS Fall 1990)."

Cappers: Paying for medical referrals is known as capping (California Department of Insurance Website 10-3-97). The people who stage accidents designed to make false insurance claims are know as cappers (Adamson 2-24-98).

Check Inclusion: A bookkeeper embezzled from his employer "...by including checks made out to himself in stacks of legitimate business checks prepared for the owner's signature. The bookkeeper took the checks for signature at times when the owner was busy (*WSJ* 10-2-95).

Check Kiting: "A Kite exploits the float in the banking system, the day or so lag between the time you deposit a check in your bank and the time the check clears the bank it was written on...If the swindlers write fast enough and get their timing right, they can keep the cycle going for a while before the banks realize that one of them is short $50,000 (Smith 7-10-95)."

Chop Stocks: Stocks illegally purchased from wholesale brokers at deeply discounted prices and then resold to retail customers. The sale is illegal because these stocks are restricted by Rule 144 of the Securities and Exchange Commission. Making "book" entries of the stocks into customer accounts as opposed to issuing certificates conceals the illegal nature of the sales. The certificates are not issued because their restricted nature is noted on the paper (Weiss 12-15-97).

Collusive Bidding: The coordinated effort by two or more contract bidders to effect the outcome of a competitive contract bid (Listing, without definition, taken from The Financial Crime Investigator Website).

Commodities Pool: A securities trading account that groups various investor's funds. Because they are subject to abuse, these accounts are the source of frequent enforcement action by the Commodities Futures Trading Commission, a US regulatory agency (CFTC Website).

Conflict of Interest: The deliberate concealment, by one or more contract participants, of a pre-existing, or on-going interest, a party or parties have in a contract or other business or government operation (Listing, without definition, taken from The Financial Crime Investigator Website).

Counterfeit Parts: The aerospace industry is plagued by unscrupulous manufacturers and suppliers who mislabel and counterfeit parts. In one case, a parts repair station "fraudulently repair[ed] and overhaul[ed] aircraft starters and generators and falsely certified them as meeting original equipment manufacturer specifications (DOT OIG 10-1-94 thru 3-31-95)." Other serious part counterfeiting involves fasteners (bolts). used in "highway, mass transit, and aviation industries; materials used in construction of bridges, airport runways, and FAA towers; parts used in commercial airplane engines and USCG helicopters (DOT OIG 10-1-94 thru 3-31-95)."

Counterfeit Products: Criminals defraud manufacturers of their trademarked and patented goods by making copycat items. Typical of these frauds, the Orange County Register (Hardesty 12-9-97) reported that a counterfeiter made about $19,000,000 in fake Oakley designer products like sunglasses.

Cramming: The unauthorized billing for telephone services not requested by the customer. These services may include Internet access, voicemail, paging, 900-number calls, or personal toll-free-number services. These services are often tacked-on as part of telemarketing sweepstakes or contests (Oldham 1-26-98).

Credential Fraud: Individuals or organizations may misrepresent their education, certification, or experience to unjustly gain contracts, benefits, or awards.

Credit Profile Reports: A report about individuals and businesses that is maintained by credit information companies (Visa Corporation 1995). Criminals may obtain the reports by fraudulent means to gain an individual's credit card number or loan history: Employees of a New Jersey auto dealership used the dealer's access to credit reports to fraudulently obtain 2,500 credit files which they used to make more than $800,000 in fraudulent charges (*Kiplinger's Personal Finance Magazine*).

Cross-Charging: A scheme employed in contract fraud where a business allocates costs to an un-related contract. Typically the contractor will assign costs incurred on a fixed-price contract to a cost-plus contract, thereby defrauding the customer who agreed to the fixed-price (Ramsey Website). This is especially prevalent in government contracts.

Curb Trading: "Trading by telephone or by other means that takes place after the official market has closed. Originally it took place in the street on the curb outside the market. Under CFTC rules, curb trading is illegal (CFTC 1997)."

Curbstoning: A practice used by dishonest car dealers whereby cars are sold on street corners, creating the impression that the car for sale is owned by an individual. A title search may reveal the owner (ABC 6-30-95)`

Daisy Chain: "A series of purchases at successively higher prices and sales at lower prices of the same issue by the same group of people. Its purpose is to manipulate prices and draw unsuspecting investors into the market, leaving them defrauded of their money or securities (NASAA 1986)."

Data Diddling: The unlawful practice of changing computer data to further a fraudulent scheme (Judson 1994).

Death Vultures: Or hearse chasers, are unethical salesmen "...who victimize the bereaved by selling them flowers, bibles, and other things, falsely claiming that they had been recently ordered or purchased by the deceased. Sometimes they render bills when nothing is owed. Sometimes they claim the deceased has made partial payment and endeavor to collect the alleged balance (Senior Consumer Resources Bulletin September 1984).

Defalcation: "Misappropriation of money held by an official, trustee, or other fiduciary (Random House 1973)."

Dilution: A variety of products, including medicine, food, and fuel, may be diluted using lesser ingredients to defraud buyers.

Dirt Pile Scams: A mining fraud in which an investor buys a specific amount of soil or "ore" which allegedly contains an economic quantity of metal. Dirt pile scams often work out of boil rooms, using telemarketing techniques. In the scam, the dirt pile never has an economic metal value (New Mexico State Securities Division 1989).

Drop Houses: Credit card thieves, and other mail frauds, may use empty houses, rented mail drops, or un-related people's houses as locations to divert victim's credit cards so that the criminal can use them (NFIC Website).

Dummy Corporation: "(1) Any corporation created for effect and not for substance. (2) A captive leasing company acting primarily as an agent for a particular manufacturer in coordinating product leases and raising necessary financing (NASAA 1986)."

Dumpster Diving: The legal practice of scouring dumpsters to gain personal and private information about a person or company. The practice may be used in the furtherance of credit card theft or identity fraud (Judson 1994).

Equity Skimming: The fraudulent practice of purchasing distressed properties through quit claims, then selling or renting the properties without paying the underlying mortgages, thereby eventually causing financial hardship to both the original owner and the buyers (USPIS Fall 1990).

Equity Stripping: The marginal to criminal tricking of homeowners into borrowing more than they can afford so that the homeowner loses title to their home when they can no longer make the loan payments (Heady 5-31-98).

Escape Security Firms: The unlawful creation of multiple securities firms to allow brokers to escape to a second firm if the SEC for securities shut them down violations (USPIS Winter 1990-91).

Expense Shifting: The fraudulent moving of present-term expenses to a future accounting period or of future expenses to the present accounting period. This accounting falsification is designed to manipulate a business's current or future financial statement (Schilit 1993).

Factoring: "The purchase of accounts receivables at a discount from another to provide that person with cash and/or to relieve him of subsequent collection losses (NASAA 1986)."

False Claims: A scheme that uses oral, written or implied deception to claim something of value.

Fat-Fingered Scales: Any method used to cause a scale to read falsely (Kilzer 11-13-94). Generally applied when causing items to appear to weigh more than they actually do.

Fictitious Revenue: The addition of fake revenue to a business's balance sheet. This falsification is designed to artificially improve a business's financial statement (Schilit 1993).

Fictitious Trading: "Wash trading, bucketing, cross trading, or other device, scheme or artifice to give the appearance of trading. Actually, no bona fide, competitive trade has occurred (NASAA 1986)."

Flip Sales: Questionable, rapid sales of properties (particularly raw land) that may undermine the due diligence of lenders by not allowing the lender to investigate the property and its value (Asbury Park Press Website).

Form 990: IRS form filed by charitable organizations. An auditor's review of the form may show if a charity is legitimate (*WSJ* 7-5-95).

Fraud: "...consists of any false representation of a matter of fact, whether by words or by conduct, by false or misleading allegations or by concealment of that which should have been disclosed, which deceives or is intended to deceive another so that he shall act upon it to his legal injury (Baker v Rangos, 229 Pa. Super. 333,___,324 A 2d. 498, 505 (1974). (civil case). in Patten and Edward J. Shapiro 1984)," also, "The intention, or unintended, gaining of something of value by deception."

271

Futures Contract: "...negotiable contract to make or take delivery of a standardized amount of commodity or financial instrument during a specific month... (Fitch 1990)."

Ghost Employees: A perpetrator may submit fictitious payroll certificates to his client, charging time for employees who do not exist. In a political corruption case in Chicago, a politician received pay for his job as a traffic sign investigator, but he performed no duties. (*Chicago Tribune* 9-7-95).

Ginzy Trading: A non-competitive commodities trading practice where floor traders split large trades to manipulate the transaction price (CFTC 1997).

Honorary Authorship: The common practice in science of attaching senior scientist's names to research with which they were not directly involved (Butlet 6-15-95).

Impossible Social Security Numbers: "No SSN has ever been issued with 0000 serial number or 00 group number. Any alleged SSN showing these numbers would therefore not be valid (HHS October 1989)."

Income Shifting: Generating income then causing the money to be paid to another is fraudulent when it used to deceive the US IRS (IRS CID Website 1997), an insurance company, courts, or others. In one case, a farmer tried to hide assets from a divorce proceeding to effect their outcome (Web site http://www. communinet.org/News_ Journal/tax.html). Income shifting may also be used to falsify a business's financial statement. For example, shifting current-term income to a future period may create the false impression of earnings growth (Schilit 1993).

Inflated Appraisals: Borrowers may bribe appraisers, or take other steps, to inflate appraisals to obtain unjustified property loans, to setup a fraudulent insurance claim, or to take un-deserved tax deductions for donated items (Conklin 1994).

Insider Trading: The illegal securities trading practice where a "...person based that trading on non-public material information. And the person had access to that information by virtue of a relationship of trust or fiduciary duty that was violated by the trading (Fleckenstein 6-26-98)." Auction houses may also be guilty of insider trading is the house or its officials secretly bid for items consigned to them (Conklin 1994).

Interpositioning: A fraudulent securities-brokerage practice in which the broker-dealer deceives a customer by making undisclosed non-competitive trades. These trades are completed by using the broker-dealer's account to buy securities, then selling the securities from the broker-dealer account to the customer, in effect, charging the customer two sets of commissions. In contrast, the customary practice is to place a market order for the customer, or to directly fill the order from inventory held by the broker-dealer. These commissions can amount to 5% to 12% of the transaction, and in one case ran to 40.9% (Goldberg 1978).

Jiggle the Market: "To affect the market price of shares within a narrow range. The purchase is to encourage the public to sell their holdings and enable a stock promoter to accumulate relatively low priced stock in anticipation of future market promotion (NASAA 1986)."

Kickbacks: The payment of money, or other things of value, to a government or business employee for the purpose of effecting a contract award or the administration of a contract.

Kiting: The creation of a false bank account balance by manipulating bank deposits (*Webster's Third New International Dictionary* 1981).

Lapping: "A fraud technique involving the misappropriation of customers' payments and failure to record the receipt of such funds. To cover the situation, subsequent payments are recorded as for the first customer's account rather than the accounts to which they should be credited. A form of "robbing Peter to pay Paul [Ponzi Scheme] (NASAA 1986)."

Lien Sharks: Unscrupulous general contractors may fail to pay their subcontractors, thereby inducing the sub to file liens against a building owner. The desperate subcontractors may then sell the liens to a consolidator who colors the tile to the property. To clear the title, the property owner is forced to payoff the liens, in effect paying for the work a second time (Sifakis 1993).

Loan Flipping: The equivalent of stock churning, which is perpetrated by unethical stock or insurance brokers. In the case of loan flipping, the perpetrator encourages or induces the borrower to repeatedly refinance, each time assuming a loan with higher origination points and/or a higher interest rate (Heady 5-31-98).

Maritime Scuttling: "...is the willful casting away of a vessel with connivance of her owners for the purpose of claiming against insurance." Also known as Hull Fraud (International Chamber of Commerce 1985).

Medicaid Mills: Clinics that were set up primarily to create production-line billing of the government insurance program. The physicians in these mills commonly upcoded (see entry) diagnoses and ordered unnecessary tests (Jesilow, Pontell, and Geis 1993).

Misbranded Drugs: The re-labeling of prescription drugs, typically calling generics by a brand name.

Mississippi Christmas Tree: A series of fictitious owners of a farm or ranch, designed to obtain fraudulent farm subsidies for the US Department of Agriculture (PBS 5-5-98).

Money Laundering: "... knowingly using money obtained from an illegal source for a legitimate purpose (Pingree Website)." Laundering can often involve a second or third party where the other parties did not commit the initial crime, but they did invest the money.

Mooch Lists: Telemarketers sell one another lists with previous victims. The lists allow criminals with new schemes to target those who had lost to prior schemes (*NYT* 5-21-95).

Off-loading: The practice of one federal agency or federal contractor awarding contracts to another branch of government for the sole purpose of avoiding procurement regulations. Under some circumstances, specified by the Economy Act, off-loading is legal, but when used simply to avoid procurement regulations, while deceiving government regulators, it is not (DOD OIG 10-1-93 thru 3-31-93).

Opportunity Fraud: Like opportunity crime, is not pre-meditated, but instead occurs when someone seizes an opportunity (Coalition Against Insurance Fraud Web site).

PBX Fraud: "A PBX is a small computer that operates as an automatic switchboard for any location that has multiple telephone lines, which includes most companies of more than half a dozen or so employees." Computer hackers break into the system, making unauthorized phone calls which are billed against the victim company (*Information Plus* 1994).

Paper Accidents: "False accident reports are filed to support insurance claims for collisions that never happened (*WSJ* 5-26-95)."

Paper Recycling: Synonymous with plagiarism and may also be used to describe reuse of the same data by the same author (*Nature*, 3-15-90, "Accusations of "paper recycling," p 187).

Papering Job: "The technique used by boiler room operators prior to their making phone calls to potential customers. It involves sending teasing letters and brochures describing the alleged advantages and potential of the security the operators are promoting (NASAA 1986)."

Phantom Experiments: A commentary in *Nature* suggests some researchers engage in misconduct by citing experiments that were never conducted to fill-in inadequate or control data gaps (*Nature* 10-1-87).

Phone Phreaks: Criminals who specialize in stealing phone access by using a whistle or other device to mimic the tone used by phone company switching systems, thereby tricking the system into granting free phone service (Judson 1994).

Piece Off: "Giving a bribe or a bonus to do something to assist a [securities] manipulation (NASAA 1986)."

Pigeon Drop: Criminals defraud people, especially the elderly, by telling them they are "bank examiners," and to assist an examination the victim is to withdraw his money from the bank and give it to the "examiner." Another variation is orchestrated by having a victim "find" a wallet or case stuffed with money—counterfeit money. The perpetrators then convince the victim that the best course of action is to hold onto the money for awhile to see if anyone claims it. If no one claims it, the perpetrators say all of the finders will split the money.

In the interim, the perpetrators are asked to give a small deposit to the others to show their good faith (Nash 1976).

Product Substitution: The replacement of one specified item for another, cheaper, non-conforming item in a goods or services contract (Listing, without definition, taken from The Financial Crime Investigator Website).

Pump and Dump Scheme: Stock manipulators artificially raise the price of a narrowly traded security, and when investors step in to a surging stock, the manipulators sell their shares at inflated prices (Barrett 7-10-95).

Pyramid Scheme: Any distributorship or sales organization which relies on each new tier of distributors to find a lower tier of distributors in order to pay themselves, is a pyramid scheme: The initiator of the pyramid is paid first, and eventually, those at the bottom are paid nothing and lose their initial payments to the tier above them. Chain letters and multilevel sales organizations are variations on pyramid schemes (SEC Information for Investors and Palmeri 8-14-95).

Quackery: False claims of health benefits for unproven medications, devices, or treatments (Marvin Sept 1994).

Questioned Cost: "A cost resulting from an alleged violation of law, regulations, or the terms and conditions of the grant, cooperative agreement, or other document governing the expenditure fund. A cost can also be "questioned" because it is not supported by adequate documentation or because funds have been used for a purpose that appears to be unnecessary or unreasonable." Questioned costs are fraud indicators (NSF10-1-93 thru 3-31-94).

Recovery Room: Telemarketers who repeatedly try to scam the same victims by saying they can recover previous losses are said to run recovery rooms (OCC Website 1997).

Recycled Work: Unethical lawyers [and others such as engineers] double bill clients by submitting work already completed, from prior clients, to new clients (*WSJ* 9-18-95).

Reloading: The telemarketing fraud practice of continually contacting prior victims of telemarketing fraud. The elderly are especially susceptible to this practice (USPIS Winter/Spring 1995).

Rogue Traders: Stock or futures traders who make trades in defiance of their sponsor's guidelines. Rogues often cause huge losses and use deceptive methods to conceal their losses (Shirouza et al. 9-20-96).

Salami Slicing: "A form of data diddling that occurs when an employee steals small amounts from a large number of sources through electronic changing of data." Examples including shaving miniscule amounts off of bank accounts (Judson 1994).

Scam: "(1) A scheme to defraud investors, and/or creditors. (2) A planned bankruptcy where the bankrupt makes many sales for cash and/or purchases extensive inventory on credit and then absconds with the sales proceeds or inventory leaving his creditors (customers and suppliers) with few or no assets. A tried and true technique is to seek out a new supplier, place a small order in Month 1, and pay cash or on the approved credit terms when required. In Month 2 much larger orders are placed, payment may be on time or a little late. In month 3 very substantial orders are placed. By Month 4 the man and the merchandise are gone but the creditors are left unpaid (NASAA 1986)."

Secrete Commissions: See Kickbacks.

Security: "Any note, stock, bond, evidence of debt, interest or participation in profit sharing agreement, investment contract, voting trust certificate, fractional undivided interest in oil, gas, or other mineral rights, or any warrant to subscribe to, or purchase, any of the foregoing or other similar instruments (NASAA 1986)."

Self-Dealing: A scheme where a banker, trustee, (or other person in a position of trust,). "makes loans to insiders at abnormally favorable terms, or illegally accepts kickbacks in exchange for making a loan (Fitch 1990)." Presumably, self-dealing could also involve the awarding of contracts, privileges, or other things of value from a person in a position of trust.

Shell Corporations: A corporation without assets or apparent business activities (NASAA 1986).

Shill: A person who lures a victim into a fraud (Nash 1976) or into a gambling room.

Short Changing: Dishonest cashiers may shortchange by counting bills twice to gain a customer's confidence, then palming one bill as he passes the change to the victim. The perpetrator expects that the victim's suspicion is down after seeing the change counted twice (Sifakis, 1993).

Short Cons: Fraudulent schemes involving relatively small amounts of money and short periods of time like one day or less (Nash 1976).

Shoulder Surfing: Individuals who steal telephone credit card numbers by glancing over the rightful owners' shoulder to see the card or the code as it is punched into a touch tone phone. Shoulder surfing commonly occurs at airports. The stolen numbers may be used for the thief's exclusive use or to be resold to others.

Slamming: The "switching of customers' long distance companies without their knowledge." Many people who are "slammed" are charged higher rates by the new company (*Albuquerque Journal* 8-15-95). Another slamming scheme victimized the primary provider of the long distance service—an entrepreneur defrauded major telecom companies like ATT by selling long distance services but failing to pay the telecom companies for their share of the sale (Keller 4-23-98).

Slip and Fall Accidents: Perpetrators stage accidents in businesses to fraudulently collect insurance or government disability compensation.

Spilt Masters: Master art works have been cut in half to create two masters when there was once one, thereby increasing the total market price for the work (Sifakis 1993).

Staged Accidents: "Previously damaged vehicles are brought together to look as if the damage was caused by a real incident (*WSJ* 5-26-95)."

Straw Buyers: A buyer who acts instead of another in order to deceive a third party.

Structured Cash Transactions: Federal law requires those who make cash transactions of $10,000 or more, and those who split up cash transactions that would otherwise exceed $10,000, to file notifications with the IRS. Some criminals structure their transactions to try to avoid government scrutiny of illegal activities (USPIS Spring 1991). Also called structuring.

Stuffed Flat: Unscrupulous furniture sellers may use an apartment as a front for selling used, or low quality furniture to unwitting buyers. The store continually replenishes the apartment, deceiving buyers into thinking they are getting a good deal by buying furniture at distressed prices (Sifakis 1993).

Telemarketing Fraud: The use of telephones to sell misrepresented goods, investments or charities. The Federal Trade Commission estimates consumers lose over $1billion each year to telemarketing fraud (FTC 4-94).

Toxic Waste: A slang term for "stripped" high-yield bonds. By stripping the bonds of the principal payment, they become highly volatile investments. Failing to disclose this volatility to buyers may be fraudulent (Knecht 12-20-94).

Trading Ahead: The illegal practice where securities brokers make trades in advance of customer trades, using their foreknowledge to benefit themselves (CFTC 1997)

Travelers: American-based clans of English, Scottish and Irish descent, many whom are involved in organized crime. They specialize in home repair and trailer sale frauds, but are also involved a great variety of other schemes (Wright 1996).

Trojan Horse: An internet-downloaded computer program that allowed criminals to use the victims telephone lines to charge long distance telephone calls to the victim's phone account. The victim was enticed into downloading the program, and, once in place, the program disconnected the victim's regular Internet Seville provider and connected it to a different provider (NFIC Website).

Truth-in-Negotiations Act: A Federal law that requires sole-source vendors to reveal all relevant information prior to receiving a contract award. It is fraudulent to holdback information (Ramsey Website).

Turnaround Deal: "(1) A manipulation whereby a promoter prearranges an underwriting sale to go to reliable or nominee buyers for a specified period of time in order to show that a public distribution has been made. What the public does not know is that the promoter has put up his own money with the nominee or had guaranteed the purchaser(s). that he will buy the stock back at a small profit to enable his own dealings later. (2) Another variation is the use of nominee companies to purchase the underwriting. The object is that the promoter ends up with all the stock hidden from the authorities and also controls the money that he has paid for the stock because it is now in the treasury of the company he controls. He can then get his money back by management fees, phony or inflated invoices for work not done, or by selling the company worthless assets at inflated prices. In the end he receives the stock at virtually no cost to himself. Offshore and overseas banks are often used to launder the turnaround and the securities are registered in street names, usually the underwriting broker's in order to avoid transferring registrations at the transfer agent and leaving a record of the turnaround (NASAA 1986)."

Unbalanced Bidding: A complex contract fraud scheme involving variable-quantity, variable item, procurement contracts. In this scheme, one bidder is given prior knowledge of specific quantities of items that are likely to be purchased over time through a procurement contract. With the competing bidders only having more generalized knowledge of the procurement, the fraudulent bidder is able to tailor its bid to both win the contract award and to make a higher profit on the sales (Model Procurement Code Project Staff 1984).

Unbundling: The fraudulent medical billing practice in which health care providers "bill a single operation as many small procedures to increase reimbursement (Langreth 10-23-97)."

Undercarated Jewelry: Unscrupulous retailers misrepresent the gold content in jewelry, thereby defrauding the public (*NBC* 9-12-95).

Upcoding: The fraudulent medical billing practice of "exaggerating the severity of a condition," in order to bill insurance companies for more money (Langreth 10-23-97)."

Uttering: To put forged checks, counterfeit money, counterfeit coins or note (Random House Inc. 1973).

Vote Buying: The giving of money or gratuities to voters to sway the way the cast their votes (Sabato and Simpson 1996).

Wash Sales: Securities trades completed without the intent to complete a transaction. Wash sales may be completed by brokers as a method of churning (CFTC 1997). Wash sales may also be used to create unrealized securities losses in a tax fraud. Tax wash sales defraud the US government when the seller posts a sale at the end of a tax year, and then re-purchases the same security within 30 days.

Washed Postage: Criminals literally wash used stamps then reuse or sell them, thereby defrauding the Postal Service (USPIS Summer 1990).

White Plastic Fraud: "...A scheme in which the merchant submits phony sales drafts to a processing bank and then splits the sales draft income with the person supplying the account numbers that were charged (Fitch 1990)." Presumably, the cardholder never intends to pay the credit card bill.

BIBLIOGRAPHY

AARP, January-February 1995, "Fraud Alert," *Modern Maturity,* p 72.

ABC, *20-20,* 6-30-95.

ATSDR Web site http:Latsdr1.atsdr.cdc.gov:8080/HAC/PHA/summit /sum _p1. html.

Abrams, Steven, 9-27-97, "'Soft dollar' case charges filed," *NYT* in Academic Index, v147 pB2-D2.

Acello, Richard, 11-3-94, " Identity theft takes big toll on taxpayers," *San Diego Transcript* in ProQuest Business Dateline, pA1.

Adamson, Deborah, 2-24-98, "Allstate Files Suit To Recoup Millions; 45 Named In Action To Counter Fraud," *Daily News,* in Proquest Business Dateline

Albuquerque Tribune, 8-13-95, "Stop Payment Checks Backfire in Business Flaps," pB9.

Albuquerque Journal North, 9-1-95, "Caller poses as grandson, asks for cash," pB1.

Anderson, Alun, 9-29-88, "First scientific fraud conviction," *Nature* v335 p389.

Anderson, Christopher, 11-28-91, "The case of the amazing shrinking scandal," *Nature,* v354 p 258.

Anderson, Christopher, 1-9-92, "US government targets indirect cost agreements," *Nature,* v255 p.

Anderson, Christopher, 10-1-93, "Michigan Gets an Expensive Lesson," *Science,* v262 n5190 p23.

Anderson, Christopher and Traci Watson, 7-16-92, "US drops Imanishi-Kari investigation; Baltimore withdraws Cell retraction," *Nature,* v358 p177.

Ann Landers Column, 6-23-98, "Don't fall for 'phone test' scam," *DP,* p6E

Armbrister, Trevor, June 1995, "Vote fraud: a national disgrace," *Reader's Digest* in Academic Index, v146 n878 p85.

Asbury Park Press Web site, "Ex-executives at S.C. bank alleges cover-up of real estate fraud," http://www.autoinjersey.com/news/cards/story/1,1449, 32097,00.html.

Autosistance/Top Rip Off's Web site, http://home.earthlink.net/~auto sistance /ripoff.html.

Ayres, Ed, July/Aug 1996, "The Expanding Shadow Economy, *World Watch,* p10-23, in IRS Researcher.

BBB We site http://www.bbb.org/library/first.html.

Bachler, Christopher J., June 1995, "Resume fraud: lies, omissions and exaggerations," *Personnel Journal* in Academic Index, v74 n6 p50-58.

Baker v Rangos, 229 Pa. Super. 333,___,324 A 2d. 498, 505 (1974). (civil case). in Patten, Thomas L., and Edward J. Shapiro, 1984, "Prosecution For Fraud

And False Pretenses," in Identifying And Prosecuting Fraud And Abuse In State And Local Contracting, American Bar Association.

Barker, Robert, and Neal Templin, 10-95, "Car Repairs: how to avoid getting ripped off," *Reader's Digest* in Academic Index, v147 n882 p105.

Barrett, Amy, 7-10-95, "Deals Too Sweet To Be True," *Business Week*, p122.

Baum, Bob, 2-11-95, "Thieves Get Over $346,000 at ATMs," *Albuquerque Journal*, pA1-A2.

Benke, Alan, 6-15-98, Personal communication.

Betts, Mitch, 4-18-94, "Computer matching nabs double-dippers: database comparisons to fight welfare fraud in N.Y., N.J.," *Computerworld* in Academic Index, v28 n16 p90.

Blair, Jason, 7-4-98, "Scam a new twist on phone fraud," *DP*, p8A.

Blue Cross and Blue Shield Web site http://www.bluescares.com/new/this_week/general_articles/archives_dir/FBI_investigates.html.

Bobic, Michael, 11-5-97, Web site, Mbobic@siucvmb.siu.edu.

Borrus, Amy, 12-4-95, "Exports That Aren't Going Anywhere," *Business Week*, p121.

Boselovic, Len, 11-16-97, "Friend of Fraud? Unscrupulous Invention Marketing Find a Steady Flow of Willing Customers," *Pittsburgh Post-Gazette*, in Proquest Business Dateline.

Bond.Ins.Fraud, Web site http://www.pimall.com/nais/n.ins. bond.html.

Bomer, Elton, 1997, The Texas Department of Insurance Web site http: //www.tdi.state.tx.us/commish/help.html.

Braga, Michael, 3-8-96, "Scam artists find Sarasota brokerage no easy mark," *Tampa Bay Business Journal* in ProQuest Business Dateline, v16 #11 p3.

Brauchli, Marcus W, Nicholas Bray, and Micheal R. Sesit, 3-6-95, "Broken Bank Barings PLC Officials May Have Been Aware Of Trader's Position," *WSJ*, pA1-A5.

Brannnigan, Martha, 6-26-98, "Sunbeam Auditor Is reviewing 1997 Finances," *WSJ*, pA4.

Broad, William and Nicholas Wade, 1982, *Betrayers of the Truth: Fraud and Deceit in Science*, Oxford University Press.

Bryant-Friedland, Bruce, 2-16-98, "Grand jury finds fraud in insurance program," *Florida Times Union* in Proquest Business Dateline, p6.

Burks, Susanne, 3-2-95, "Meat Co. Suspected of Food Stamp Scam." *Albuquerque Journal*

Burks, Susanna, 8-16-95, "Melloys, State Settle Claims," *Albuquerque Journal*, p5D.

Burns, Gary, 4-17-95, "What's A Small Investor Like You...," *Business Week*, p83-84.

Busch, Richard, March-April 1995, "Anatomy of a travel scam," *National Geographic Traveler*, p6.

Butler, Declan, 6-15-95, "Uproar greets new blood scandal indictment," *Nature*, v375 p526.

Butters, Robert D., "Builder's Competence," The Risk Management Reporter, March 1997, Web site, http://www.schinnerer. com/ Builder's Comp.htm.

CBS, 7-13-95, *48 Hours*.

CBS, 6-25-95, *60 Minutes*.

CBS, 8-24-95, *Eye to Eye*.

CFTC, 1997, *Glossary*.

CFTC, 1-10-94, "News Release."

CFTC, Web site, http://www.cftc.gov/annualreport 96/en96.html.

CFTC, 7-10-92, "WEEKLY ADVISORY," p8.

CFTC, Web site, http://www.cftc.gov/opa/ rutman0515.htm.

Calavita, Kitty, Henry N. Pontell, and Robert H. Tillman, 1997, *Big Money Game*, Berkeley: University of California Press.

California Department of Insurance, 10-3-97," Doctors, Wife, Cappers To Face Fraud Charges," California Department of Insurance Web site, http://www.insurance.ca.gov/PRS/ PRS1996/Pr047-96.htm.

California Department of Insurance, 7-15-97, "Former Insurance Agent Charged With Fraud," California Department of Insurance Web site, http://www.insurance.ca. gov/PRS/PRS1996/Pr047-96.htm.

Car & Driver, 7-94, "Have Screwdriver, Will Steal," p 165.

Cervantes, Miguel, 1604, *Don Quixote*, translated by J.M. Cohen, 1968 ed., Baltimore: Penguin

Chase, Alston, 6-19-98, "Why government 'junk science' refuses to die," *DP*, p11B.

Choquette, Kara, 7-6-98, "Unwitting investors fall victim to ATM scam, " *USA Today*, p3B.

Cheung, Nicholas Web site, http:www.coinmasters.org/texts-docs/pub22.tx and pub20.tx.

Church, George J., 9-25-97, "Elderscam: reach out and bilk someone," *Time* in Academic Index, v150 n8 p54-57.

City of Denver, September 1984, "Be Alert For Schemes...Con Games...Rip Offs," *Senior Consumer Resources Bulletin* , 2p.

Conklin, John, 1994, *Art Crime*, Westport, Conn.: Praeger Publishing, 322p

Connors, Phil and Bernard Nelson, Aug 1995, "Calling all cellular phone users," *Kiplinger's Personal Finance Magazine,* p97.

Consignment Fraud, Web site, http://heads-upoanet.com/pub 008.htm

Consumer Reports in Academic Index, April 1996, "Pension safety: do you know where your benefits are?" v61 n4 p86.

Consumer Reports, Jan 1998, "You've won!...or have you?," v 63 n1 p62-64.

Consumer's Research, 12-94, "Air Ticket Frauds Grounded," v. 77, no. 12, p 37.

Cotton, Paul, 2-12-92, "Harassment Linked to Fraud, Lawsuit Alleges," *JAMA*, v270 p783-4.

CreditComm Services, Web site http://credit comm.com/ assistance/phony.html.

Cyphert, Laura, 3-20-98, "Fraud Detection In The Construction Industry," *San Diego Daily Transcript* Web site, http://the source.net/reports /98/03/ Surveying/tr.html.

DOD OIG, April 1992 thru September 1994 [various], "Semiannual Report to Congress."

DOE OIG Web site, http://www.vais.net/~ edoig/semian 33/ investng.txt.

DOT OIG, April 1991 through March 1995 [various], "Inspector General Semiannual Report to the Congress."

DOT, 1978, "Recognizing Fraudulent Identification, " Washington: U.S Government Printing Office.

Dalton, Rex, 3-19-97, "Dating in doubt as researcher is probed," *Nature*, v392, p 218-219.

Davis, Kristin, Aug 1995, "Guarding Your Financial Privacy," *Kiplinger's Personal Finance Magazine,* p 38-45.

Davis, Kristin, July 1998, "The Bonnie and Clyde of Credit Card Fraud." Kiplinger's Personal Finance Magazine, 65-71.

de Wit, Maarten J., Letter to Editor, 3-1-94, "Censorship in geology?" *Nature*, v368 p10.

DeBoth, James R., 1998, "The Importance of Being Aware of Mortgage Fraud," Mortgage Market Information Services, Inc. Web site. http://www.interest.com/editorial/Mortgage _column /mtg_story_980210.htm.

DeGeorge, Gail, 3-21-94, "Who Pays $25,000 For A Fax Machine? You," *Business Week*, p8.

Deichmann, Ute, and Benno Muller-Hill, 5-14-98, " The fraud of Abderhalden's enzymes," *Nature*, v393 p109-11.

DP, 8-9-95, "McInnis receives 'ghost' telegrams," p3B.

DP, 10-7-95, "3 guilty in $300,000 scam," p8B.

DP, 4-18-98, "Internet name scam ruled law violation," p7A.

DP, 8-12-98, "Workplace theft rising, survey says," p9C.

Dixon, Jean, 9-4-95, "GAO: Social; Security Slack in Nabbing Disability Crooks," *Albuquerque Journal*, pA7.

Dopp, Paul. 1996. "Procurement Fraud." CGA Magazine Online. http://www. cga.canada.org/CGAMagazine/may96/ fraud_e.htm.

Dobrzynski, Judith H., 1-28-97, "Art Dealers, Outraged, Question Works to Be Auctioned in Florida," The New York Times, C9, C19.

Dow Jones Newswire, 9-16-98, "FBI Says New Technology Causing Bulge In US Banking Fraud," Web site http:www.sims.berkeley. edu/~cbutler/ news 6.html.

Dunkin, Amy, 10-19-92, "When Your Broker Leads You Down The Garden Path," *Business Week* , p 116-7.

Durant, Will, 1950, *The Age of Faith*, New York: Simon & Schuster.

Dwyer, Paula et al., 7-1-96, "Descent Into The Abyss," *Business Week*, n3482 p28-29.

Economist in Academic Index, 7-30-94, "Incredible Edibles," v332 n7874 p46.

Economist, 5-11-96, "Policing the cops," v339 n7965 p26.

Economist, 12-23-95, "Financial disasters," v337 n7946 p5.

Eichewald, Kurt, 6-20-95, "Prudential Settles Broker Case With US," *NYT,* pD6.

Emshwiller, John R., 10-2-95, "Worker Theft Seen Targeting Small Business," *WSJ* p.

Emshwiller, John R., 6-1-95, "Hot Specials at Small Stores: Food Stamp Fraud," *WSJ*, pB1-B2.

Emshwiller, John R., and Andy Pasztor, 3-31-95, "Grand Jury Investigates the Collapse Of Orange County's Investment Pool," *WSJ*, pA4.

FBI, 1989,"White-Collar Crime A Report to the Public."

FBI, 1994, "Federal Bureau of Investigation Health Care Fraud Program."

FTC, 1-92a, *Art Fraud*, leaflet.

FTC, 1-92b, *Facts For Consumers*, leaflet.

FTC, 2-94, *Telemarketing Travel Fraud*, leaflet.

FTC, 4-94, *Telemarketing Fraud*, leaflet.

FTC, 5-96, *High Rate, High Fee Loans*, leaflet.

FTC, 8-96, *Fair Debt Collection*, leaflet.

FTC, 10-96a, *'Gold' and 'Platinum' Cards*, leaflet.

FTC, 10-96b, *Secured Credit Card Marketing Scams*, leaflet.

FTC, 6-97, *File Segregation A New Credit Repair Scam*, leaflet.

FTC, 1-98, *Medical Billing, Business Opportunity Schemes*, leaflet.

FTC, 4-98, *Cramming: Mystery Phone Charges*, leaflet.

FTC, 5-98., *In the Loupe: Advertising Diamonds, Gemstones and Pearls*, leaflet.

FTC, Web site http://www.ftc.gov/bcp/conline/pubs /buspubs /supplies.htm.

FTC Web site, 2-93, http://legalelectric.com/Libraray/Gene/89.html.

Financial Crime Investigator Web site, http://www.cci2. com/fci_ sch.htm.

Fitch, Thomas, P, 1990, *Dictionary of Banking Terms*, New York: Barrons.

Fitzgerald, Mark, 10-94, "Postal Service takes action against bogus ad invoicing scheme," *Editor & Publisher*, v127, n44, p25.

Fleckenstein, Loren, 6-26-98, "Market Got Wind Of TCI-AT&T Deal," *IBD*, pA21, quoting John Heine.

Frankel, Max, 4-13-97, "The frauds of April," *NYT* in Academic Index, s6 p30.

Franz, Douglas, 5-10-98, "Fraud accompanies boom in hospice care," *DP*, p17A.

Gasparino, Charles and John Connor, 8-17-98, "Progress Is Seen in 'Yield Burning Probe," *WSJ*, pB2.

Geison, Gerald, 1995, *The Private Science of Louis Pasteur*, Princeton N.J.: Princeton University Press.

Gellene, Denise, 7-12-94, "State study finds widespread fraud in auto body repairs," *Los Angeles Times* in ProQuest Business Dateline, pD1.

Goldberg, Jeffrey, 6-7-93, "All the wrong moves: are some Isreali-owned moving companies taking customers for a ride?" *New York*, v23, n23, p44.

Goldberg, Stuart C., 1978, *Fraudulent broker-dealer practices*, New York: American Institute For Securities Regulation.

Goodstein, David, Autumn 1991, "Scientific Fraud," *American Scholar*, v60 n4 p505-11.

Goldstein, David, "Conduct and Misconduct in Science," Web site, http://www.caltech. edu/~goodstein/conduct.html.

Gove, Philip Babcock, ed., 1961, *Webster's Third New International Dictionary*, Springfield MA: G&C Merriam Co.

Greenberg, Herb, 8-17-98, "The Auditors Are Always Last to Know," *FORTUNE*, P228.

Grunbaum, Rami , 12-9-94, "Promoter draws SEC inquiry," *Puget Sound Business Journal* in Proquest Business Dateline, v15 #30 p1.

Grabner, Lynn, 3-27-98, "Feds will seek Hoyt indictment," *Business Journal-Sacramento* in ProQuest Business Dateline, v15 issue2 p1.

Graves, Scott, 11-20-94, "Fraud haunts stores over the holidays," *News Chronicle* in Proquest Business Dateline, pB10.

Green, William and Katherine Bruce, 8-11-97, "Riskless crime?" *Forbes* in Academic Index, v160 n3 p100-103.

HHS - OIG, October 1989, "Social Security Number Fraud," p7.

HHS Web site, 12-19-94, http://www.sbaonline.sba.gov/ignet /internal/hhs /sfa/ 121994.html.

Hahn, Brad, 10-9-96, "Top fraud on list: Unused cars," *Sun Sentinel Ft. Lauderdale*, in Proquest Business Dateline, pA3.

Hamilton, Denise, 11-21-94, "Fakes send sales of jade plunging: Gem merchants fight back with high-tech detection methods," *Los Angeles Times* in Proquest Business Dateline, pD1.

Hardesty, Greg, 12-9-97, "Oakley says N.Y. raid netted shady shades," *Orange County Register* in Proquest Business Dateline, pC1.

Hays, Constance L., 5-21-95, "If the Hair Is Grey, Con Artists See Green," *NYT*, pF1.

Heady, Robert, 5-31-98, "Beware of home-equity scams," *DP*, p10-I.

Heinzl, Mark., 5-6-97, "Bre-X Probe Intensifies as tests Find Little Gold," *WSJ*, pA3.

Henkel, John, Nov-Dec 1997, "Record fine imposed on generic drug maker," *FDA Consumer*, v31 n7 p38-39.

Herbert, Alan, 1995, *Coin Clinic*, Iola WI: Krause Publications Inc.

Hight, Philip J., 5-19-95, "A University and 4 Scientists Must Pay for Pilfered Work," *NYT* , pA20.

Hilts, Philip J., 5-19-95, "A University and 4 Scientists Must Pay For Pilfered Work," *NYT*, pA20.

Hirezy, Wofgang, 1996, Web site http://mlm.kentlaw.edu/archives /election-law/ index/96/jul_dec/msg00116.html.

Holden, Constance, ed., 11-26-93, "HHMI Cuts Cardiologist Loose," in "Random Samples," *Science*, v262 #26 p1369.

Holden, Constance, 4-29-94, Fired Mobil Scientists Awarded $7 Million," *Science*, v264 p656.

Holland, Kelly, 9-4-95, "Bank Fraud, The Old-Fashioned Way," *Business Week* , p96.

Holland, Kelly, and Paul M. Eng, 5-31-93, "An Alarm Goes Off At The Cash Machine," *Business Week,* p 39.

Horn, Michael, 3-23-98, "The Death Care Business," *US News & World Report*, p51-58.

Hoving, Thomas, 1996, *False Impressions*, New York: Simon & Schuster.

Hudson, Mike, Fall 1993, "The Poverty Industry," *Southern Exposure* in SIRS Researcher, p16-27.

Hyten, Todd, 12-23-94, "Food Brokers Probed," *Boston Business Journal* in Proquest Business Dateline, v14 #45 p1.

Hyten, Todd, 8-9-96, "Biocode uses invisible ink to reveal fake products," *Boston Business Journal* in Proquest Business Dateline, v16 #26 p6.

IBD, 7-30-98, "Perspective - Tax Cheats," pA6.

IBD, 6-10-98, "A Black Market For Tobacco," pA6.

IBD, 7-29-98, "EPA: Environmental Propoganda Agency," pA34.

IRS CID, 1997, "Fraudulent Foreign and Domestic Trusts," Web site http://www.tres.gov/ irs/ci /tax_ fraud/trusts.htm.

IRS CID, 1997, "Enforcement Activities," Web site http://www. tres. gov/irs/ci/ media/toc.htm.

Information Plus, 1994, *Crime A Serious American Problem*, p123.

Ingersoll, Dave, Oral communication, 7-10-98.

Institute of Certified Financial Planners, 1994, "Avoiding Investment and Financial Scams: Seeking Full Disclosure Is The Key," pamphlet.

International Chamber of Commerce, 1985, *Guide to the prevention of international trade fraud*, Paris: ICC Publishing S.A., n420.

JAMA, 4-15-92, "Physician Fraud and Medicaid," p 2037.

Jacobs, Margaret A., 9-18-95,"Lawyers and Clients Problem of Overbilling By Many Large Firms Is Confirmed in Surveys," *WSJ*, pB8.

Jesilow, P, H. N. Pontell, and G. Geis, 1993, *Prescription For Profit (How Doctors Defraud Medicaid)*, Berkeley: University of California Press, 247p

Jensen, Edythe, 1-23-98, "Homestead Scam Letters Resurface Similar Gimmick Shut Down in' 94," *Arizona Republic* in Proquest Business Dateline, pE1.

Judson, Karen, 1994, *Computer Crime*, Enslow Publishers, Inc., Hillside, N.J., p 48.

KUSA News, Denver, 6-8-98.

Kaye, Steven D. and Richard J. Newman, 9-14-92, "Avoid Made-Up Auto Maintenance," *US News and World Report,* p124-126.

Keller, John J., 4-23-98, "How a Minister's Son Discovered 'Slamming' And Then Disappeared," *WSJ*, pA1-A6.

Kelly, Dennis,7-13-95, "Millions looted from Pell loans, senator says," *USA Today*, pD1.

Kerry, John, Sept 1991, "Where Is The S&L Money?," *USA Today (Magazine),* p20-21.

Kilzer, Lou, et. al, 11-13-94, "Concrete tests faked at airport: Fort Collins company admits results tainted," *DP* in Proquest Business Dateline, pA1.

Kimelman, John, 9-1-94, "Too Charitable to Charities?," *Financial World* in SIRS, p46-51.

Knecht, G. Bruce and Jeffrey Taylor, 5-19-95, "SEC Charges New Era and Bennett With Fraud on Charities, Investors," *WSJ*, p A1-A4.

Knecht, G. Bruce, 12-20-94, "Derivatives Dregs Houston Firms Sold Risky 'Toxic Waste' For Wall Street Giants," *WSJ* , p A1-A11.

Knight, Mike, New Spirit Jewelers & Crystal Gallery, Web site http://www.wehug.com/ diamondalert1.html.

Knott, David, 3-6-95, "Beware of Nigerians bearing deals," *Oil and Gas Journal,* p37.

Knutson, Lawrence L., 10-10-97, "Ruby Ridge Officer Sentenced," Associated Press.

Koerner, Brendan I., 4-14-97, "Another tale of a rat," *US News & World Report* in Academic Index, v122 n14 p14.

Koestler, Arthur, *The Act of Creation*, in Schilit, Howard M., 1993, *Financial Shenanigans: How To Detect Accounting Gimmicks And Fraud*, New York: McGraw Hill.

Kracher, Beverly and Robert R. Johnson, Nov 1997, "Repurchase announcements, lies and false signals," *Journal of Business Ethics* in Academic Index, v16 n15 p1677-86.

Kuehn, Wolf, 1997, Gemmology World Web site http://www. ci-gem.ca/357.html.

Kuntz, Phil, 8-1-95, "Hard Rock Cafe Founder Is One of Many Caught Between Rock and Hard Place of Election Laws," *WSJ*, pA12.

L.A. County Department of Consumer Affairs Web site http://www. co.la.ca.us/consumer-affairs/real estate/index.htm.

LI Business News in Proquest Business Dateline, 1-23-97, "Postal fraud prompts high tech meters,"p19.

Landers, Ann, 6-23-98, "Don't fall for 'phone test' scam," *DP*, p6E

Landwehr, Rebecca, 2-27-98, "Regulators brace for blitz of Y2K fraud," *Denver Business Journal* in Proquest Business Dateline, v29 #26 p3.

Langreth, Robert, 10-23-97, "The Payers - GOTCHA! Health insurers go all out in their effort to ferret out bogus claims," *WSJ*, pR20.

Lederman, Douglas, 5-24-97, "IRS audits of colleges continue to find violations of tax laws," *The Chronicle of Higher Education* in Academic Index, v42 n37 pA27

Lehman, Jane H., June 1995, "Scammers target hard-to-sell land," *Consumer's Research Magazine* in Academic Index, v78 n6 p21-23.

Lehman, Peter and Mark Dion, August 1996, "Stealing trash: gray-collar crime," *The Police Chief* in Academic Index, v63 n8 p39-43.

Leiren, Hall, Jan 1996, "They've got your number," *BC Business* in ProQuest Business Dateline, v24 #1 p42.

Lemke, Bob, 1983, *How To Get Started In Coin Collecting*, Summit PA: Tab Books Inc.

Liu, Caitlin, 7-27-97, "The Stone-Cold Facts Gem Buyers Should Know," *Washington Post*, pH1.

Los Angeles Times, "FBI Investigating Fraud by Foreign Doctors," in Blue Cross Blue Shield Web sites.

Lord, Mary, 9-28-98, "Sheepskins fleecers," *US News and World Report*, p72-73.

Love, Alice. A., 5-27-98, "Report finds identity fraud on rise," *DP*, p 2C.

Lovitt, Jonathan T., and Richard Price, 6-23-95, " Burial scam a 'disgusting' find," *USA Today*, p3A.

Lowe, Peggy, 6-13-98, "Denverite held in fraud case," *DP*, p 3B.

Lowry, Tom, 7-22-98, "SEC judge bars Jett Former trader must return $8.2M," *USA Today*, pB1

Lutterbeck, Deborah, Spring 1995, "Food Stamp Fallout," *Common Cause* in SIRS, p8-11.

Lynch, David J., 7-19-95, "Entrepreneurs lose in get-rich scheme," *USA Today*, pB1.

MOJO WIE, Web site http://www.mojones.com/MOTHER _JONES/MA 95/davis3.html.

MacDonald, Heather, 1-20-95, "SSI Fosters Disabling Dependency," *WSJ*, pA12.

Maddox, John, 11-19-92, "Conflicts of interest declared," *Nature*, v360 p205.

Maddox, John, 6-10-93, "Contaminated blood case nears end," *Nature*, v363 p491.

Mannix, Margaret, 6-1-98, "Stolen Identity," *Newsweek*, p48-50.

Maremont, Mark, 9-16-96, "Anatomy of a fraud," *Business Week*, n3493 p90-93.

Maremont, Mark, 4-25-94, "Burned by Merrill," *Business Week*, p122-125.

Margasak, Larry, 10-12-97, "Confused by All Those Fund-Raising Inquiries?," *Sun-Sentinel* (Ft. Lauderdale, FL) in SIRS Inc., p6A.

Mark, Erika R., ed., March 1995, "How car repair shops cheat women (and how to fight back)," *Good Housekeeping*, p201-202.

Marlins, Antoinette L. and Antonio C. Bonanno, 1995, *Jewelry & Gems [-] The Buying Guide*, Woodstock VT: Gemstone Press.

Marsa, Linda, June 1992, "Scientific Fraud," *Omni*, p38-43, 82.

Marvin, Mary Jo, Sept. 1994, "Swindlers in the 1990's:Con Artists Are Thriving," *USA Today Magazine* in SIRS p80-84.

McEnaney, Maura, 7-2-95, "Ex-Forger's Checking Advice," *Albuquerque Journal*, pF2.

McFadden, Kay, 6-26-95, "Cellular-phone fraud losses near $1billion," *Albuquerque Journal* Business Outlook, p7.

McFarlane, Walter A., 1984, "Anti-Trust In State Government," in *Identifying And Prosecuting Fraud And Abuse In State And Local Contracting*, American Bar Association, 123p.

McGourty, Christine, 8-31-89, "Bitter dispute reaches NIH," *Nature*, v340 p668-669.

McMahon, Bill, 4-4-98, "State sues Shell Oil over royalties [-] Company defends gas sale prices," *Advocate-Baton Rouge*, in ProQuest Business Dateline, p1C.

McMahan, Pauls, and Mele, Christopher, "Voter fraud hard to catch," *The Times Harold Record*, 10-18-97, Web site, http://www.th-record.com/10-17-97/pmcmkjsa.htm.

McMenamin, Brigid, "Your trust has a hole," *Forbes*, 6-15, 1998, p240-242.

McMorris, Francis, , 10-26-94, " Travel Agents in 4 States Arrested In 'Operation Free Travel' Sting," *WSJ*, pB5.

McRae, Mathis E., 2-94, "Policing the guardians: combating guardianship and power of attorney," *The FBI Law Enforcement Bulletin*, v63, n2, p1.

Mehlman, Ira, 3-24-97, "Funding Fraud," *National Review* in Academic Index, v49 n6 p30-31.

Milloy, Steven J., and Micheal Gough, 8-7-98, "Silencing Science In The Climate debate," *IBD*, pA28.

Model Procurement Code Project Staff 1984, "Overview Of The Procurement Process, Related Frauds, And The Model Procurement Code," in *Identifying And Prosecuting Fraud And Abuse In State And Local Contracting*, American Bar Association.

Monealegre, Mellissa, 12-12-97, "AG's office warns of credit card insurance scam," *Montgomery Advertiser* in Proquest Business Dateline.

NASA OIG, 4-1-94 thru 9-30-94, "Semiannual Report."

NASA OIG, 10-1-92 thru 3-31-93, "Semiannual Report."

NASAA, 1986, *Glossary.*

NCAHF Newsletter, 11→12-97, Web site http://www. ncahf. org/newsltt/n120- .html.

NBC, 8-2-95, *Dateline NBC.*

NBC, 9-12-95, *Dateline NBC.*

NBC, 7-20-98, *Dateline NBC.*

NFIC Web site, 1997, http://www.fraud.org elderfraud /eldertbroch.htm.

NFIC, 3-27-96, "What Is A 'Private Sovereign Entity,'" Web site http://www.fraud.org/news/1996/mar96/032796.htm.

NFIC, 5-22-96, "Bi-Monthly Mortgage Deals On The Rise," Web site http:www.fraud.org/ news/1996/ may96 /052296.htm.

NSF OIG, 4-1-1991 thru 9-30-1991, "Semiannual Report to the Congress."

NSF OIG, 10-1-93 thru 3-31-94, "Semiannual Report No 10."

NSF OIG, 4-1-94 thru 9-30-94, "Semiannual Report to the Congress."

NYT, 5-4-78, "California And GM Agree In Engine Switching Case,".

NYT, 2-20-98, "US enters suit on oil payments," v147 pC2-pD2.

Nando Times, 3-5-98, "Agencies working to combat fraud in child tax credits," Web site http://wedge.nando.net/newsroom/ntn/politics/030598/politics4_ 7756_noframes.html.

Napier, Kristine, Mar 1994, "Unproved Medical Treatment Lure Elderly," *FDA Consumer*, p32-37.

Naretti, Raju, 1-6-95, "IE Is Accused in Ex-Employee's Suit, Recently Unsealed, of Improprieties," *WSJ*, pB6.

Nash, Jay Robert, 1976, *Hustlers and Con Men*, New York: M. Evans and Company, Inc..

National Geographic Traveler, March-April 1995 "Buyer, beware of travel scams," p22.

National Whistleblower Center Web site, 4-14-97, http://www. whistleblowers. org /nwcpr001.htm.

Nature, 10-1-87, "Getting to grips with fraud,"v329 p377.

Nature, 3-10-89, "Accusations of 'paper recycling,' " p187.

Nature, 5-23-91,"Overheads cost research dear," v351 p255.

Nature, 9-12-91, "Indirect costs again," in News, v353 p196.

Nature, 6-15-95, "Honorary Authorship,: v375 #6532 p532.

New Mexican, 9-14-95, "Foundation must stand trial," pB4.

New Mexican, 9-30-95, "Residents sue car dealership," pB3.

New Mexico State Securities Division, "1989 Grant Application The Goldbrick Project Association," p7.

Newborn, Ellen, 6-3-96, "Burned retailers are fed up, clamping down," *USA Today*, pA1-A2.

Niggs, Herbert N, and Gabriela Radulescu, 7-13-94, "Scientific Misconduct in Environmental Science and Toxicology," *JAMA*, v272 n2 p168.

Nordenberg, Tamar, March-April 1998, "Selling drug samples lands doctor in prison," *FDA Consumer*, v32, n2, p39.

Novack, Janet, 11-8-93, "The tax cheater handbook," *Forbes*, p202.

Novack, Janet, 4-11-94, "You know who you are, and so do we," *Forbes*, p89.

Novak, Viveca, 5-26-95, "FBI Probe of Auto Insurance Fraud Nets More Suspects," *WSJ*, pB2.

OCC Web site, http://www.occ.treas.gov /chckfrd/ clsdacct.htm.

O'Connor, Matt, 9-7-95, "'Investigator' pleads guilty in payrolling," *Chicago Tribune*, Section 2 p2.

Oldham, Jennifer, 1-26-98, "Group Targets False Charges on Phone Bills," *Los Angeles Times* in Proquest Business Dateline.

O'Neill, Peggy Lee, 7-8-95, "Suit: Blue Cross Shifts Costs," *Albuquerque Tribune*, pA2-A4.

OSEPP Web site, http://www.amandla.org/osepp/news/54.htm

Overstreet, James, 5-9-97, "New technology boosts counterfeiting business crimes take \$10 billion bite out of industry," *Denver Business Journal* in ProQuest Business Dateline, v48 #35 p17c.

PBS, 5-18-98, "Secrets of an Independent Consul,"*Frontline*.

Packer, Lynn, 3-9-95, "Can Deedee Skate?" *Private Eye Weekly* (Salt Lake City), p7-10.

Palmeri, Christopher, 8-14-95, "The aloe juice man," *Forbes*, p98.

Patel, Tara, 5-21-94, "Real juice, pure fraud?" *New Scientists* in Academic Index, v142, n1926, p26.

Pennisi, Elizabeth, 9-5-97, "Haeckel's embryos: fraud discovered," *Science* in Academic Index, v277 n5331 p1435.

Plotkin, Howard, 9-93, "The Port Oxford Meteorite Hoax," *Sky and Telescope* , p35-38.

Pool, Robert, and Peter Alduos, 8-8-91, "Standford counts cost of overhead scandal," *Nature*, v352 p459.

Plantech Corporation Web site http://www.plantech corpcom /serpr51.htm.

Racker, Efriam, 5-11-89, "A view of misconduct in science," *Nature*, v339 p91-93.

Rafi, Natasha, Aug 1998, "A 401(k) mystery is revealed," *Money*, p30.

Ramsey, William R., Web site http://www.ramsey-law.com /011DEF.html.

Random House, 1973, *College Dictionary*.

Rechtin, Mark, 8-93, "Nevada Chevy dealer denies racketeering, fraud charges," *Automotive News*, n5512, p6.

Rivero, E., 12-23-97, "Insurance Agents Face Fraud Charges," *Daily News* in Proquest Business Dateline.

Robinson, Marylin, 4-17-98, "Many fall for tow truck scam," *DP*, p2B.

Rose, Luis J. and William H. Freivogel, 1-15-95, "Fertile for Fraud," *St. Louis Post Dispatch* in SIRS, pB+.

Rossiter, E.J.R., 6-11-92, "Reflections of a whistle-blower," *Nature*, v357 n6378 p434-436.

Russell, Judi, 3-17-97, "Breaking the bar code: Retail victims are not amused," *New Orleans City Business* in ProQuest Business Dateline, v17 #37 p8.

SEC, no date, *How To Avoid Ponzi and Pyramid Schemes*, Leaflet.

SEC Web site, http://www.sec.gov/enforce /alerts/ltdtreas.htm.

Sabato, Larry and Glenn Simpson, 6-96, "Vote Fraud," *Campaigns & Elections*, p22.

San Francisco Chronicle, 5-11-98, "Man Accused of Bilking Elderly Now on Internet."

Santa Fe New Mexican, "Artful Scam," in Express Line Section, p5.

Sberna, Robert, 10-23-95, "Electronic tax cheats the latest IRS target," *Crains Cleveland Business* in Proquest Business Dateline, p39.

Schatz, Thomas A., 8-25-95, "Medicare Fraud: Tales From the Gypped," *WSJ*, pA8.

Schiffres, Manual, "Dispatches From the Dragnet Files," *Kiplinger's Personal Finance Magazine*, July 1998, p27-28.

Schilit, Howard M., 1993, *Financial Shenanigans: How To Detect Accounting Gimmicks And Fraud*, New York: McGraw Hill.

Schmid, Randolph E., 4-22-98, "Disaster scam warnings given," *DP*, p2C.

Schmit, Julie, 2-14-95, "Business travelers' risky game: Expense reports," *USA Today*, pA1.

Schreiner, John, 1-15-97. "Placer Woos Bre-X With $6.4B Merger," *Financial Post-Toronto*, p1.

Second Opinion Web site, http://tor-pw1.netcom.ca/~secondop/pre-employment.html.

Securities Division, Washington State Department of Financial Institutions, Web site http://www.wa.gov/dfi/securities /publications.html.

Segal, Marian, Oct 1995, "Food broker sentenced in export diversion scheme," *FDA Consumer*, v29 n8 p29-30.

Seniors Site, Web site http://seniors-site.com/fraud/bulletin.html.

Shaffer, David, 6-20-93, "Phony Fund-Raisers Under Fire," *St. Paul Pioneer Press* in SIRS, p1B+.

Shernoff, William M., Sanford M. Gage, and Harvey R. Levine, 1995., *Insurance Bad Faith Litigation*, Oakland, CA: Time Mirror Books.

Shirouza, Norihiko, et. at., 9-20-96, "Sumitomo Puts Its Copper Losses At $2.6 Billion, Will Sue Ex-Trader," *WSJ*, pC1 and C18.

Sicherman, Al, 9-4-95, "Flaky counterfeiters take lots of time to make shampoo," *Minneapolis Star Tribune*, pE1-3.

Sifakis, Carl, 1993, *Hoaxes and Scams*, New York: Facts on File Inc.

Sinkankas, John, 1959, *Gemstones of North America*, New York: Van Nostrand Reinhold CO, v I.

Sloan, Alan, 2-16-98, "Books, cooked D.C. style: 'saving' Social Security by borrowing from it," *Newsweek*, v131 n7 p42.

Smith, Adam, 1776, *The Wealth of Nations Books I--III*, New York: Penguin Books.

Smith, Lee, 7-10-95, "The Wrecking Crew," *Fortune*, p58-64.

Smithsonian Institution OIG, 10-1-92 thru 3-31-93, "Semiannual Report," p11.

Smithsonian Institution OIG, 4-1-93 thru 9-30-93, "Semiannual Report," p13.

Snow, Toney, 7-10-95, "Take Profit Out of Fraud Suits," *USA Today*, p10.

Sprint, no date, "Phone Fraud [-] We All Pay," pamphlet.

Spurgeon, David, 7-21-94, "Audit backs jailed professor's allegation," in News, *Nature*, v370 no6486 p166.

Staples, Ed. "Experts Assess Fraud Risk In Mortgage Credit Scoring." Real Estate Finance Today, Web site http: //www.newcitysys. com/Articles/ experts_assess_fraud_ risk_ in_mor.htm.

Stecklow, Steve, and Rebello, Joseph, 5-24-95, "IRS Is Studying Whether New IRA's Donor's Committed Fraud," *WSJ* in Academic Index, pA3-2.

Stretch, Greg, 6-98, personal communication.

Stevens, Amy, 1-13-95, "Ten Ways (Some) Lawyers (Sometimes). Fudge Bills," *WSJ*, pB1-B6.

Stewart, Walter W, and Ned Feder, 1-15-87, "The integrity of the scientific literature," *Nature*, p207-214.

Stipp, David, 5-27-96, "Farewell, my logo: a detective story," *Fortune* in Academic Index, v133 n10 p128(8).

Stone, Richard, 2-18-94, "Aids Scandal Embroils Top French Biologist...," in Science Scope, *Nature*, v263 p907.

Stone, Richard, 2-25-94, "The Perils of Biotech Consulting," in Science Scope, *Science*, v370 no6486 p1079.

Sullivan, Suzanne, July 1996, "Put a lock on your bank account," *Kiplinger's Personal Finance Magazine*, p84.

Swinbanks, David, 12-23-93, "Survey battle leads to plagiarism verdict," *Nature*, v366 n6457 p715.

Taubes, Gary, 2-4-94, "A Costly Settlement Ends Whistle-Blower Suit, *Science*, v263 n5147 p605.

Thatcher, Rebecca, 2-8-98, "Pet-locating scam preys on vulnerable families// BBB warns owners - to beware of out-of-town 'finders' asking for money," *Austin American Statesman*, in Proquest Business Dateline.

Thompson, Jim, 1990, *The Grifters*, New York: Vantage Books.

Thrasher, Ronald R., July 1994, "Voice-mail fraud," *The FBI Law Enforcement Bulletin*, in Academic Index, v63 n7 p1.

Topolnicki, D, and E.M. MacDonald, Aug. 1993, "The Bankruptcy Bonanza!" *Money,* in Proquest Business Dateline.

Troester, David, 3-2-98, "Paxon Continues Battle To Dump Federal Tax Code," *Business First-Buffalo*, v14 n21 p4.

Twain, Mark, 1885, *The Adventures of Huckleberry Finn*, New York: Random House, 1993 ed.

US Chamber of Commerce, 1977,*White Collar Crime.*

US News & World Report, 7-29-96, "Worthless phone cards," v121 n4 p62.

USA Today, 7-13-95, "States turn to high-tech to fight fraud," pA1-2.

USA Today, 7-6-98, "Phone scams rise; FCC leaves consumers on hold," p12A.

USPIS, Winter/Spring 1989 through Summer 1998 [various], "Law Enforcement Report."

USSS Web site http://www.treas.gov/usss/investigation /index 419.htr.

USSS Web site http://www.treas.gov/usss/money/altergec.html.

Valdmanis, Thor, 7-15-98, "Cendant disclosure triggers meltdown," *USA Today*, p3B.

Viles, Peter, 5-3-93, "Hackers plead guilty in contest fraud," *Broadcasting & Cable*, v123 n18 p42.

Visa Corporation, 1995 "Credit Cards: An Owner's Manual," leaflet.

von Grimmelshausen, Hans Jacob Christoffel, 1669, *The Adventures of a Simpleton (Simplicius Simplicissimus),* 1963 ed. New York: Frederick Ungar Publishing CO., 249p.

Waldman, Peter and Jay Soloman, 5-6-97. "Gold Fraud Recipe? Bre-X Workers Saw Mine Samples Mixed," *WSJ*, pA1-A12.

WSJ, 5-19-95, "SEC Charges New Era and Bennett With Fraud on Charities, Investors," pA3-A4.

WSJ, 6-13-95, "Ex-Air-Charter Official In New Jersey Gets 18-Month Sentence," pA4.

WSJ, 7-28-95, "A Painful Lesson On Dealing With Pirates," pB9.

WSJ, 9-18-95, "Lawyers and Clients," pB7.

WSJ, 8-29-95, "Federal Investigation Puts Cloud Over Sun Health Care," pB4.

WSJ, 5-26-95, "FBI Probe of Auto Insurance Fraud Nets More Suspects," pB2.

WSJ, 9-29-95, "Legal Beat [-] Teyibo Sentencing," pB4.

WSJ, 10-2-95, "Worker Theft Seen Targeting Small Business," page unknown.

WSJ, 9-13-96, "Ex-Currency Trader At Chemical Pleads Guilty In Peso Case," pB7.

WSJ, 2-26-97, "Thirty Brokers Plead Guilty To Hiring Test-Takers," pC24.

Walsh, Sharon, 10-13-94, "Prudential close to settlement on partnership sales," *Washington Post* in ProQuest Business Dateline, pB9.

Web site, http://www.thonline.com/th/news/1996/ th0514/ stories/10738.htm.

Web site http://rs7.loc.gov/cgi-bin/lexl.script.

Webb, Ben, 9-28-89, "False accusations at London hospital," *Nature*, v241 p268.

Weiss, Gary, 12-15-97, "Investors beware: chop stocks are on the rise," *Business Week* in Academic Index, n3557 p112-128.

Wesier, Benjamin, 7-15-98, "Busy lawyer accused of being a phony," *DP*, p14A.

Western, Ken, 11-19-95, "Sheet tips off hotels to scams," *Arizona Republic*, in Proquest Business Dateline, pD1.

Westlaw, 1994, Federal Criminal Codes and Rules, St. Paul: West Publishing CO.

Willette, Anne, 8-10-95, "FBI going undercover on mortgage fraud," *USA Today*, pA1.

Wilson W. Crook, III v. Board of Regents of the University of Michigan, et al., 9-17-85, Washington D.C.: Wilson - Epes Printing Co., Inc.

Women's Connection Online, Inc., 1997, "Barter Exchange Tax Fraud Case Helps Small Business," Web site http:www. women connect. Com /info /business/ nov1897a_ bus.htm.

Wright, Don, 1996, *SCAM!, Inside America's Con Artists Clans*, Elkhart IN: Cottage Publications.

Wyatt, Edward, 7-2-95, "Rogue Trader Is Named In Investment Fund Loss," *NYT*, pD14.

INDEX

PLEASE, IF THIS IS A LIBRARY HOLDING
COPY THIS FORM - DO NOT DAMAGE THE BOOK
Order Form For
The Fraud Identification Handbook
FROM:

_____
_____
_____
_____

Phone Number (_____) _____ _____

Quantity of books ordered:_____

Total Price of Books Due $_____
(Cost: 1 copy $22.95 2 copies $40.00)

Shipping and Handling Costs $_____
(1 copy add $2, 2 copies add $3.00,
priority mail add $5 to each book)
Add 3.2% for all books shipped to   *$_____*
a Colorado address.

Grand Total Enclosed $_____

Please Pay by Check or Money Order
Allow 30 days for delivery, 10 days for priority.

Remit to:
    George B. Allen
    2343 W. Hyacinth Rd.
    Highlands Ranch, CO 80126   Telephone (303) 508-7898

    Upon receipt of payment your book(s) will be promptly sent.

PLEASE, IF THIS IS A LIBRARY HOLDING
COPY THIS FORM - DO NOT DAMAGE THE BOOK
Order Form For
The Fraud Identification Handbook
FROM:

_____
_____
_____
_____

Phone Number (_____) _____-_____

Quantity of books ordered:_____

Total Price of Books Due $_____
(Cost: 1 copy $22.95 2 copies $40.00)

Shipping and Handling Costs $_____
(1 copy add $2, 2 copies add $3.00,
priority mail add $5 to each book)
Add 3.2% for all books shipped to   *$_____*
a Colorado address.

Grand Total Enclosed $_____

Please Pay by Check or Money Order
Allow 30 days for delivery, 10 days for priority.

Remit to:
        George B. Allen
        2343 W. Hyacinth Rd.
        Highlands Ranch, CO 80126   Telephone (303) 508-7898

        Upon receipt of payment your book(s) will be promptly sent.

PLEASE, IF THIS IS A LIBRARY HOLDING
COPY THIS FORM - DO NOT DAMAGE THE BOOK
Order Form For
The Fraud Identification Handbook
FROM:

_____

_____

_____

_____

Phone Number (_____) _____-_____

Quantity of books ordered:_____

Total Price of Books Due $_____
(Cost: 1 copy $22.95 2 copies $40.00)

Shipping and Handling Costs $_____
(1 copy add $2, 2 copies add $3.00,
priority mail add $5 to each book)
Add 3.2% for all books shipped to $_____
a Colorado address.

Grand Total Enclosed $_____

Please Pay by Check or Money Order
Allow 30 days for delivery, 10 days for priority.

Remit to:
    George B. Allen
    2343 W. Hyacinth Rd.
    Highlands Ranch, CO 80126   Telephone (303) 508-7898

Upon receipt of payment your book(s) will be promptly sent.

4552